HEROES OF THE SAS

HEROES OF THE SAS

Barry Davies BEM

This paperback edition first published in
Great Britain in 2007 by
Virgin Books Ltd
Thames Wharf Studios
Rainville Road
London
W6 9HA

First published in paperback in 2000 by Virgin Publishing Ltd

2 3 4 5 6 7 8 9 10

A catalogue record for this book is available from
the British Library.

ISBN 978 0 7535 1247 0

Typeset by TW Typesetting, Plymouth, Devon

Penguin Random House is committed to a sustainable future for
our business, our readers and our planet. This book is made from
Forest Stewardship Council® certified paper.

Printed and bound in Great Britain by Clays Ltd, St Ives plc

When tired, wet and cold, exhausted beyond all sense of reasoning, the SAS soldier continues to operate. When operating deep behind the enemy lines, and faced with overwhelming odds, he will stand and fight. When wounded, captured or in solitary confinement, he will endure the pain. For his deeds are but a grain of sand in a desert of achievements won by heroes of the SAS past, present and future.

CONTENTS

INTRODUCTION

Although this book is called *Heroes of the SAS*, it is more about certain men who have passed through the years of the Regiment's history. While most of this book is confined to the British SAS (Special Air Service) there are several stories from the worldwide SAS family and the odd one or two from those men who have been closely linked with the SAS.

It is sometimes difficult to define a single person as the hero of a particular situation, for in many cases the operation or action in question involved many SAS soldiers. The Gulf War incident explored in the acclaimed book *Bravo Two Zero* concerns the exploits of Andy McNab, yet there were seven soldiers in the patrol. So the reader will forgive me if I choose to name but one person for the heading of each section. Likewise there are those characters whose stories may seem more farcical than heroic, yet in their way they were men of the SAS – every one a hero. Likewise, some stories are short, while others are more detailed, yet this difference does not reflect on the efforts of any individual.

The reader must also forgive me if I have included more personal incidents involving those soldiers I knew well, trusting that those still alive will remember and see the funny side. As is only to be expected with the SAS, many of those mentioned in this book have died, either in battle or through the normal activities of the reaper of time, but some remain and are still serving with the SAS. Those whose identities are in the public domain I have named but in other incidents, such as the shooting in Gibraltar, I have simply supplied an alias.

There is no chronological order to the book other than in placing the two founding fathers, David Stirling and Paddy Mayne, first. The deeds of the individuals who have passed through the ranks of the SAS would fill a library, so it is regrettable that many individuals get only a short mention, some none at all.

Finally, to help the reader avoid getting confused about the identity of any particular SAS unit I have given below a brief history of how the SAS family developed over the past sixty years or so. Take a few minutes to read it and you should be able to avoid any subsequent bewilderment over different unit names such as 'SRS' and 'SAS'.

THE SPECIAL AIR SERVICE FAMILY

1941: The Special Boat Section carried out its first raid on the night of 22nd June; prior to this it had been known as Floboat Section.

1941: David Stirling was given permission in July to raise the SAS (Special Air Service) from members of 'L' Detachment. The SAS was stated to be a Brigade; however, there was at that time no SAS Brigade: this was a ruse to deceive the Germans.

1941: On the night of 16/17th November the SAS carried out their first raid, which was not successful.

1943: In January Lieutenant Colonel David Stirling, founder of the regiment, was taken prisoner and sent to Colditz Castle in Germany. Lieutenant Colonel R.B. 'Paddy' Mayne took over command, by which time the SAS had developed considerable water-borne raiding skills and at the conclusion of the African campaign 1 SAS was renamed SRS (Special Raiding Squadron). The Special Boat Section became the SBS (Special Boat Service) and was under the command of Lieutenant Colonel the Earl Jellicoe. While the SBS operated in the Aegean and Adriatic, the SRS carried out commando-style raids in Sicily and Italy.

1943: The 2nd SAS regiment was created by the founder's brother, Lieutenant Colonel W.S. Stirling.

1944: By January the SRS units, less SBS, were re-formed into SAS Brigade, under the command of Brigadier R.W. McLeod. It comprised:

1 SAS (Lt. Col. R.B. Mayne) – the former SAS and SRS.
2 SAS (Lt. Col. B.M.F. Franks).
3 SAS (French) Lt. Col. J. Conan.
4 SAS (French) Lt. Col. P. Bourgoin.
5 SAS (Belgian) Lt. Col. E. Blondeel.
'F' Squadron from Phantom (GHQ Reconnaissance Regiment).

1945: At the end of the war in July, 1 and 2 SAS (British) were disbanded, with 3 and 4 SAS (French) going to the French Army; likewise 5 SAS went to the Belgian Army.

1945: The SAS Regimental Association was formed in November.

1947: 21 SAS (Artists') TA formed under the command of Lieutenant Colonel B.M.F. Franks.

1950: 2 SBS was formed from a detachment of the Amphibious School attached to the Royal Navy Rhine Squadron in West Germany.

1950: Malayan Scouts formed under the command of Lieutenant Colonel J.M. Calvert. Joined by volunteers from 21 SAS (Artists') TA.

1951: In March the Southern Rhodesia Far East Volunteer Unit was raised for service in Malaya. The unit was designated C (Rhodesia) Squadron Malayan Scouts (SAS). A and B Squadrons were already in existence, A Squadron having been formed from volunteers from units in Malaya and B Squadron from volunteers from 21st SAS Regiment (Artists') TA. 264 (SAS) Signals Squadron's origins also date back to 1951 when, as a signals troop, they were attached to the Malayan Scouts (SAS).

1952: The Malayan Scouts were officially redesignated 22nd SAS Regiment (22 SAS).

1952: C Squadron (Rhodesia) returned to Rhodesia where it was disbanded shortly afterwards.

1957: NZSAS Squadron returned to New Zealand and was disbanded.

1957: The Australian SAS unit was formed.

1958: The SAS were sent to Oman where they were involved in the assault on Jebel Akhdar.

1959: The SAS left Malaya. They settled temporarily in Malvern but then transferred to permanent camp at Hereford (1960).

1959: The New Zealand Squadron was re-formed. In May 1962, a detachment was deployed to Thailand where its two troops assisted US Army Special Forces. In 1963 the squadron was redesignated 1st Ranger Squadron, New Zealand SAS.

1959: 23 SAS TA formed in London, but were later transferred to Birmingham.

1962: A small team from Rhodesia were sent to train with the SAS, enabling them to restart the Rhodesian SAS.

1962: Regimental Headquarters transferred from Euston to Chelsea.

1963: 22 SAS were committed to Borneo together with TK.

1964: The Australian Special Air Service Regiment (SASR) was formed on 4th September.

1964: The Regiment had a permanent Squadron operating in Aden.

1966: In July 264 (SAS) Signals Squadron was formed as a fully independent unit co-located with 22 SAS in Hereford.

1966: In June an Australian SAS Squadron (SASR) was deployed to South Vietnam.

1967: The SAS withdrew from Aden.

1968: In December a detachment, designated 4 Troop, of 1st Ranger Squadron NZSAS was deployed to South Vietnam on attachment to the Australian SAS Squadron based at Nui Dat in Phuoc Tuy Province.

1969: SAS troops were committed in Northern Ireland, albeit in a small way. By 1971 a whole Squadron was operating Province-wide.

1970: The Oman War began, with two Squadrons leading the main assault onto the Jebel Massif.

1971: In February the New Zealand SAS withdrew from Vietnam. Subsequently, the 1st Ranger Squadron NZSAS was redesignated the 1st NZ SAS Group

1971: The Australian SASR withdrew from Vietnam.

1974: The SAS anti-terrorist team was raised in Hereford to counter the growing international terrorist threat.

1977: Two SAS anti-terrorist team members assisted the Germans with a hijacked aircraft.

1978: 1 Special Air Service Regiment (Rhodesia) officially renamed.

1980: 1 Special Air Service Regiment (Rhodesia) was disbanded. Many members went on to join the South African Defence Force (SADF).

1980: The SAS were called in to deal with the Iranian Embassy siege in London.

1982: Two plus SAS Squadrons are sent to the war in the Falklands, which cost the Regiment 21 men.

1989: As part of a joint Anglo/American effort to defeat the drugs barons, a Squadron of SAS was sent to train the Colombians in anti-terrorist tactics.

1991: Three SAS Squadrons were sent to fight in the Gulf War where they operated for the full duration of the war, deep inside Iraq.

1994: SAS soldiers were sent to Bosnia.

1998: The regiment moved to its new base in Credenhill, Hereford.

1. THE MAKING OF AN SAS SOLDIER

Have you ever wondered where SAS soldiers come from? What makes an SAS soldier? Are they born killers? Having known many of the men mentioned in this book I can put your mind at rest: for the most part they are normal. True, some of the SAS soldiers I have known have told me tales that would make a saint go ballistic. Take 'Nobby', for example. At the age of seven he came home from school to find that his mother and father had moved house without telling him. He eventually went to live with his aunt. Yet a more stable person I have yet to meet. Then there was Steve. He was nine years old when his mother died. His father began drinking heavily and became a down-and-out. With no home life, Steve took his seven-year-old sister and went to live rough in the streets of Manchester – it was two years before the authorities caught up with them. A few years later, Steve joined the army and finally made his way to the SAS. Once he was established in Hereford he sent for his sister. These are extreme cases. I would say that my own story of how I came to be in the SAS is a more typical one.

I was born, just as the Second World War was coming to an end, in Wem in the beautiful countryside of north Shropshire. My arrival was free of significant omens other than that I was born on the cusp between Scorpio and Sagittarius – thus my subsequent life has always seemed to be guided and protected by some strange fate. My early years were simple. I came from a poor but very loving family, and all my early memories are happy ones. My fondest recollection is of being coerced downstairs by my two older brothers early one Christmas morning to ask our parents if we could have our presents. Creeping down the staircase, I saw the kitchen door was ajar and I could hear my mother and father talking. As I peeped round the corner, there was my mother sitting on my father's lap, having a kiss and a cuddle. At that moment my father enquired, in a very tender voice, 'Do you still love me?'

'I expect so,' replied my mother.

Totally embarrassed at this intimacy I quickly slipped back upstairs, much to my brothers' annoyance.

Our family became quite large, swelling to four sons and two daughters – not uncommon in a rural community such as ours. At fifteen I left school without achieving a single certificate in any subject. It was a good school, but no one had encouraged me to aspire – except for one of the senior girls. So, having received my first sex lesson on the back playing field, I left Madely Secondary Modern school, now renamed Charles Darwin Comprehensive, and went forth to seek my fortune. Actually, I went to work in a butcher's shop.

While my employer's wife, Mrs Coleman, served in the shop, Mr Coleman would instruct me on the finer points of gutting dissection. As he demonstrated the skills of butchery to me he would tell me thrilling stories of his Army days, which for some reason all seemed to be about wonderful adventures full of daring deeds. Looking back, I think that these stories were the seeds that, once planted, germinated in my mind and led to me becoming a soldier.

One bright Sunday morning, at the impressionable age of seventeen, I broached the subject of joining the Army with my father. My enquiry was met with a flat 'No' and, despite my pleading, I got no further. What the hell, I ran away and joined the Army anyway.

A few weeks later, having finished work at about two o'clock in the afternoon, I clandestinely visited the Army recruiting office in the nearest major town, Shrewsbury. After I had completed the written test the recruiting sergeant seemed most impressed, and informed me that my results might possibly get me into the Welsh Guards. I was easily taken in. I discovered that he was actually a Welsh Guards recruiting sergeant, and would receive a bounty payment for every man he recruited. Still on a naive high, I was told by the sergeant to report next day to Sir John Moore's barracks in Shrewsbury, where I would be given a thorough medical examination. If I passed, he said, there was no reason why I should not join the Army immediately.

At home that evening I played it very low-key, said nothing about going to the recruiting office, and went to my bed early. Next morning, while the rest of the family were still asleep, I got up as normal – butchers start work early. On this occasion, however, I dressed in my best casual clothes, robbed the bathroom of a few toiletries and made my way to Shrewsbury again.

At around 10 a.m. I was standing stark naked while a tall dark stranger in a white coat held my testicles and asked me to cough as he assessed my fitness for Her Majesty's Service. The time came to measure my height, 'Five foot six,' called out the orderly assisting the doctor. I interrupted, informing the doctor that the recruiting sergeant had said I was to mention the minor fact that I was joining the Guards Division. 'Five foot eight,' shouted the doctor, and obediently the orderly adjusted his notes. I was really impressed by my first contact with the army – not only had my testicles been groped copiously but, in the space of a few seconds, I had grown two inches taller.

I returned to the recruiting office where, in an upstairs room, I raised my hand and was 'sworn in'. Things got even better – I was given £30 and a one-way ticket to Pirbright barracks in Surrey. What a great place the army is, I thought to myself as I journeyed down to Surrey. Then I reached the guardroom at Pirbright.

'Good afternoon, sir, I've come to join the Army.' I was cheery and light-hearted and spoke with a smile on my face. Unfortunately the man who owned the face to which I was talking didn't think it was a good afternoon – not that day, nor any other day.

'I'm not a fucking sir, I'm a fucking sergeant!' he bellowed at me from a distance of two inches, spraying my face with spittle. He then turned and bellowed at some poor little man in uniform who was sitting in the guardroom. Immediately, the soldier shot to attention and his feet started to move at a funny speed, just like those of a cartoon character. Like a bat out of hell he went flying past me as if he was being chased by the devil himself. The sergeant turned his attention back to me: 'Follow him, c**t.'

Despite this confrontation I settled in rather well. Two days later, my mother found out where I was. I was asked if I would like to stay or go home. I stayed, of course. Army life suited me and I took to it like a duck takes to water. While all around me other trainees moaned and groaned at the rigid discipline, I loved it. Then, just three weeks into the sixteen-week basic training, I was given a real gun to fire. Prince Philip was to visit the depot and had asked to see young recruits firing on the range. Our squad was selected.

On the appointed day we marched to the firing range and I jumped into the slit trench. Big mistake. Being only seventeen and a half years old and not yet fully developed, I needed to stand on three full sandbags in order to see properly down the range. The rifle felt big and heavy, but we had practised the drill in the barrack room and I had the hang of it.

Prince Philip finally arrived and we were given the order to load our weapons and start shooting in our own time. I sighted at the target one hundred yards away and squeezed off my first shot. The rifle kicked hard against my shoulder and the barrel pumped a little – 'whaw'. What a feeling. I was in awe of the weapon's power. I felt elated. At the time I saw nothing wrong with that. To me the rifle was a tool of my trade, much as I was an implement for my superiors, trusting as I did completely in the democratic fairness of our politicians and generals. Happily, I trained well, enjoyed the camaraderie and strove to be the best, to build myself into a gladiator whose disciplined fury could be sent into the arena to challenge the beast that threatened our society. A somewhat romantic notion that was modified when I finally finished up with the 1st Battalion Welsh Guards, who were at that time stationed in Germany.

What can I say about the Welsh Guards other than that they are a fine family regiment? With good mates and the chance to stand outside Buckingham Palace, what more could a man want? Lots, in fact. I will confess that I was never very enthusiastic about parade-ground soldiering, much preferring to don my camouflage uniform and play soldiers. My wish was granted when the Regiment was posted to Aden. That same year I was transferred to the Reconnaissance Platoon. Army life was getting better.

Aden was a shipping port of some importance and had been under British control since 1839. In 1962, the Soviet Union supported internal strife in neighbouring Yemen that led to the overthrow of the ruling Imam. Britain covertly supported the Imam, who was now operating out of Aden. The problem was, Yemen had laid territorial claims to Aden. A situation such as this leads to what governments like to call 'a confrontation'. To soldiers 'confrontation' loosely translates as 'action'.

My first taste of action came when the 'Recce' platoon was stationed up-country close to a small Arab village called Al-Mella. Our assignment was to safeguard the Royal

Engineers who were constructing a road. Several times our camp at Al-Mella came under 'Adoo' (the Arabic word for 'enemy') fire, but most of it was stand-off stuff. That is to say, the enemy would sneak up on us, mostly at night, and from a range of three hundred metres blast away for all they were worth. We in turn would happily respond.

One day, while enjoying 24 hours' relaxation, I and other members of the platoon were playing volleyball on the concrete pitch that also served as a helicopter landing pad. The game was interrupted by the arrival of an unexpected incoming chopper. Fate was doing its own thing again and interfering. That chopper was to change my life. We stood, watching idly as it landed, shielding our eyes from the dust cloud caused by the down draught. Finally, the 'copter came to rest and two soldiers leaped down from the doorway.

I say 'soldiers', but these men were different. At first it was difficult to define that difference. Although they seemed, at first glance, like giants, they were, in fact, of ordinary size. They looked intensely professional but were, for military men, irregularly dressed. Above all, they moved with an air of supreme confidence. Then came the second surprise. Both soldiers reached into the chopper. Between them they pulled out the body of a dead Arab and unceremoniously dragged it to the nearby medical tent. They then returned to the chopper and repeated this routine with a second body. They deposited both corpses in an untidy heap.

By this time some of our senior officers had arrived at the medical tent. Normally they would expect to be saluted and deferred to there but there was something about these two strangers that demanded respect. There were no salutes, no handshakes, just plain instructions from the two extraordinary strangers. After a few moments they got back into the helicopter and departed. That was when I first heard those magic letters: SAS.

For the remainder of that day our camp was full of whispered conversations about our clandestine SAS visitors.

I kid you not, when I say that the letters 'SAS' were whispered, indeed they were. The myth lived, even then.

A month or so later, back in the permanent barracks of Little Aden, I was reading the customary orders for the following day – and what did I read on 'Part One Orders' but the magic words: 'Volunteers required for the SAS'. I was hooked. Next morning, at the first opportunity, I visited the Company office and applied. Thereafter I trained solidly for four months. You would not believe the hell I put myself through but, again, it was this 'destiny thing'. I knew I had to train hard.

When I was up-country at Al-Mella, I would shoulder my heavy rucksack, sling a GPMG (general-purpose machine-gun) around my neck and stagger like a man demented back and forth up and down the runway. It wasn't safe to go too far outside the village. When back in barracks, I would run the roads until I was so knackered I could have died. The worst thing was that I heard nothing. All my enquiries were met with: 'What the fuck do you want to join the SAS for? You don't have a dog's chance of passing.' Despite this I persisted, and carried on training. This was now becoming part of my daily routine.

One lunchtime, as I stood sweating in the cookhouse, queuing for my meal, the Company clerk slid casually up behind me and whispered, 'You lucky bastard, you're booked on a flight to the UK tomorrow night.' Just like that, I was going to try my luck at the SAS selection course in Hereford.

To all would-be suicide candidates, SAS selection is hard. There is no other way to say it. I recently read in a book about what makes a ideal candidate for the SAS and I quote: 'The ideal candidate should be intelligent, assertive, happy-go-lucky, self-sufficient and neither extremely intro- not extroverted. He should not be emotionally unstable but rather be a forthright individual who is hard to fool and not dependent on orders.' That is as good a description as any of the typical SAS soldier that I served with. It is what makes the SAS so unique: a whole bunch of individuals with the capacity to act as one.

Anyway, I finished up in Hereford. SAS selection is certainly not easy, in fact it is almost downright impossible. Out of 140-odd starters, thirteen of us finished up wearing the famous winged dagger. Thereafter life really started. Real adventurous training and operations came in one continuous surge and I was happy doing what I had always wanted – being a soldier. Which brings me to my one pet hate. When people find out you are an SAS soldier, they all ask the same stupid question: 'Have you ever killed anybody?' I mean, what do they want me to say? 'Yes, thousands, and it was really enjoyable' – get real! Being in the SAS is just a profession. Different from most, I will grant you, but still it is essentially a job. I always wanted to be a soldier and, as with any other profession, I discovered that there are different levels of professionalism. For me, being in the SAS was the pinnacle of achievement. And it wasn't easy. I worked hard getting fit enough to go on selection. When I had passed, I worked even harder at improving my SAS skills and took pleasure in my achievements. Such is the nature of SAS operations that they require high standards from each individual soldier to carry them out. It is this emphasis on individuality that makes the SAS so unique and it helps to explain why I wanted to be a member.

During those SAS years I worked alongside many brave men whose names you will never hear. So as a mark of respect to the many who do not make the headlines I have included a few of their stories in this book in the hope that the reader will get a better understanding of what the SAS is truly like.

2. LIEUTENANT COLONEL DAVID STIRLING

David Stirling was a Scottish laird and the founding father of the SAS. He was a man with a vision, a man who became a legend.

Before the Second World War, David Stirling, as an adventurous young man, had trained to climb Everest. He was a tall man, standing some six feet, five inches in height, who conducted himself with an air of great calmness. In 1940 Stirling joined the Scots Guards as a subaltern but soon volunteered for 8 Commando, named 'Layforce' after its commander, Captain Robert Laycock. Believing that a small band of dedicated men could operate successfully behind the enemy lines, Stirling managed to present his plan to General Richie, who at the time was Deputy Chief of Staff. Stirling's memorandum in which he set out his idea finally reached the Commander-in-Chief of British forces in the Middle East, General later Field Marshal Auchinleck, and the SAS was born.

As the founder of the SAS, Stirling's main strength came from his ability to select and enlist those men who had both daring and vision, such as Paddy Mayne and Jock Lewes. Lewes, an Australian by birth, was a powerful and energetic man: it was said that he could march fifty kilometres in a night and survive in the heat of a desert day on just one water bottle. He is also credited with originating the SAS motto 'Who Dares Wins', but unfortunately he was killed in December 1941 when his jeep convoy was strafed by a Messerschmitt Bf110.

David Stirling has been quoted as saying, 'We believe, as did the ancient Greeks who originated the word "Aristocracy", that every man with the right attitude and talents, regardless of birth and riches, has a capacity in his own lifetime of reaching that status in its true sense. In fact, in our SAS context, an individual soldier might prefer to go on serving as an NCO rather than leave the regiment in order to obtain an Officer's commission. All ranks in the SAS are of "one company" in which a sense of class is both alien and ludicrous.'

The first SAS raid was part of Operation Crusader and took place on 17 November 1941. This operation, devised by General Claude Auchinleck, was intended to evict General Rommel, commander of the Afrika Korps, from Cyrenaica. 'Crusader' was the largest armoured operation to be undertaken by British forces at this time. The role of the SAS was to raid the airfields at Tmimi and Gazala.

L Detachment was divided into five aircraft – provided by 216 Squadron – whose SAS 'cargoes' were commanded by David Stirling, Paddy Mayne, Eoin McGonigal, Jock Lewes and Lieutenant Bonnington respectively. The aircraft took off from Bagoush airfield on the night of the 16/17 November but navigation was hampered by strong winds and the planes encountered heavy flak. The actual drop was disastrous, with the men being scattered over a wide area on landing and several injuries being sustained – Stirling himself was knocked unconscious. One of the aircraft actually landed on a German airfield, resulting in the crew's and SAS men's deaths. The mission was abandoned as a result, individual soldiers having to make their own way to a pre-arranged rendezvous with the Long-Range Desert Group (LRDG). Only 22 of the 64 men dropped made it successfully. Luckily for Stirling, much of Operation Crusader was plagued with difficulties and those in high positions of command had little time to analyse individual failures. However, the problems encountered on this first mission prompted a radical rethink about transporting troops to their targets on future SAS missions.

The next SAS raid was carried out on the German airfield at Agheila and Sirte on 6 December. Stirling sent a small party, led by Captain Lewes, to Agheila while he and Paddy Mayne attacked targets at Sirte and nearby Tamet. Lewes and his party were transported by the LRDG to a point some twenty miles from the target from where they approached it on foot. The airfield proved to be abandoned. However, some success was achieved when the frustrated raiding party came across a large number of Italian vehicles at Mersa Brega near a roadhouse, which they destroyed. Jock Lewes used a captured Italian truck, complete with machine-gun mounted on the back, to shoot up the roadhouse.

Stirling and the rest of his men were flown to the Gialo oasis from where the LRDG transported them to their targets. Sirte, which was recced by Stirling, proved to be abandoned but Mayne had better luck, destroying some 24 aircraft. From there on in the luck of the SAS changed and successive raids with the aid of the LRDG proved extremely fruitful.

In January 1942 Benghazi fell to the British, an event which led David Stirling to believe that Bouerat, a port on the North African coast some three hundred miles to the west, would become the new supply centre for the Afrika Korps. He therefore decided to mount a raid against the port to blow up shipping in the harbour. Stirling and twelve SAS men, accompanied by two Special Boat Section personnel and transported by the Long-Range Desert Group, set off on 17 January. The navigator was Mike Sadler and the LRDG commander was Captain Hunter. Their equipment included a collapsible canoe that they intended to use to plant bombs on the ships.

The first stage of the journey involved a trip to the Wadi Tamit. All the vehicles were overloaded with supplies, and once at the wadi the trucks had to be manhandled down the rock-strewn defile. However, they were spotted by an Italian aircraft and the convoy was dispersed to lessen the risk of losses once enemy fighter-bombers appeared. The wireless truck and its crew disappeared, but Stirling decided to carry on with the mission. Once they were sixty miles from Bouerat, the raiding party loaded into just one truck – sixteen SAS and SBS and four LRDG personnel – and headed off for the target. However, the truck carrying the party ran into a gully during the journey and the canoe, which was wedged between the soldiers, was damaged. Undeterred, they carried on and entered the port on the night of 23 January. They split into small groups and moved cautiously towards the waterfront.

To their surprise the raiders found that there were no enemy sentries around the town – and, unfortunately, no shipping in the harbour. The SAS did manage to blow up a number of warehouses, petrol tankers and the harbour radio station before retreating with no losses. By this time Rommel had launched an offensive that would push the British Eighth Army back to the Egyptian border. This meant that Jalo had to be evacuated, which meant Stirling's party had to strike for Siwa, another oasis but two hundred miles further to the east. This was reached without too much hazard.

On another occasion David Stirling, accompanied by Sergeants Johnny Cooper and Reg Seekings, led a series of raids on Benina, a major aircraft-repair base. On the first two occasions, they found the base deserted, but in June 1942 they achieved success. During an RAF bombing raid on Benghazi, they once again made their way past the enemy sentries and succeeded in placing Lewes bombs (so named after Jack Lewes, their inventor) on a number of aircraft, some new aircraft engines in crates and some machinery. As a *coup de grâce*, Stirling attacked the enemy guardroom with grenades as he and his men withdrew. On reaching the rendezvous with the LRDG, he met the patrols of Captain Paddy Mayne and Lieutenant Andre Zirnheld, who had attacked Berka Satellite and Berka Main airfields respectively.

Not content with the results achieved that night, however, Stirling decided to mount a further raid on the area. On the following night, accompanied by Captain Mayne's patrol and a number of other individuals, he drove down the escarpment in a borrowed LRDG vehicle towards Benina. Having bluffed their way through a German checkpoint, Stirling and his party encountered a number of Italian troops who opened fire but couldn't stop the SAS vehicle as it sped on. Shortly afterwards, a number of enemy vehicles were spotted by a filling station. These soon had Lewes bombs planted on them. By now the entire area was alive with enemy troops and Stirling decided to withdraw.

Heading across the desert, successfully avoiding enemy patrols despatched to intercept them, the SAS men succeeded in reaching Djebel Akhdar. As they reached the top of the wadi that led up the escarpment, however, Corporal Bob Lilley spotted that the pencil fuse of one of the remaining Lewes bombs was burning. Thanks to his split-second warning, all the occupants of the vehicle succeeded in baling out from the vehicle, which was blown to bits a few seconds later. Stirling and his men thus had to complete the journey to the rendezvous with the LRDG on foot.

By June 1942 the problem of constantly relying on the LRDG was overcome when David Stirling managed to acquire and assemble twenty three-ton trucks and fifteen newly arrived American Willy's jeeps. The latter were soon 'married' to the Vickers-K (a machine-gun, several of which were found abandoned in a disused RAF hangar). The combination produced formidable firepower mounted on a robust and reliable platform, resulting in a highly effective mobile fighting machine. The Vickers-K was originally designed for aircraft and would fire a mixture of ball, tracer and armour-piercing ammunition. These jeep/machine-gun hybrids proved their worth during the raids carried out by the SAS. Stirling himself greatly preferred to travel in his 'Blitz Buggy', a much-battered staff car he shared with Corporal (later to become Colonel) Cooper and Corporal Seeking. The 'Blitz Buggy' was a Ford V-8 staff car modified for SAS desert operations. The roof and windows had been removed. Armed with a Vickers-K machine-gun in the front, and twin guns in the rear, it was also equipped with a long-range fuel tank, sun compass and radiator condenser. Painted in the drab desert camouflage of the Afrika Korps, it always sported the current air-recognition decal on the bonnet. The vehicle was used on several missions, including two forays into Benghazi.

Not long after, on the night of 7 July 1942, both Stirling and Mayne were active again, this time targeting the airfield at Bagoush. After an overland approach in vehicles, the initial attack on the airfield was carried out by a group of four men under Captain Mayne while Major Stirling established a roadblock nearby to intercept and attack any enemy vehicles. Lewes bombs were placed on a total of forty aircraft but only twenty exploded, because of faulty primers. A further fourteen aircraft were then attacked and destroyed by the whole force mounted in Major Stirling's Blitz Buggy and in three jeeps, each vehicle armed with twin Vickers-K machine-guns. Major Stirling and his men then withdrew without loss. Unfortunately, Stirling's Blitz Buggy met an untimely end in the aftermath of the raid on Bagoush airfield. During the raid the Blitz Buggy, accompanied by two jeeps, had led the way over the airfield, its Vickers guns and those of the jeeps setting aircraft ablaze. On the morning after, however, as the SAS were withdrawing to a rendezvous, the three vehicles were spotted by two Italian aircraft which attacked, destroying the Blitz Buggy and one of the jeeps.

On 26 July 1942 the SAS raided Airfield 12 at Sidi Haneish in the Fuka region of North Africa. This particular landing strip was usually crammed with a variety of German aircraft. Under cover of darkness, David Stirling led eighteen jeeps from their hideout across the desert towards the airfield. As always, Sadler, one of Stirling's soldiers who possessed an uncanny knack for directional accuracy, did the navigation. Finally Sadler stopped the column, indicating that they were very close to their target. The area seemed extremely quiet and almost deserted, when suddenly the runway lights lit up the whole area.

At first the SAS thought they had been detected but the noise of an approaching aircraft indicated the real reason for the sudden illumination. It was a moment of opportunity and Stirling gave the order to attack. The unit split into two columns, each of nine jeeps, commanded by George Jellicoe and Paddy Mayne with Stirling at the head. Onto the airfield they drove with a total of 68 guns blazing. The parked aircraft were riddled with gunfire, many of them bursting into flame. At one stage the flames became so hot that many in the columns suffered singed facial hair. Stirling's jeep was hit and he was forced to abandon it and climb into another. Then, as quickly as it had begun, the SAS raid ended and the jeeps left the airfield, disappearing into the desert night. In just a few short minutes they had destroyed forty aircraft. The SAS casualities were light, with the loss of only one man and two jeeps. The column split up into smaller groups and made their way back to the rendezvous, burying their fallen comrade along the way.

By November 1942 David Stirling, with B Squadron, was operating in an area called Zem Zem located south-east of Tripoli. Their task was to try and badger enemy forces as the Eighth Army advanced west after the battle of El Alamein. At this time the SAS depot was at Benghazi, though B Squadron's forward base was situated at El Fascia.

By 13 December the squadron had a total of 24 jeeps and was in place and ready for action. At the same time a squadron headed by Major Paddy Mayne was operating along the road between Agheila and Bouerat. Unfortunately for Stirling's men the area was full of enemy soldiers and the locals were hostile. In a couple of days most of the patrols were captured or killed.

Compared to the SAS's earlier successes, its operations in Tunisia were disappointing. This wasn't really surprising because German and Italian forces were being squeezed into very small pockets of territory by US and British forces. Consequently, the SAS had to operate in a pretty small area. The reason that so many jeep-mounted patrols, including that of David Stirling at Gabes Gap, encountered difficulties was that the countryside was filled with columns of retreating Axis forces.

Stirling had navigated through Gabes Gap, having completed his recce, when his party of five jeeps was spotted by a German reconnaissance aircraft. Thinking that the German pilot would radio for ground support his patrol hid in a shallow bush-covered wadi just off the Gafsa road. Stirling and several of his fourteen men were taken prisoner, but their German captors were inexperienced and Stirling managed to escape. Unfortunately he was betrayed by an Arab and recaptured by an Italian unit. He was sent to an Italian prison at Gavi from which he escaped at least four times. This resulted in his transfer to the notorious German prison fortress of Colditz where he waited out the rest of the war.

Stirling's career after the war was almost as flamboyant as his wartime activities and a detailed account would fill several books. In 1984 the new SAS barracks was completed on the site of the old Bradbury Lines in Hereford and was officially opened and renamed Stirling Lines. David Stirling did the honours himself and the day ranks as one of the best get-togethers in the regiment's history. In 1990 he was knighted for his services. Sadly, Sir David Stirling died in the same year.

3. LIEUTENANT COLONEL BLAIR 'PADDY' MAYNE

Paddy Mayne was one of Stirling's first recruits into the SAS. The nickname 'Paddy' was due to his Irish ancestry, and before the war he was well known for his accomplishments in the world of sport. In battle he possessed qualities of leadership that set him apart from most men. His reputation was based on his personal bravery, which at times was characterised as reckless and wild – although this 'recklessness' got him credited with the destruction of more enemy aircraft than any Allied airman.

Stirling invited Mayne to join the newly formed L Detachment SAS Brigade at its formation in July 1941. He proved to be a valuable asset, playing a large part in missions in North Africa, and later, after Stirling's capture, taking over as Commanding Officer and overseeing the SAS's operations in Europe.

In March 1942 Captain Paddy Mayne mounted an operation involving a number of attacks on Benghazi and the airfields in the area, with Berka Satellite field being the objective of a four-man patrol that he led personally. The other members were Corporals Bennett and Rose, and Private Byrne. Travelling with an LRDG patrol via the Siwa Oasis, Mayne and his men arrived at Djebel Akhdar from where they could observe the area of coastal plain on which Benghazi and the airfields were located. Under cover of darkness on the following night, they left the wadi in which they had been lying up and made their way down the escarpment to their target. Moving on to the airfield, they placed Lewes bombs on fifteen aircraft, a number of fuel dumps and twelve large bombs, before withdrawing and making their way during the rest of the night to a rendezvous where they were collected by the LRDG.

Another raid on the Berka airfields took place on 13 June 1942. This coincided with a raid on Berka Satellite by the RAF whose bombers arrived overhead as Mayne, accompanied by Corporals Lilley and Warburton and Private Storey, was moving across the airfield towards some aircraft. There was little they could do but seek what little cover there was on the airfield until the raid was over. With the enemy on full alert, Mayne withdrew after planting some bombs on a fuel dump. Avoiding enemy patrols already scouring the area, he led his men to the rendezvous with the LRDG where he also met Major David Stirling who attacked a nearby aircraft-repair base at Benina. Also at the rendezvous was Captain Zirnheld and a patrol of L Detachment's Free French troop that had attacked Berka Main, destroying eleven aircraft.

The success of the new unit led to its expansion and its renaming as 1st SAS Regiment (1 SAS). Mayne was given A Squadron to command, and for his accomplishments on the battlefield was awarded the DSO. On 29 November 1942 Mayne established his new base in the wadi at Bir Zalten, sixty miles south of enemy positions at Agheila. Its task was to attack enemy transport on the road between Agheila and Bouerat and it proceeded to do so, mounting some sixteen raids a week at night and thus forcing the enemy to use the road by day. Vehicles were attacked, telegraph poles blown down and the road mined or cratered.

Such was the effect of these operations that the Germans were forced to divert troops to carry out operations against the SAS. In some respects this stepped-up German activity was partly responsible for the capture of David Stirling on 27 January 1943. Mayne was promoted to Lieutenant Colonel and assumed command of the regiment. In July and August 1943 both the Special Raiding Squadron (SRS) – 1 SAS temporarily renamed – and 2 SAS were party to the Allied capture of Sicily. The SRS successfully assaulted Capo Murro di Porco first, followed by Augusta two days later.

On 4 September 1943 the Special Raiding Squadron (SRS) landed at Bagnara, north of the Straits of Messina that the Eighth Army had crossed from Sicily on the previous day prior to landing in the area of Reggio. The SRS had been tasked with cutting lines of communication in the enemy's rear.

The squadron met little opposition in the area of Bagnara itself but soon came under artillery and mortar fire from German units in the surrounding hills. It took up positions to block any enemy counter-attack and held the town for three days until the arrival of leading elements of the Eighth Army that had advanced from Reggio. Casualties suffered were five killed and seventeen wounded. Shortly after being relieved by the Green Howards, the squadron withdrew to Sicily prior to embarking on another mission.

Following its operation at Bagnara in September 1943, the SRS was then tasked with the capture of Termoli to aid the Eighth Army's breaking of the German Termoli Line north of Bari, codenamed Operation Devon. The SRS was part of a combined force that also included two Commando teams and various support units. The 207-strong SRS sailed from Monfredonia in a large landing craft on 2 October and arrived off Termoli the following morning. After No. 3

Commando had seized the beach, the SRS went in using smaller landing craft.

The Germans were occupying the surrounding countryside, and very soon a series of small battles developed. Paddy Mayne pulled his men back into the town that evening, by which time Roy Farran and twenty soldiers from 2 SAS had also arrived at Termoli.

The next day was quiet, with troops from the 78th Division arriving and the Commandos taking their leave. It was the lull before the storm, for on 5 October the Germans launched a strong counter-attack. Mayne and his men plugged the gaps in the line as the enemy tried to retake Termoli. During the savage action a shell hit an SAS lorry, killing eighteen men. The fighting, which went on through the night and into the following day, was particularly heavy around the cemetery and beside the railway line. The landing of the Irish Brigade in the harbour tipped the scales in favour of the British and the town was eventually secured. It was a sobering experience for the SRS and turned out to be the unit's last action in Italy.

Upon returning to England in March 1944, the SRS was changed again. Once more it was expanded and its title returned to its former designation of 1 SAS. The Regiment saw further action in France, Scandinavia, the Low Countries and Germany, all with Lieutenant Colonel Paddy Mayne at the helm. One such action was Operation Howard, a jeep-mounted SAS probing exploration involving B and C Squadrons, 1 SAS.

The party left Tilbury on 6 April 1945 and arrived at Nijmegen in Holland the next day. Mayne's task was to carry out reconnaissance ahead of the Canadian 4th Armoured Division towards Oldenburg in north-west Germany. There were forty jeeps in all, travelling in two columns, though the going was slow through terrain containing many rivers and dykes. During the advance B Squadron was caught in an enemy ambush, and it was during this action that Mayne won his fourth DSO. Though managing to fight their way out of one ambush, the 'Howard' party soon found itself being ambushed again and again. Major Bond, a member of 1 SAS, who, under Colonel Mayne, commanded B Squadron, died during the advance towards Oldenburg.

The operation, which meant confronting stiff German resistance with relatively lightly armed jeep troops, was not a normal SAS task and several times they ran into serious trouble. Major Bond and his driver, Trooper Lewis, were both killed attacking a German position near Borgerwald. The main problem arose from the speed at which the SAS jeeps could move forward in advance of the Canadian Sherman tanks. In reality jeeps moving at any speed offered little protection against fortified German positions for their SAS occupants. The problem was resolved when Mayne halted, waiting for the Canadians to catch up.

The steady toll of casualties forced the SAS soldiers to pull back to refit. It was soon clear that the mission could not continue and so, after reaching Oldenburg on 3 May, the SAS soldiers were withdrawn to Belgium. 'Howard' was one of those operations that were only partially successful: there were too many enemy troops concentrated into a small area. Stories of Paddy Mayne abound and are too numerous to mention in a single volume. Needless to say, this phenomenal soldier led the SAS until the end of the war by which time he had added two more bars to his DSO. The SAS was disbanded on 1 October 1945 and Mayne soon found himself demobilised and having to return to civilian life again. He was killed in a traffic accident in Newtownards, Northern Ireland on 15 December 1955.

4. SERGEANT 'GEORDIE' BARKER

Geordie Barker was one of the funniest and best-loved characters ever to join the SAS, and like so many of his peers his deeds were not trumpeted by some sensational media headline. Geordie joined the SAS from the Royal Engineers, passing selection in 1968. He was posted to G Squadron, Air Troop where he became a free-fall expert – and a man who could raise everyone's spirits. Between 1971–75 he served with his Squadron through the Oman war as part of the BATT force (British Army Training Team) commitment. During this conflict one of the major problems was to keep the enemy forces, the Adoo, from getting near the edge of the mountain escarpment. From such a vantage point they were able to bombard the town of Salala and the nearby RAF base below. In the end, the only solution was to build a series of small defensive encampments along the escarpment. These positions became known as 'Dianas'.

On one tour Geordie was stationed at Diana 5, a location that came under frequent fire from a small hill some eight hundred metres away. The only weapon the SAS men possessed that could effectively reach such a distance was a .50 calibre Browning heavy machine-gun. To compensate for this shortcoming Geordie decided it was time to use a bit of improvisation. His idea was that we should make a launch ramp out of a wooden pallet and fire five 66mm rockets from it at a 45-degree angle. Given that the effective range of the rockets was around 350 metres, the plan required that the launcher should be carried and secured out in no man's land between the Diana position and the enemy hill. Cutting the fuses and rewiring them to one central electrical detonator would make it possible to launch all the rockets, using a single control wire back at the Diana 5 position.

The launch ramp was completed. Under cover of darkness Geordie and a friend named Barry walked out to a spot where the Adoo position was in range and set up the rocket apparatus. Of course, there was always the chance that the Adoo would spot the rockets, come down, dismantle the launcher and then turn the missiles against the Diana position. To prevent this, Barry set up several jumping mines around the launch site. The mines were particularly nasty bits of ordnance because, when triggered, they would pop up out of the ground attached to a cord. The cord was only waist-high in length and once it had reached its limit it would pull out the safety pin, instantly detonating the mine. The resulting damage to a nearby human body was devastating. And, to make matters worse, the mines Barry was using were old and therefore rather unreliable. It was a tense, nerve-racking job, removing the safety bolts.

Barry had just finished removing all the bolts, thus arming the mines, when Geordie put his torch directly in Barry's face and switched it on.

'Can you see OK?' he said jokingly to Barry who instantly lost his night vision. Not a desirable situation when surrounded by a whole mess of armed and extremely dangerous mines.

'I saw this First World War movie once where guys were blind and they had to put their hands on the shoulders of the man in front to be led through a minefield. So come on, I'll save your life,' Geordie said, grinning.

Despite the situation, Barry had to laugh. It was Geordie's way of creating a joke, one which he would be able to tell many times over: how he, Geordie, had led his friend from the minefield – not bothering to mention that he had caused the temporary blindness in the first place.

Some weeks later, while in the base camp on R&R (rest and recuperation), Geordie related the story of the rocket ramp in great detail. By all accounts, the enemy had turned up at the hill and started firing, at which point every man in the Diana 5 position had tried to pull the firing lever that Geordie had devised to launch the rockets. Geordie got there first. The rockets went off, smashing into the hill in a blaze of glory. Two of the Adoo were killed and the rest driven away, never to return.

Years later, on a day in March 1978, Aldo Moro, the leading Italian Christian Democrat politician, was attacked in his car while driving down a busy street. The car was stopped by a blockade before gunmen opened fire with their automatic weapons, killing Moro's bodyguards. The attackers were members of the Red Brigades (*Brigate Rosse*), extreme left-wing Italian terrorist groups. They took Moro and held him hostage for 54 days, all the time making demands of the Italian government. The demands were always refused. Realising they were not going to get anywhere, the terrorists executed Moro with a shot to the head. His body was eventually found on 10 May, dumped in the boot of a car in a Rome street.

While the so-called guerrillas were holding Moro, the Italian authorities decided on a crackdown on terrorist activity. Raids were mounted on Red Brigade safe houses, suspected terrorists were arrested and much ammunition and weaponry was seized. However, the Italian counter-terrorist agencies found nothing that would tell them where Moro was. By a coincidence, during this time a four-man SAS team was in Italy trying to gather information on the Red Brigades. Geordie Barker and his friend Barry were two of the team members. Obviously, in the interests of security, no operational details about their task can be given, but what happened to them vividly illustrates what can occur when there is a lack of communication between intelligence services.

On this particular occasion, the SAS men had been led to a small hut on the side of a wooded hill. It was a safe house used by the Red Brigades and it was thought that some contact might be made. The SAS men usually only moved around at night, but on that morning they were late and were spotted in the early dawn by an over-vigilant villager. Suspicious of their motives, the villager called the police. At around ten in the morning, the SAS men had just settled down to get some sleep when the door burst open to reveal a fat, sweating *carabiniere* (policeman) waving a pistol. He seemed as surprised to see them as they were to see him. As the SAS men jumped to their feet, all the policeman could manage was a muttered 'Good morning. What are you doing here?' – all spoken in Italian.

The men, not being able to speak Italian, replied in English. This, as well as the scene around the hut – sleeping bags and half-eaten food – seemed to unnerve the policeman. He ran for the door and back down the hill. Not thinking much of it, the SAS men had a laugh and then went back to sleep.

Two hours later, Geordie went outside the hut, needing to relieve himself. He wasn't gone long before he burst back into the room, announcing that there were armed policemen surrounding the hut. Upon hearing this, the rest of the men went outside to take a look and were met by a hail of bullets from more than one sub-machine gun. Instinct took over and they all made a run for it, not stopping until they had put as much space between them and the armed policemen as they possibly could. Once they were clear, the SAS soldiers made contact with their controllers and were quickly placed in a safe house and from there returned to England. The breakdown in communication between the Italian intelligence groups had almost cost them their lives.

Before returning to England the four were held in a storeroom for security. After several days this became a bit much for them and the SAS men demanded to be let out on the town for a couple of hours. It was agreed, however, that they were to leave in twos and return very quietly so as not to blow the cover of the safe house supplied by the Italian agency responsible for the SAS operation.

Needless to say, Geordie and Barry paired up and left the building, making it not further than the first bar a hundred metres away. Within the hour Geordie was drunk and insisting that British footballers were brilliant and the Italians crap. He proceeded to give a demonstration of ball control with a plastic football. So funny was his act that the Italians gathered in the bar bought Geordie and Barry beer all night. Some hours later the pair staggered back to the safe house, singing 'Just one cornetto' at the top of their voices.

Sadly, Geordie Barker died in Oman, not from a bullet but when his parachute failed to open. It was a great blow for everyone, and Barry, in particular, found his friend's death difficult to come to terms with. Geordie is often in Barry's thoughts and now Barry continues to tell the tales of the rocket ramp and the rest of Geordie's antics. Those who remember Geordie's catlike grin and wicked sense of humour will think of him not just for his work in the SAS but for his effect on the human race. Without doubt the world would profit greatly if we had a few more Geordie Barkers.

5. SERGEANT PETER TOWNSEND (PSEUDONYM)

Pete arrived in Hereford in December 1986 and joined the ranks of 22 SAS where, for the duration of his service, he was a member of A Squadron's Mobility Troop. While Pete is chosen as the main character of this chapter purely because he actually killed the first Iraqi of the ground war in the Gulf, it must be remembered that this operation involved half a Squadron of SAS who were deployed behind the Iraqi lines for the entire duration of the Gulf War. All of the names used here are pseudonyms since many of those concerned are still serving with the SAS.

Their story started in earnest when the half-squadron slipped quietly over the border into Iraq. The patrol, consisting of eight heavily armed Land Rovers and a UNIMOG (Universal Motor Gerat), plus a number of motorcycles, pushed slowly forward into the barren landscape. They moved during the hours of darkness, lay hidden under camouflage during the day and met no resistance.

A week later, they had progressed one hundred kilometres into hostile territory without being detected by the Iraqis. The senior members of the mobility troop were on the bikes, giving the newer members time to get used to the difficult driving conditions.

These conditions were not what the SAS men had been led to anticipate by their intelligence briefings. Expecting a desert area to be always hot, they had dressed in thin clothes. However, the Iraqi desert at this time of year was proving to be cold. Bitterly cold. Exposed skin began to suffer, crack, and show signs of frostbite. To make matters worse, the raw flesh began to get infected and painful. The terrain wasn't much better than the climate: there were no sand dunes, only bare, flat, hard ground, rocks and ravines. Cover was just about non-existent.

Early one morning, the patrol found a place to lie up for the day. As usual, the location wasn't ideal but it was better than nothing. The vehicles were covered up with overhead camouflage nets and the men prepared to spend the rest of the day either sleeping, mending kit or cleaning weapons. Apart from the sporadic clank of a spoon against a mess tin or the occasional low mumble of voices, the camp was silent.

Suddenly there came the low rumble of a powerful motor. A vehicle was moving towards them. Heads looked up, trying to locate the sound as the sentry frantically signalled that the enemy was approaching. Men ran around in a state of organised chaos, grabbing weapons and finding good firing positions as the Iraqi truck, a Gaz 69, drew closer. Despite the camouflage nets that concealed the vehicles from aircraft overhead, the column still stuck out like a sore thumb on the ground. It was obvious the Iraqis had spotted them since the truck was driving directly for the camp. The SAS men, crouched behind their weapons, silently watched and waited.

The vehicle finally stopped twenty metres away. From the behaviour of the driver and the other men on board, they had mistaken the patrol's camp for one occupied by friendly forces, not thinking that hostile troops could be this close to Baghdad. The driver and the man beside him got out. The driver walked around to the front of his vehicle and opened up the bonnet. The other man, smart and with the ubiquitous Middle Eastern style of moustache, kept on walking towards the patrol's position. He wore a blue beret with an eagle's emblem on it and the insignia of a captain. It wasn't until later that the men of the patrol found out that, in fact, he had the authority of a lieutenant colonel or of an even higher rank.

As the Iraqi got nearer, one of the men from the patrol, Mel, decided that a welcome was in order. Telling the others to cover him, he walked out from under the camouflage net, his weapon held to his side away from the Iraqi's line of vision. The Iraqi officer looked bewildered but it wasn't until the men stood three metres from each other that he realised he had come face to face with an enemy. Mel immediately brought his rifle up and fired. Nothing happened. As Mel dropped to his knees to clear his gun's blockage, one of the others, Pete, was able to line up the Iraqi in his sights. Pete fired and the man fell to the ground, dead. Pete didn't know it at the time, but his shot had just initiated the first ground contact of the entire Operation Desert Storm. The first kill of the conflict was down to Pete.

A battle erupted around them as bullets flew both ways, some coming from the back of the Iraqi vehicle. Obviously there were some more soldiers there, although the number was unknown. In the hail of fire, the driver was killed almost immediately and the back of the truck was riddled with bullet holes. In the uneasy lull that followed, a few men from the patrol ran forward to check out the back of the truck. Mel pulled out a man who was seriously injured, the biggest wound being just above his hip. He had been lying on the floor of the truck in such a way that the pressure had held back any bleeding. Now that Mel had dragged him out, blood spurted from his wound in an arc of two to three metres. Obviously a bullet had hit a main artery. Mel let him slump back down onto the floor, his knees underneath and his backside stuck incongruously in the air. Remarkably, despite his injuries he was still alive. But he was obviously dying.

The only other surviving Iraqi soldier was hysterically begging Sam, another member of the patrol, for mercy. Sam managed to hold the half-crazed man against the side of the truck with one hand whilst also pushing a rifle into his face. This soon shut the man up and he was quickly hauled off to the Officer Commanding's (OC) wagon to be interrogated by two of the patrol's interpreters. The whole incident had taken seconds from start to finish. The rest of the camp suddenly erupted into chaos: men who had previously been asleep were now out of their sleeping bags and wondering what the hell was going on.

The badly wounded Iraqi was taking a long time to die; the sounds coming out of his mouth were those of mortal agony. Slowly slipping from this world, he began to lose control of his bodily functions: the stench of urine and faeces rose from his trousers. Mel rolled the man over and checked him for weapons and any maps that could be of use, but apart from a pistol there was nothing of value. Pete wanted to put the dying man out of his misery but this was not allowed: it was decided to leave the Iraqi to die in his own time.

Meanwhile, under interrogation, the prisoner was telling everything he knew. He didn't even need much persuasion; he was just glad to be alive. He told them that there were about three thousand Iraqi soldiers heading for the patrol's position. And they were not far away, either. Everyone got stuck into packing up, throwing the cammo nets into the backs of the wagons before grabbing hold of bergens and ammo boxes. It was time to make a quick exit.

Then another problem came to light. It appeared that the OC was losing it in the stress of the moment. He dithered about what should be done before finally settling on getting back over the border. Although this seemed a sensible option on the surface, most of the men thought it strange. After all, killing Iraqis was what they were in Iraq for and one little contact shouldn't be allowed to scupper the whole mission. All that was necessary was to retreat to a place where they wouldn't be as easily discovered. However, it was the OC's decision and the others had no choice but to go along with it.

Before they set off, the bodies needed to be disposed of. Some of the men tried to dig a hole, but got no further down than six inches before hitting solid rock. Making the best of a bad job, they laid the bodies in and covered them up as well as they could; even so, limbs still stuck out of the ground like a macabre new crop. Needless to say, this was not good. The men were on a deniable mission and leaving dead bodies around would soon give away the sort of Allied soldiers that were on Iraqi soil. When the OC saw the shallow grave, he demanded that the bodies be dug up again and placed in the back of the Gaz 69. Getting someone to drive the Gaz, dead bodies and all, was, surprisingly, no problem. A volunteer put himself forward immediately. This was not so much a case of dedication to duty but rather an astute realisation that the truck had a cab and a heater – a smart move when the air temperature hovered around freezing point.

The dead bodies and the mortally wounded man were thrown into the back of the truck. Meanwhile, the OC was panicking about which way to go. Eventually Pete made the decision for him, deciding that they should head east for about ten kilometres, then south before finally turning west to box their last position. The POW was bagged, tagged and thrown on to the UNIMOG before, finally, forty minutes after the contact, the convoy moved off. The move was done in such a rush, however, that they nearly left behind the two men on sentry duty. On hearing the vehicles' engines, they came flying down from their positions, convinced they were about to be left. It was lucky they did.

As planned, the column headed east. Darkness was falling and it seemed lights from columns of Iraqi trucks and tanks were everywhere. At least avoiding the road meant that the patrol could stay far away enough from the enemy so that, in the dim light, they looked just like them. The cold grew more intense, made worse by the occasional rain and the wet clothes acted to increase the chill factor, creating another danger for the men: hypothermia.

After a while, somebody spotted something strange through his PNGs (passive night goggles). This was checked by using the sight of a Milan weapon with its greater powers of magnification. What the patrol saw was a small group of Iraqi soldiers about one hundred metres directly in front of them. They were in full battle order, carrying weapons and equipment, but walked with their heads down, not alert to anything around them. Behind were a number of vehicles but they were too far away to be identified properly.

Not wanting to risk another contact, the patrol quickly turned and headed in another direction. This happened more than once, but after a while the men realised that none of the Iraqis they encountered seemed to notice them. The patrol probably looked just like another Iraqi column going about its legitimate business.

At approximately midnight, the column found a place to hide up. It was a depression in the ground, large enough to allow the vehicles to turn around, and it also had a good escape route in an emergency. The HQ vehicles were placed in the middle of the depression, with the rest on higher ground. A contact report was sent to HQ to relay what had happened and to request further instructions.

Meanwhile, another attempt was made to bury the bodies. By now there was one more: the mortally wounded soldier had, at last, died. The same problem with soil depth was encountered, but here there was more time to make the graves wider and to pile soil and rocks on top. Nevertheless, as before, the OC decided he didn't want the dead Iraqis left there, so once more, now looking a little worse for wear, the bodies had to be dug up and put back into the Gaz 69.

After receiving the contact report, the column moved off once more, continuing south. The intention was to get within 25 kilometres of the border so that a resupply by helicopter could take place. Just before first light the patrol located what seemed to be a disused Scud site. It had good defensive possibilities so the decision was made to lie up there for the day, since moving around in daylight this close to the border was too risky.

The vehicles were set up in their usual positions and the men went through their standard operational procedures: setting sentries; laying anti-tank and anti-personnel mines on approach routes; setting up mortars and camouflaging vehicles. Those tasks done, the men began to clean their weapons before seeing to themselves. Any vehicle maintenance that needed to be done was carried out, the bodies were put into body bags and then the men who weren't on sentry duty got some sleep. Not that there was a great deal to be had: because of the cold, sentries had to be changed more frequently than normal.

The resupply was expected at 04.00 hours but, as was often the case, it happened when it happened. When the men finally heard the distinctive sound of a Chinook helicopter in the distance, they prepared for its arrival, only to have it fly straight past (much to their consternation). As radio silence had to be maintained during the resupply times, no one knew what was happening; they could only hope the helicopter was resupplying another call sign further north first. Some of the men were definitely not amused. They had had to push the Gaz vehicle out to the landing site in readiness for it to be taken away. Now they had to push it all the way back again.

Just as they had begun to give up all hope of a resupply, the Chinook was heard again. It was coming in low and fast, between about ten and twenty feet from the ground.

The ability of RAF pilots to fly at this dangerously low height with only night-vision goggles to help them has always been seen as the best possible evidence of the kind of consummate skill so vital to Special Operations work. The SAS men once more struggled to get the Iraqi vehicle out to the landing site.

As the helicopter landed, its rotors flared. The clouds of dust kicked up by the down draught made contact with the blades, creating a weird blue friction-induced glow – an amazing spectacle, although the noise and glow would have advertised the Allied presence to any hostile force that might have been in the area. Once the helicopter had touched down, its rotors still turning in case it needed to make a quick getaway, the tailgate dropped. A man stood there, in silhouette, but clearly carrying a weapon and a bergen. The SQMS (Squadron Quartermaster Sergeant) jumped off the Chinook and started to organise the resupply – six fifty-gallon oil drums, fourteen days' rations for thirty-six men, ammunition and a large pile of blankets all had to be offloaded. The patrol put their backs into the job, all except for the OC and Mel who were having a conversation with the mystery man on the tailgate. Once the supplies had been dealt with, it was time to get rid of the vehicle, the bodies and the POW. The SQMS shook his head. 'Sorry, we can only take the POW,' he declared.

Seconds later, the men were in for another shock. The OC had been relieved of his command and was on his way back to Hereford and an ignominious end to his career. His replacement, the silhouette on the tailgate, was Brian, the RSM, unfortunately not the most popular man in the Regiment at that time.

So now there were a number of problems to deal with: a sudden change of command, disposing of the Gaz 69 and the bodies, and the resupply. The latter problem was caused by the way in which the new fuel had arrived. The men had been trained to expect the fuel to arrive in jerrycans. Now they had to work out how to refuel nearly two hundred cans from six oil drums with just one handpump. With all hands to the work, the entire resupply operation took one and a half hours.

With that completed, all that was left was to dispose of the vehicle and the bodies; they certainly couldn't be taken any further. Two of the men got their demolitions kit out and placed two anti-tank bar mines fitted with XM122 timers to the truck, one underneath and the other on top. The timers were set, giving the column enough time to get well clear of the area. The truck was then pushed into a nearby ditch and doused with fuel and diesel that hadn't been used. Considering that one bar mine is enough to completely destroy a 56-ton Chieftain tank, it was a certainty that two mines should vaporise the vehicle and its contents without leaving much evidence.

With everything reloaded and refuelled, the column set off again – four vehicles in front, the UNIMOG in the middle and four more vehicles behind. They drove on until nearly dawn, covering 35 kilometres under cover of the night until a lying-up position was found and the men started to camouflage the vehicles. It was just before 05.30 hours.

A couple of minutes later, exactly on time, there was a dull red flash on the horizon in the direction from which the men had just travelled. Seconds later there was a thud as the sound of the explosion finally caught up with the light. At last, the dead Iraqis could rest in peace.

6. MAJOR IAN CROOKE

Major Ian Crooke was a rare exception to the normal type of officer serving with the SAS: he was more at home drinking with the NCOs than in the Officers' Mess. In early August 1981, while most of the nation was still celebrating the wedding of Prince Charles to Lady Diana Spencer, Ian Crooke was acting executive officer at the Hereford base, working under the SAS Commanding Officer, Lieutenant Colonel Michael Rose. As Colonel Rose was spending a few days at home with his family, any demands on the SAS were to be fielded by Major Crooke. So when a call came from the highest levels of government, informing him that the small African country of Gambia, once a British colony, was undergoing a *coup d'état*, Crooke went into action.

From information received, it seemed that the rebels had taken the opportunity to seize power while the country's president, Sir Dawda Jawara, was in London, attending the royal wedding. Such an important occasion had drawn heads of state from all around the world to attend – a wonderful opportunity for any terrorist group to launch an attack.

Upon receiving the call, Crooke immediately contacted Rose to let him know about the situation. At first Rose was keen to go himself, but realised that it would take too long for him to make arrangements for his children. He would also have to be picked up by helicopter to return to base which would all take too much time. Eventually he accepted that he couldn't do the job and asked Crooke to choose a suitable man to accompany him, select whatever weapons and equipment he needed and to get to Gambia as soon as was humanly possible.

Gambia is in west Africa. It is a narrow country that straddles both banks of the Gambia River and is bounded on the west by the Atlantic Ocean and on the remaining three sides by Senegal. The capital city, Banjul, is situated on St Mary's Island, close to the mouth of the Gambia River. The terrain consists of sandy beaches along the coast giving way to low-lying swampy ground along the river valley of the interior.

The coup had been masterminded by a young Marxist called Kukoi Samba Sanyang, the leader of the Gambian Socialist Revolutionary Party. In the local Mandinka language 'Kukoi' means to 'sweep clean' and was a name he had chosen for himself. He had been groomed for the revolt by Colonel Gaddafi of Libya, who had a vision of a confederation of Islamic African states, all under his guidance.

The rebellion broke out on Thursday, 30 July, at 5.00 a.m. Usman Bojang, a former deputy commander of Gambia's three-hundred-strong Police Field Force, managed to persuade the Bakau-based contingent – about a third of the force – to join the coup. These men disarmed the rest of the police, who insisted on remaining loyal to Jawara, and then took over the radio transmitter for Radio Gambia. On the way into Banjul, they freed prisoners from the country's largest prison and gave them weapons liberated from the police armoury. Not long after dawn, Banjul was subjected to widespread riots and looting. Indiscriminate shootings followed and in the next few hours the streets became littered with bodies. Sanyang immediately closed the country's borders, as well as its airport at Yundum. He then issued a proclamation of a dictatorship of the proletariat, charging the overthrown government with corruption, nepotism and injustice.

Europeans and Americans in Gambia, either there because of their work or on holiday, were guided to various places of safety by some of the rebel policemen who, sensibly, saw no gain in the harming of Westerners. One such place was the residence of the ambassador of the United States, Larry G. Piper. He sheltered 123 foreigners, 80 of whom were Americans. Most of the Europeans found sanctuary in the Atlantic Beach Hotel on the edge of the city. Even this place was not entirely safe: during the riots, two armed looters raided the hotel safe, taking the manager hostage. As they ran from the hotel, gunshots were heard. A short while later, the two looters were found, dead, in the lobby. As there was every chance more looters would attack them, the hotel 'guests' planned to defend themselves as best they could. They organised around-the-clock sentries and posted 'guards' armed with fire extinguishers.

Meanwhile, Jawara tried to take control of the situation as best he could from London. He telephoned his vice-president, who was being protected by loyal troops in the police headquarters in Banjul, to find out what exactly was going on. He then managed to control all news of what was happening in Gambia by allowing himself to be interviewed by the press. In this way he was able to downplay the whole situation and the full truth of the coup, including what was happening to the foreigners, never reached the world at large. If it had done so, the incident would have become more serious, giving further credibility to the rebels. Leaving for Dakar, the capital of Senegal, on a private jet, it looked as if Jawara was going back to retake control of his country.

By now, Crooke and another SAS soldier, Sergeant Tony Mayers (not his real name), had assembled the weapons and equipment they thought they'd need and were preparing to leave for Gambia. They had chosen to take with them Heckler and Koch sub-machine guns, Browning 9mm automatic pistols and a supply of ammunition and grenades. The first flight available was an Air France commercial flight to Dakar and, casually dressed, Crooke and Mayers joined the rest of the passengers, mostly reporters and television crews. However, in their bags they carried their arsenal of weapons, walking through check-in and Customs without being detected. This was not unusual. Even if they had been stopped, most airport anti-terrorist teams would only need to make a few phone calls and then all the normal channels would be ignored.

Crooke's and Mayers's first problem came when they arrived in Senegal. British diplomats there refused to allow them to get involved with the coup, despite British Prime Minister Margaret Thatcher's wishes. Officials in both Dakar and Banjul considered that the SAS men's presence would only serve to make matters even more dangerous, especially for the trapped British citizens. Banjul officials also wanted to let the Senegalese army handle the problem on its own. That way, if they succeeded they could be cheered and if they failed they could be admonished.

Deciding to ignore the British officials, Crooke arranged to get a couple of seats on the next plane bound for Gambia's Yundum airport, which had now been reopened. Having landed, they were met by Lieutenant Colonel Abdourah-man N'Gom, the Senegalese paratroop commander. By his side was a six-foot-six retired SAS major, Clive Lee. Lee had been out in Gambia, working as a civilian adviser to the Gambian Pioneer Corps, training youths in rural areas in agriculture and construction. When he heard about the coup on the radio, in true SAS style he gathered together 23 of the Pioneer Corps, armed them and set off for the capital.

To get there they had to cross the Gambia River, the problem being that ferry services had been suspended. Not having time to mess around, the retired major, in his own inimitable style, soon persuaded the ferryman to take them across. Once on the other side, the Pioneers stealthily made their way through the mangrove swamps, thereby avoiding the rebel checkpoints on the road to Banjul. Arriving in the city, Lee's party headed straight for the police headquarters where they added their support to the small group of loyalists defending the building. They soon had the area completely under their control by barricading the surrounding streets.

Many ex-SAS soldiers are scattered around the world, working for foreign governments or in various security jobs. Nevertheless, they still carry with them a tenuous link with the Regiment wherever they go. If any situation arises where their services may be required, they are honour-bound to go to the aid of any associated SAS operation. The bond of brotherhood between SAS men of any age is extremely strong.

Yundum airport had only been recaptured after a hard battle between the Senegalese paratroopers and the rebels. During the assault, 120 paratroopers were either wounded or killed. Once the airport had been secured, the Senegalese troops set about clearing the whole of Banjul of rebels; this was achieved within a few hours. Denton Bridge, across Oyster Creek, was also now controlled by the Senegalese, making it all but impossible for the insurgents to re-enter the city. The rebels were now concentrated in two areas only: Bakau and Fajara.

By the time Crooke and Mayers arrived, the whole conflict had reached an impasse. N'gom had strengthened his forces within Gambia and had reached the outskirts of Bakau. However, here he was forced to stop since Sanyang had taken over a hundred hostages, among them Lady Chilel N'Jie, one of the President's two wives, and a number of his children. Members of the Gambian cabinet had also been captured. Through a mobile transmitter (N'Gom had recaptured Radio Gambia from the rebel forces), Sanyang forced Lady Chilel to make an impassioned plea for the Senegalese to withdraw, otherwise all the hostages would be executed. Her almost hysterical appeal was followed up by Sanyang himself repeating the threat.

Crooke decided it was time to make a reconnaissance. On 5 August, he and his two comrades moved carefully forward of the Senegalese outposts. The three casually dressed Europeans with sub-machine guns stuck out like a sore thumb, despite their subterfuge. However, they didn't seem to be in much danger; the rebels were keen to leave any foreigners alone. They also lacked any sense of the need for security and were totally unaware of any threat to their positions. Crooke decided that they would be no match for the better-motivated and -trained Senegalese troops. What he did not know at the time was something that may have accounted for the rebels' lack of morale: Bojang had been killed during the second day of the coup, thus leaving them without a leader.

Returning from the recce, Crooke convinced N'Gom that he could advance his troops into Fajara and Bakau immediately. Accompanying the Senegalese force, the British men threaded their way through the suburbs of Fajara. A British engineer working for an American crane company saw them as they arrived at his hotel. He later recalled: 'Ten Senegalese troops and a British army officer arrived at the hotel. With him were two men who I can only describe as the most vicious-looking professionals I have ever seen.' He was, of course, referring to Crooke and Mayers. The British officer, dressed in khakis but without insignia, was most likely Clive Lee. The men were told that the rebels were holed up along a creek near the beach. Lee, Crooke and Mayers went off in search of them, there was some gunfire and then the three men returned, having calmly wiped out the rebel position.

At the house of Larry Piper, the United States Ambassador, a UN aid worker remembered when he first saw the rescue party. 'The house was on a bluff sloping to the beach. I went out and saw a wave of Senegalese come running up the hill in full camouflage-type gear led by three whites, one of whom had on an Australian hat, khaki shorts and a knife strapped to his leg. It was literally like living in a movie.' Once the party had checked that everything was all right, a few soldiers were left behind to keep it that way and then they disappeared.

Crooke and his men made their way to the offices of the British High Commissioner. There he discovered that Lady Chilel and her four children had been taken to a British clinic by armed guards the day before. Her children, one of whom was only five weeks old, were ill and needed treatment. The British clinic was a disease-research facility and stood only a couple of blocks from the High Commissioner's building. They had treated the children and asked that Lady Chilel should be allowed to bring them back again in 24 hours. While Crooke was there, the High Commissioner received a telephone call from one of the British doctors at the clinic to say that Lady Chilel had returned and that her children were being treated at that moment. The doctor was duly informed that armed SAS men would be in the building in minutes.

Crooke, Mayers and Lee headed for the clinic while doctors spun out the treatment as much as they dared to give the men more time. They even managed to persuade Lady Chilel's guards to put their weapons out of sight, telling them that it was frightening the other patients.

There were two more armed guards at the door of the hospital. Handing his weapon to Mayers, Crooke told the other men to make their way silently behind the guards. He then casually walked up and engaged them in conversation. What he said and how he managed to distract them so well and for so long has never been revealed, but whatever it was, it worked. The two guards never suspected that anything was wrong until they felt the muzzles of two guns at the backs of their heads.

The two captives were left with Lee and Mayers while Crooke entered the building and proceeded to where Lady Chilel's children were being treated. Their unarmed guards were caught totally by surprise and Crooke was able to take them prisoner. He then escorted Lady Chilel and the children to safety at the British High Commissioner's office. Their mission over, Crooke and his two men returned to N'Gom's headquarters at the airport.

The day before, Sanyang's mobile transmitter had been found and destroyed by Senegalese troops. Sanyang himself managed to escape but was eventually arrested in the neighbouring country of Guinea Bissau. With Sanyang's disappearance in Gambia, the coup began to fall apart. However, there were still some diehard rebels holed up in a police barracks with hostages, as well as a few bands of criminals and disloyal policemen at large. These needed to be dealt with.

N'Gom decided to move against the rebel-held barracks first, but he needed to advance slowly so as not to frighten them into killing their hostages. The rebels had already planned a mass execution a few days earlier, but one of their men, apparently having changed his mind about his allegiance, started shooting at some of the rebel guards. He was shot dead immediately, but his act of defiance served to delay the hostage killings. The Senegalese advanced slowly on their target and surrounded one side of the barracks. They left some of the exits unguarded so that the rebels could get away, hopefully without inflicting any innocent casualties. They had to wait anxiously for an hour while nothing happened, but then the hostages walked free – and the rebels fled, only to be rounded up later.

In all, it took eight days to quell the rebellion, with the loss of over a thousand lives. President Jawara was able to return to his country and rule as before. The Gambian government demanded that Sanyang be extradited from Guinea Bissau to face justice, but to their disappointment the socialist leadership of that country refused and later released him. More than a hundred insurgents, including convicts, were caught by the Senegalese forces and tried for their crimes. Seven were executed for their part in the coup. It was never proved that Libya had been the motivating force and Gaddafi managed to keep from being implicated in any of it.

The involvement of the SAS was also kept quiet. In press interviews, President Jawara was seen happily kissing his baby son, but denied that European soldiers had been involved in the rescue of his wife and child. This was exactly what the British government wanted: after all, it was a deniable operation. The only voice that let on about the SAS presence there was a Senegalese officer who told reporters that the SAS had indeed been instrumental in putting down the coup.

Crooke and Mayers stayed in Gambia a little longer, just to make sure that the British citizens would be safe. Their actions had proved that even a small number of skilled, confident and well-trained men could take on an opposition far superior in numbers and win, before disappearing as if they had never been there.

Upon his return, Crooke took part in the annual debrief, where every SAS member was able to find out what other members had been up to. Of course, only SAS soldiers were present at these meetings. Crooke gave a very detailed account of what had happened in Gambia and it was considered a shining example of the Regiment doing what it did best. Although Crooke and his men had much help from the Senegalese, and the enemy they were up against was disorganised and incompetent, there was no denying that much of the operation's success had been due to Crooke's initiative and common sense. His decision to ignore the British officials at Dakar and carry on with the mission could have been disastrous for him if things had gone wrong. However, his judgement had been spot on, and anyway, in those days, the SAS could do no wrong in Margaret Thatcher's eyes.

7. TROOPER 'RIP' REDDY

Rip Reddy joined the SAS in 1967 and was a member of G Squadron's Air Troop. His service with the SAS was short for, like so many young men before him, he was taken before his time. However, the events that led to his death place him in the unique position of being the first fatality of any SAS Halo (High Altitude, Low Opening) operation.

It all started in November 1969 when British Intelligence warned that Iraqi-backed forces were training guerrillas in villages of the Musandam Peninsula, Oman, and it had picked up information on a huge arms shipment due to arrive at the tiny coastal village of Jumla. This shipment was to be accompanied by a group of Iraqis with communist tendencies. British Intelligence translated this as the start of a major communist push into the area to take advantage of the turmoil of the time.

G Squadron 22 SAS was dispatched via Cyprus to the British airbase in Sharjah, near Dubai. The move from the UK had been rapid and many of the soldiers were still wearing their best suits since most had been attending a wedding when the fast-ball started. Without leaving the confines of the Sharjah airport they were loaded, together with their bergens and weapons, onto several three-ton trucks and driven out into the desert. Later that evening several choppers arrived and ferried the men over to a campsite on the eastern coast of the peninsula. This had been done for several reasons. Firstly, the area was similar to the one they would attack, although it lacked a village. Secondly, a Royal Navy minesweeper, complete with several rigid raiders manned by the SBS, was due to arrive offshore the following day.

The plan was for the SBS to insert the SAS onto the small beaches both north and south of Jumla. This would be done during the hours of darkness and would allow enough time for the SAS men to scale the high rocky peaks that towered out of the sea and hemmed in the entire village on its landward side. By dawn, with the SAS in place to stop any enemy running away, a combined force from the local Arab states would attack the village and capture the Iraqis and their equipment. Each SAS soldier was given six different-coloured *shamaghs* (Arab headdresses). The thinking behind this was simple, based mainly on the assaulting Arab force being made up of several different local forces, all with a different-coloured *shamagh*. To avoid any question that the SAS might be mistaken for the enemy, as the different Arab units approached the SAS positions they would change headdress to comply with that unit. In reality, some forty SAS soldiers were all converted into Tommy Cooper lookalikes as they dived frequently into their bergens looking for the correct *shamagh*.

On the surface this was a sound plan: not only would it protect the Straits of Hormuz, through which half the world's oil passes, but it would stop a major political and military catastrophe in the area. However, things didn't work out that way. Due to bad weather the whole plan was delayed for twenty-four hours – but only after the SAS and SBS had put to sea. By the time the men were due to leave the minesweeper and get into the rigid raiders, most were suffering from acute sea-sickness. They finally approached the beach in total darkness, with nothing to see other than a few faint lights coming from the village. Immediately the SAS were ashore they started to climb the cliff face, with Mountain Troop members leading what was a difficult and dangerous assault. They made it to the top one hour before dawn, with the only casualty being a broken finger and with everyone in position, overlooking the village to the open sea beyond.

As the light improved it was possible to see the main landing force about a mile out to sea, rapidly heading for the village beach at full speed. The landing craft ran up the beach and several shots rang out, waking up the villagers who slowly started coming out of their homes to greet the Arab soldiers. Strangers and visitors were rare in this remote area and soon tea and coffee were distributed and everything seemed very amiable. Then one of the officers got tough and inquired about the whereabouts of the Iraqi rebels, stating that he knew they were in Jumla. At this the villagers looked confused, pointing out that their village was called Gumla. Due to an intelligence mix-up the SAS had invaded the wrong village. By the time headquarters had confirmed this, and sent them racing across the Jebel top to the correct village, it was too late. The rebels had gone and so had most of their equipment. The SAS were pulled back to the British base at Sharjah, from where they launched an assault on the Wadi Rhawdah, intelligence believing that this was the route the enemy had taken.

The topography of the Wadi Rhawdah needs some explanation. It is roughly an egg-shaped depression in the high coastal mountain range that juts up from the sea. The walls of the depression tower up some three hundred metres from the wadi floor to form a natural barrier. The only entrance to the wadi is through a narrow break on the seaward side, a gap hardly large enough to let a Land Rover through. This small enclave is home to an isolated but friendly people known as the Bani Shitoo, who live in stone houses and catch rainwater in cisterns carved out of the rock.

From their secure base in Sharjah the SAS assembled two Air Troops with the intention of carrying out a high-altitude free-fall night drop directly into the wadi. While this sounds straightforward, one must remember that the men were to parachute from 10,000 feet, each carrying heavy equipment secured to their bodies, and plunge earthward at an average speed of 120mph. Their target was a small depression in a mountain range whose peaks reached above 4,000 feet – and all this had to be done in total darkness. This SAS recce team would carry out a search and locate the rebels who had escaped during the raid on the Musandam Peninsular. Once they had been located the rest of the SAS men would be helicoptered in to secure the area.

The free-fall drop was the first such official night operation the SAS had ever undertaken and the recce team landed without incident, apart from Rip Reddy who did not respond to their radio calls. Thinking he had drifted off course the recce unit carried out their orders until the arrival of reinforcements next morning. By early dawn it was obvious that Reddy, who had still not made radio contact, was missing, and a search was initiated. Spotting his parachute a short while later, they came across his body. From evidence at the scene, Reddy had been carrying too much equipment, making him overweight for the parachute. In addition he had landed on a scree fall that was slightly higher than the wadi bottom. The chute had opened but only seconds before he made contact with the ground, impacting with instantaneous and fatal effect. The area was finally secured – but the enemy were not in the Wadi Rhawdah, and never had been.

8. SQUADRON SERGEANT MAJOR BILLY WALDOCK (PSEUDONYM)

Once more, 'Billy' is a pseudonym for a man who truly deserves full recognition of his outstanding bravery. Faced with certain death this man drew on his years of experience as an SAS soldier and, guided by the motto 'Who Dares Wins', made it through.

Like most of the SAS, Billy, a Squadron Sergeant Major (SSM), was working in a fighting column during the Gulf War. On 9 February 1991, while one half of A Squadron were about to be involved with the attack on Victor Two – a key Iraqi radar installation – the other half, under Billy's command, were carrying out a CTR (close target reconnaissance) on a communications station. During the night, the fighting column had moved close in on its target. Using the MIRA (Milan Infra-Red Attachment), the SSM stood in the back of one of the Land Rovers to see what they were up against. The installation was ringed with barbed wire that the column had already cut through and now they moved further into the base, leaving one Land Rover at their entry point to act as cover.

The place was much larger than they had expected but no one wanted to pull out halfway through the job, especially as they were now so far in. Billy told his driver, Keith, to keep going; they would deal with whatever came their way as it happened. At the top of a small slope, Billy picked out what appeared to be movement through the MIRA. The enemy was all around them, and even though the SAS men hadn't been spotted yet it was surely only a matter of time. Billy decided the best option was sheer audacity: they would drive quietly through the Iraqi positions, hoping the darkness and the enemy's lack of alertness would play in their favour.

Their luck held for a while as they threaded their way past the defences, until suddenly they were confronted by an Iraqi soldier who stepped out in front of the Land Rover, gesturing for it to halt. The third man in the vehicle, John, who was manning the GPMG (general-purpose machine-gun) in the front passenger seat immediately opened fire and the Iraqi went down in a hail of 7.62mm fire. There wasn't much of him left.

The sound of the gunfire alerted the Iraqis that they were under attack and suddenly the Land Rover seemed to be targeted from all sides. For those inside it was the firefight from hell as bullets flew at them from all directions. Billy took a bad hit in his upper thigh, the bullet knocking him off balance and throwing him into the back of the Land Rover. Keith put his foot hard down onto the accelerator and rammed the vehicle forward, hoping that they could punch a way out of their predicament by sheer speed and aggression alone. With John hammering the opposition with the GPMG and Keith driving like a lunatic, they came close to escaping, managing to smash through the camp gates and beyond. However, three hundred metres later, the vehicle came to an abrupt and bone-jarring halt as it smashed into a tank ditch. Unfortunately, just moments before, Billy had managed to pull himself upright, trying to man the rear gun. The force of the impact threw him forward, over the roll bar, so that he ended up lying half across the bonnet and half across the laps of the two men in the front. He now looked in a very bad way: his wounded leg was lying up across his chest.

Desperate to escape, John and Keith jumped out of the wrecked vehicle, Keith flinging Billy across his shoulders. They ran into the darkness, John covering their retreat with his weapon. Once a reasonable distance had been put between them and their abandoned Land Rover, which was still being hit by Iraqi gunfire, the three men stopped to wait-up in some rocks on a small incline. Billy's condition was becoming critical. Although a big and extremely tough man, the damage inflicted on his body was serious: blood was flowing freely from his leg wound, despite attempts by the other men to staunch it.

Billy's state wasn't the only thing that was critical. Below the SAS men's position it appeared that the Iraqis had at last organised themselves and were advancing towards the men's hiding place. The men only had one rifle between them as Keith had left his in the wagon when he realised he was going to have to carry the SSM. Nevertheless, with John firing into the darkness, they managed to hold off the onslaught for a little longer.

Billy's condition was worsening fast; he was slipping in and out of consciousness. Realising that the men stood a better chance of escaping without him, he ordered them to leave him there and to take their chances while he gave them covering fire. Keith and John realised they had no other choice. If they stayed with him it meant certain capture and even death for all of them. Billy looked as though he was dying anyway, so it made sense that the two others should now concentrate on saving themselves. Even so, it was still not an easy decision to make.

Keith offered Billy a quick way out with a bullet to the head. It was not the first time in the Regiment's history this offer had been made, although only one man had ever accepted it. Billy refused to give in so easily, saying that he was going to fight until the end, so Keith and John left him with a 66mm rocket that John had managed to grab from the Land Rover. They took the rifle for themselves since, with the SSM about to pass out again, they felt that they would be able to make more use of it. With one last look back at their now unconscious friend, they quickly made tracks into the protective darkness of the night.

When Billy became conscious again, he realised that a group of Iraqi soldiers were standing around a vehicle not too far from where he was lying. It was their voices that had brought him back to awareness. He realised that he was being presented with a target opportunity that was almost too perfect to pass up. He aimed the 66mm rocket at the truck and was just about to fire when two Iraqi soldiers came from behind, jumping on him and pulling the weapon from his hand.

They demanded to know who he was. Reluctantly he admitted he was English, now fearing, at the best, a beating. To his surprise, however, on the orders of an officer, a stretcher was brought and he was taken to a hospital to receive treatment. The Iraqi doctor who fixed his leg did so with the utmost skill and consideration. Even so, his interrogation continued in the hospital.

Although Billy was fluent in Arabic, since the moment of his capture he had not let on that he could speak any more than a few words. Now, as his interrogators stood over him as he lay in his hospital bed, arguing over what to ask him next, Billy answered one of the proposed questions flawlessly, giving away that he knew their language. Angered at having been fooled, the two interrogators ripped the drips and tubes out of him and proceeded to beat him mercilessly. The medical staff tried to intervene to stop this brutality but their protests went unheard.

In spite of the rough treatment Billy received at the hands of the interrogators, with the expert care he got from the doctors in the hospital his injuries soon improved enough for him to join other prisoners of war and he was paraded around the city like a trophy.

Keith and John, after their frantic escape from the communications installation, managed to keep going – walking by night and hiding by day, until their position was discovered by an American A10 aircraft. From there, they were given instructions how to find the other half of their squadron. They had finally reached safety, but their elation was tinged with great sadness: they firmly believed that Billy must have died where they left him.

With the end of the Gulf conflict, the prisoners of war were released and it soon became clear that Billy was alive and well. It must have come as a shock, albeit a wonderful one, to those friends and family who believed that he was dead. For his bravery Billy was awarded the Military Cross. This was an unexpected honour as the decoration is usually only bestowed upon commissioned officers. In fact, the SSM was only the second NCO in the whole history of the Regiment to be awarded the MC.

9. CAPTAIN ROBERT 'BOB' NAIRAC

Sometimes, in the course of duty, men put themselves into such dangerous situations that it is impossible to rescue them. One example of this happened in Northern Ireland during the early 1970s, when an undercover unit called the Military Reconnaissance Force (MRF) set up an operation that was to be known as the Four Square Laundry. This 'laundry' operated a local service, collecting washing from house to house. Their rates were set far lower than those of their rivals, so the service became very popular. Once the washing had been collected and taken back to the laundry, the clothes would undergo forensic tests before being washed. These tests were done to see if any traces of explosives could be picked up. Such discoveries would indicate those houses where bombs were being made. Unfortunately, this clever means of collecting intelligence proved vulnerable to betrayal. Some of the members of the MRF unit had once been members of the IRA before being 'turned' to work for the British. Unbeknown to the British forces, they had changed their allegiance again, giving the

IRA information about the laundry service. This led to the laundry van being ambushed and shot up. In the ambush the male driver was killed but the woman with him managed to get away. They were both British soldiers.

Lone operatives like these often found themselves exposed by the IRA and having to make a break for it as a result. Captain Robert Nairac got himself into such a perilous situation in Northern Ireland in May 1977. While working alone he was discovered, captured and murdered by the IRA.

Having been educated at Ampleforth, a top Catholic public school, and at Lincoln College, Oxford, where he read history, Nairac joined the Grenadier Guards. He was both intelligent and a keen sportsman with a boxing blue, a combination that made him an excellent soldier. After Sandhurst, he had served a number of tours in Northern Ireland and in 1977 he was based at Portadown, spending several nights each week at the SAS base in Bessbrook Mill in County Armagh. It was widely rumoured at the time that he was a member of the SAS. In fact, he was never a member of the SAS: he was seconded to the army's undercover intelligence-gathering unit, known as 14 Intelligence and Security. However, he did work closely with the SAS, gathering information for men from the Regiment to act upon.

Nairac had convinced himself that he could pass himself off as an Irishman, speaking with an Irish intonation that was good but not perfect. He had developed a Belfast accent that he could mimic fluently and enjoyed going to local pubs, driving there in his brown Triumph Dolomite, to chat to the locals and join in the evening sing-songs. He went by the name of 'Danny Boy', a name which many SAS soldiers called him. However, it is extremely difficult to pass yourself off as an Irishman and thus become accepted by the local community if you are not actually Irish. In his favour, though, it must be said that Nairac did have bravado, which to some degree must have helped him survive for a time.

Still, anyone who is willing to get up and sing songs in the local bars of 'Bandit Country' is sure to come under scrutiny, and it would be an extremely foolhardy gesture by any member of the security forces to act in this way, especially while alone. Many of the locals liked Nairac and those that had anything to do with the terrorist organisations actually believed him to be some form of 'plant' working for the Official IRA. (Such a plant was known as a 'Sticky'.)

In fairness, Nairac did gather much basic information but his method was crude and dangerous. Moreover, many think he enjoyed the idea of being a lone undercover agent. This may seem an unfair comment but he did forgo standard operating procedure for any covert operation, often working without adequate back-up.

On the night of 14 May, Nairac went to the Three Steps Inn at Drumintee in County Armagh. The pub is isolated, set on a lonely hill out of range of any immediate help and three miles from the border with the Republic. A couple of days earlier he had purchased the songsheets of two well-known Republican songs and had practised them at Bessbrook Mill until he knew them off by heart. Feeling confident, he left the barracks at around 7.30 p.m., making his way to the Three Steps Inn – he told no one of his plans or where he was going, only arranging to telephone the SAS desk operator at around 11.30 p.m. The pub was packed that night with around two hundred people, and after an evening of steady drinking the songs began. Nairac had been on stage and had finished his versions of two favourite IRA tunes, 'The Broad Black Brimmer' and 'The Boys of the Old Brigade'.

Eventually Nairac decided that he had had enough and made his way out into the car park. He was followed and questioned about his identity. A fight started: Nairac should have been able to handle it as he was a keen boxer and could easily take care of himself. However, while the fists were flying his Browning 9mm pistol fell onto the ground. This was grabbed by one of his attackers and he was quickly overpowered and knocked unconscious. His captors bundled him into a car and immediately took him south, over the nearby border.

For a short time Nairac was left unconscious in a house with only a single guard. He recovered and attacked his guard, knocking him down and grabbing the guard's revolver just as another IRA man rushed into the room. Pointing the guard's pistol at the newcomer, Nairac pulled the trigger. The weapon misfired. Nairac pulled the trigger again and it misfired once more. He pulled the trigger a third time and once again the gun misfired. Then the guard he had originally attacked moved behind him and knocked him unconscious. His detention at the house gave his captors time to summon an IRA unit, after which his original captors were dismissed.

Nairac was swiftly moved from the house and taken into Ravensdale Forest near the border. He was bundled out of the car and carried into a small field beside a bridge. For several hours he was brutally tortured by his captors who wanted to find out details of current SAS operations. The interrogation took the form of a severe battering about the head and body with a fence post. Despite the torture Nairac refused to speak. Knowing he was about to die, and being a staunch Catholic, he asked his captors for a priest. In a final and macabre humiliation, one of the terrorists played the part of the priest to hear the officer's confession. Thereafter, realising they would not get anything out of him, his IRA captors shot him with his own pistol.

Nairac's capture meant that he failed to make his 11.30 p.m. call back to base at Bessbrook Mill and, because of his maverick loner attitude, this was not thought to be abnormal. Thus the alarm was not raised until 6 a.m, by which time he was already dead. SAS units were deployed to search the area but without any success. Two days later, the IRA issued a statement saying that Nairac had been killed. His body was never recovered.

* * *

Author's note: Some years after the event I was privy to information about the disposal of Nairac's body. Later in 1977 a twenty-four-year-old joiner from Meigh in County Armagh, Liam Patrick Townson, was arrested by the Irish police on suspicion of being involved in Nairac's murder. Under close questioning Townson gave an accurate account of how Nairac's corpse was disposed of. The method used was so horrific that it has never been made public, but suffice it to say that Townson's story involved a strong rumour about a certain animal-feed processing plant. Townson also drew a detailed sketch of the scene of the killing, pointing out where the terrorists had hidden Nairac's Browning and clothing in the nearby forest. Strangely enough, Townson, as he related the story, had nothing but the greatest respect for the way in which Bob Nairac had suffered in silence. Townson and five other men from the north were jailed for life for their part in Nairac's killing. Two months later, in February 1978, Bob Nairac was awarded the George Cross, the highest peacetime honour a serviceman can receive. As a result of his death new procedures were put in force by the SAS, with auto-alert transponders being issued in order to locate any SAS member who might find themselves a captive of the IRA.

Nairac's name has surfaced several times since his death. In 1984, seven years after his murder, allegations that linked him to the 1975 murder of John Francis Green, an IRA commander in North Armagh who was shot dead at a remote mountainside farmhouse in County Monaghan in the Republic, were made. Other allegations led some to believe that Nairac was actively assassinating terrorist suspects, thus supporting the idea that the British had a shoot-to-kill policy. This is disputed by those who worked with him, and the denial is backed up by the fact that, although armed on the night of his capture, Nairac did not use his pistol, recognising that his original assailants were not IRA.

10. TROOPER FRANK BILCLIFFE

Frank Bilcliffe had served with the SAS during the mid-1960s but, fed up with the lack of action, he decided to leave and enter civilian life. However during the early 1970s he rejoined the SAS as a member of B Squadron. Shortly after rejoining he found himself in Oman.

In 1974, as the war against Oman's left-wing rebels was coming to a close, an operation was mounted against the enemy stores complex in the Shirshitti Caves. Major General Creasey, Commander of the Sultan's Armed Forces, ordered the Iranian Battle Group to advance from the airbase at Manston and secure the coastal town of Rakyut, some seventeen miles to the south. *En route* they were to clear the Adoo (enemy) stores complex which was said to hold tons of weapons, food and combat supplies. Capture of the enemy supplies would drastically shorten the war.

The attack started in mid-December but it did not advance very far. The Adoo had seen them coming and in heavy fighting had laid waste to the Iranians. Unable to sustain the losses, the attack was called off. At this stage of

the war defeat was not an option. Almost immediately, a
decision was taken by Creasey to re-attack using the SAF
(Sultan's Armed Forces), SAS (elements of B & G Squadrons) and Firqat, a unit of trained, loyal local tribesmen.
There was a problem. All the SAF regiments in the south
were already hard-pressed with prior commitments. So it
was that the Jebel Regiment was flown down from Northern Oman. After some swift training they were sent into
battle.

By 4 January 1975, the force was ready. The plan of
attack was fairly simple: seize an old airstrip called Defa in
order to establish a supply point, then secure the ridge that
overlooked the Shirshitti depression, in which the Adoo
caves lay. As always, the SAS and Firqat led the advance.
Defa was quickly taken and the advance rapidly continued.
As the lead elements approached a landmark known as the
Zakhir Tree, they met with serious resistance. For some
reason the Firqat did not perform well, but the SAS men laid
it down thick and furious. By mid-afternoon they had
managed to reach a clearing called Point 985 whereupon a
base was established. During the night the Adoo attacked at
very close range, killing four members of the SAF and
severely wounding many more. At times it was difficult to
establish where the Adoo fire was coming from. The SAF
soldiers in the perimeter defences became extremely agitated, and fired more for relief of tension than to hit a
target.

Next day the force advanced down into the Shirshitti
region. By mid-morning, Red Company had reached the
Shirshitti wadi, but the commander realised that he had
moved too far south. In fairness to him, it must be said that
navigation in the thick bush was difficult. There also seemed
to be some confusion as to the location of the other two
companies. At this stage most of the SAS men had attached
themselves to the various command headquarters. With Red
Company was Lance Corporal Thomas. As the lead pla-
toons broke cover (against the advice of Corporal Thomas)

into an area clear of bush, the Adoo opened fire. Within seconds most of the platoon were dead, cut down by the ferocious Adoo firepower. The company commander, together with several other men, rushed forwards to get a better look at the situation. The Adoo had been waiting and the commander's group too were all cut down. Even to the hardened SAS men, the situation was clearly out of control. In such circumstances, SAS men quickly group together for support. All around them, those SAF soldiers who were still alive dropped their weapons and ran. (This did not include the white officers who tried desperately, for many at the cost of their lives, to restore control.)

By this time the Adoo were pushing their advantage, closing in on the small groups of resistance. The SAS group called for an air strike and the task of directing the aircraft fire was given to Frank Bilcliffe. Such was the confusion of running bodies, however, that the first strike came in too close and one of the rounds hit an SAS soldier in the back. Hastily the soldiers pulled fluorescent air-marker panels from their belt kits and wrapped them around their shoulders for recognition. Eventually, with massive firepower supplied by artillery, mortars and Strikemasters, the Adoo were driven back. Amid all this carnage, there were several individual acts of great courage, as men braved the horrendous fire to rescue personal friends. Although the dead were left behind, all the wounded and weapons were recovered before a tactical withdrawal was ordered. As the shaken troops made their way back to Point 985, shots could be heard coming from down in the wadi: the Adoo were confirming their kills. To offset this gruesome sound, a full-blown mortar barrage (under control of the SAS) was called down on the battle area.

Frank and his group managed to reach the top of the escarpment and establish themselves in the outer perimeter of Point 985. While the medics tended to the wounded, the rest built sandbag and rock fortifications. As darkness fell the Adoo crept up to the fortification, getting close enough to kill several Baluchi soldiers. Around midnight panic broke out in the ranks. Fearing that the Adoo would overrun Point 985, many soldiers started to fire away indiscriminately at shadows. It took the officers and the SAS several hours to calm them down. By dawn the next day Point 985 had been reinforced.

That day the Adoo had won a victory, but they were later to pay the price. As the defences at Point 985 were made stronger, it was decided to blast the Adoo out of their stronghold. So it was that for every minute of the following two days, every weapon that could reach the Shirshitti wadi was fired: artillery, the guns of armoured cars, mortars, bombs and cannon-fire from aircraft and even a bombardment from a ship lying off the coast. The air thundered, with smoke from high explosives and phosphorus weapons and dust hanging over the Shirshitti wadi like a permanent cloud.

Author's note: During the battle for Shirshitti both SAS mortar men controlling the base-line at Point 985 had been wounded, and I was withdrawn to replace them. There were six mortars in two lines of three. Each half-hour, it was our turn to fire, each tube firing ten rounds in a mixture of white phosphorus and high explosive. In the next few hours the mortars alone consumed two thousand rounds. Even with this massive barrage, the Adoo still found time to carry out night attacks on our position. Additionally, several large rockets were fired into our camp with devastating effect. Amid the carnage taking place in the wadi, the Adoo had still found it possible to launch three of these missiles. I watched in disbelief as the first one flew over our position, a great flame burning from its tail. When it fell to earth, the whole world seemed to shake. Luckily for us, only one hit the camp. Equally as unlucky, it hit the ammo bunker.

I mention Frank Bilcliffe because he was the first man I saw (air-marker panel still wrapped around his shoulders) to come over the lip of the wadi towards Point 985. Later, as they struggled to build the defences, I took a photograph of Frank and his group. They were laughing. In the end, the Shirshitti Caves were taken, and vast Adoo stores were captured. The war in Oman came to a swift end not long after.

As with so many SAS soldiers, you will rarely see Frank's name mentioned or his deeds praised, but he was there when he was needed. Frank went on to serve for many years after, and at one stage I shared a house in Hereford with him. He lost a lot of 'street cred' as a ladies' man when Mac McAuliffe and I caught him in his room blowing up a full-sized rubber doll. Whatever. He was a good friend and always out for a laugh. Sadly, Frank died in 1992.

11. REGIMENTAL SERGEANT MAJOR BRIAN MAYHEW (PSEUDONYM)

Yet again, due to the need to maintain the security of those still serving it is not possible to give real names to any of the men who took part in this operation. Needless to say, all of them are heroes, for anyone who would attack a strongly defended enemy target deep inside Iraq during the Gulf War would have had to be brave or plain mad. For the SAS, it was just carrying out orders. The assault on the Iraqi installation known as Victor Two was given to one of A Squadron's fighting columns who received their orders as they lay hidden in the vast wilderness of the Iraqi desert.

The action began when the two signallers started to decode long incoming radio messages from SAS HQ in Saudi Arabia. This feverish activity around the two signallers quickly spread to the rest of the men and soon the orders to launch an attack on an Iraqi microwave station that night became clear.

The men began to prepare for the assault, with Mountain Troop putting together a model of the radar station from whatever kit they had lying around. They built it according to the intelligence coming over the radio, intelligence that seemed quite detailed on the set-up of the station but was confused where enemy strengths and dispositions were concerned.

At 15.45 hours everyone, except for the duty sentries, made their way to the middle of the LUP (lying-up position) for a briefing. The sentries were to be briefed on their roles later – not an ideal situation as, in the rush, it was more than likely that they wouldn't get the whole story and would go into battle not completely sure of what was happening. Nevertheless, ideal or not, the column were behind enemy lines and sentries were essential.

The briefing started with the men being formed up in the groups that they would be in for the assault. Once they had settled, Brian, the RSM, and Paul, the OC designate, joined them and the briefing began. Although Paul was a major, and the new OC for the column, it was obvious to the men that Brian was still very much in charge. (SAS rank structure has little to do with who's actually in charge.)

The target radar installation was to be known by its call sign of 'Victor Two'. The plan was for the column to drive to within 1500 metres of it, place the vehicles in a fire support position and then to send out a recce team. Once the location had been confirmed, the recce team would return to their positions with the assault team and close-fire support before guiding them to the target. The aim was to completely destroy the facility, which was the main centre for guiding the Iraqis' mobile Scud missiles to their targets. It had previously been attacked by Stealth bombers but the problem was that most of it was underground and therefore safe from aerial attack. The only way to make sure it was taken out was by an attack from the ground. Once the column had achieved this objective, all vehicles were to make their way back to the fire support position.

Brian made himself the overall commander of the operation. There were to be three assault groups each of three men, plus close-fire support and fire support groups. The rest of the men were to assist with driving the vehicles.

The objective itself was a building complex with a microwave tower about 65 metres tall. The outside perimeter wall was about five metres in height while a three-metre-high internal security fence posed another obstacle. The main gate was guarded by a sentry position.

The plan was to fire two anti-tank missiles at the sentry position and the gate. An explosive charge would then be placed on the internal fence. Once this had gone off, the three assault teams were to enter the building, each taking a floor, including the levels below ground. The floors needed to be cleared and then explosive charges laid before the teams got themselves out as quickly as possible.

The men, clear about their roles, soon got to work. They were enthusiastic about the operation despite the development of some internal politics within the group. The only piece of information that wasn't clear was how many Iraqis there were at the installation, and how well-armed they were. The intelligence coming through was vague but suggested that there were more civilians than military personnel present and so there was to be no indiscriminate firing by the assault forces. A man needed to be identified as a soldier before he could be shot at. Of course, this was far from ideal in a situation behind enemy lines in the middle of a war. However, orders were orders.

It was suggested at the time that the column was being sent in because the Regiment wanted to 'blood' its soldiers; that is, it wanted to give them some experience of combat and be able to claim that one of its squadrons had led an attack in hostile territory. It was also rumoured that headquarters knew exactly how many Iraqis were at the base and how well armed they were; after all, they knew all the other details about the base. Sensing that maybe they were not being told everything, the troops started to feel uneasy.

After a final brew-up, the men formed up in their vehicles and drove for a couple of hours until they reached an Iraqi highway, or MSR (Main Supply Route) as they were known. Light was now fading. Having checked that it was all clear, the group moved off again. Before they got themselves onto the road, however, they needed to bridge a ditch so that the Land Rovers could cross over. This was done by Mobility Troop placing two sand channels, supported by sandbags, in the ditch, so that the wheels could roll across them without the rest of the vehicle getting grounded. Within seventeen minutes, all the vehicles were over, the bridge dismantled, and they were on their way again.

Five kilometres from the target and the adrenalin started to flow. All senses were alert, expecting an enemy ambush at any minute; so far it had all seemed too easy. Then the ground started to become more difficult to drive on, causing the column to make a kilometre detour to the west. Here the ground became a mass of man-made slit trenches, but as the orders were to slow down or stop only if an enemy vehicle was spotted, the vehicles carried on at the same speed.

Closing fast now on Victor Two, the MIRA (Milan Infra-Red Attachment) wagon came forward, needing to continually observe the area for enemy activity. Fifteen hundred metres away from the installation, the column came to a halt, as planned. One of the men left his bike at the location and it was logged in on the SATNAV so that the rest of them would have a position to make their way back to after the operation was over. The target was checked once more through the MIRA. It turned out that the site was huge – lots of buildings, vehicles and people; soldiers were positioned in both slit trenches and bunkers. There seemed to be little sign of the 'civilians' mentioned by RHQ.

At this point, Brian started to change the plans that had been made at the briefing. He decided that they should move forward immediately, without the services of the recce group. The column drove closer to Victor Two, internal politics changing the line-up as certain of the group decided they wanted to take the lead, no matter what. Driving along a tarmac road, they soon found themselves right in the middle of the enemy position with hostile soldiers and vehicles all around. With the previous orders changed beyond recognition, most of the men didn't have a clue what they were going to do next.

Without warning, the lead vehicles pulled over to the left side of the road and the others were obliged to form up behind them. They were now parked up alongside a small escarpment running parallel to the road. At last, the recce party was sent out to do a CTR (close target reconnaissance) and discovered the extent of the site. In all it was about a kilometre square in size, its focus being the massive control building and microwave tower bristling with communication dishes. The recce party returned quickly and a revised plan was put forward. Now it was decided that the vehicles would split into two groups and give cover from the flanks. Meanwhile, the assault teams, together with a cover party, would go on ahead by foot to carry out the business of demolishing the tower with explosives.

Their forward progress went unchallenged. On reaching the complex, three hundred metres from the vehicles, the demolition teams went forward to lay their charges whilst the covering team hung back, keeping a lookout for any trouble. One of the cover party, while waiting near the back of an Iraqi truck, heard a sound from the cab. He went around to investigate and opened the cab door to reveal the sleepy face of an Iraqi soldier. The soldier, surprised, reached for his gun, despite efforts to stop him doing so. So there was no other choice – within seconds he had been shot dead with a burst from an automatic rifle.

A firefight instantly erupted and the column felt that every gun in the compound was trained on them. Even the Russian-made anti-aircraft guns were turned on their position. The squadron fought back, giving it everything they'd got. By now the demolition teams had placed their explosives in the tower and were moving back to the rest of the column. The order was given to move out.

As the vehicles slowly regrouped and withdrew, the column drew down a heavy rain of fire from all around them. Nevertheless they kept going, punching a hole through the opposition with their own heavy guns. Finally, after an hour of battling their way through enemy positions, they disappeared into the night. Remarkably, despite the dangerous internal political manoeuvrings and the changes of plans, there were no casualties. A Squadron spent a total of 45 days behind enemy lines, during which time two of its members were killed and one was captured. The squadron received a DSM, two MCs, four MMs and four MIDs for their bravery.

12. COLONEL CHARLES BECKWITH

It may seem funny to have an American soldier featuring in a book about the SAS but, as I stated in the Introduction, this book is about heroes from the SAS *family* and, as such, Charlie Beckwith is included. A long time before Charlie became a colonel within the US Army, he served with the SAS. Between 1962–64 Charlie was a popular face around Bradbury Lines (later to be renamed Stirling Lines). He served as a normal troop member and even commanded a patrol of SAS soldiers in the Far East. His time in Hereford was not wasted, as he studied the procedure and benefits of SAS techniques, especially the system of SAS recruitment. Upon returning to the United States, he tried to get permission to set up a counter-terrorism unit run along the lines of the SAS. For many years his plans and ideas fell on deaf ears, and it was not until such events as Entebbe, Mogadishu and the Iranian Embassy siege that his superiors realised that the USA was missing out. Finally Charlie was given the go-ahead. Taking the cream from the various Special Forces units already established in the US Army, he formed his own highly secretive unit and named it 'Delta'.

Two years later, in 1980, they received their first major assignment – to rescue over a hundred Americans being held hostage in the American Embassy in Tehran. Revolutionaries in Iran had removed the West-friendly Shah from power and replaced him with a religious fanatic: the Ayatollah Khomeini. The Ayatollah's army, known as the Iranian Revolutionary Guards, soon swept through the capital. Upon entering the American Embassy, they took those inside hostage – representatives of what they saw as a country ruled by Satan.

Diplomatic negotiations were attempted. They failed, so a military rescue was considered. There were problems with this option, however: Iran was in such chaos that it was hard to get any reliable intelligence, and Tehran was far from any US airbase. Soon it was realised that the only plan that stood any chance of working was to send Delta in on an Entebbe type of raid.

The operation was called 'Eagle Claw' and required an immense amount of planning. Basically, it called for Delta to infiltrate Iran secretly, using an old airbase at Masirah Island in Oman and also the aircraft carrier *Nimitz*, which was stationed nearby. First of all, it was necessary to establish a base two hundred miles south of Tehran which would be known as Desert One. Once this had been set up, three C130 Hercules aircraft would fly Delta to the base and three more would carry fuel. A section of Rangers were also to be taken along to supply protection. Once this group landed at Desert One, it was planned that eight RH-53D helicopters from the aircraft carrier would join them.

Upon arrival, the helicopters were to refuel, take the Delta members on board and transport them to a hide area just outside Tehran. Meanwhile, back at Desert One, the C130s were to return to Masirah. At the hide area, Delta would have to wait for night to fall before going in for the attack. The helicopters, on the other hand, were to take off immediately and fly south to hide in the mountains until they were needed again to transport the soldiers out. Inside Tehran, special agents of the DOD (Department of Defence) had already been put into place to help get Delta from their hideout and into the city. Once there, Delta would make straight for the Embassy, silently make an assault and rescue the hostages. That achieved, the helicopters would then return to pick them all up.

Opposition from Iranian Revolutionary Guards was expected and Beckwith knew that it would have to be put down as soon as it began. Therefore, in addition to the assault teams, he also put a helicopter gunship on standby. Thirty miles south of the city, a force of US Rangers was to fly in to an airfield at Manzariyeh and secure it. The helicopters carrying the hostages and the assault teams would then fly into this airfield and be lifted out by a giant C141 Starlifter. The whole plan was extremely complex and relied on accurate timings and everyone doing their job. It also involved a lot of aircraft which needed to be coordinated. As a final precaution, special SAR (Search and Rescue) teams stood ready in case they were needed.

Just before the mission was about to start, Beckwith heard from Ulrich Wegener, the commander of the German GSG9 anti-terrorist force, that the Germans were planning to put a camera team into Tehran to cover the hostage situation. He asked Beckwith if there was anything he could do to help. Beckwith, keen on the idea, put it to his superiors who refused him permission to seek such cooperation. It had to be seen as an entirely American operation.

Eagle Claw began late on the evening of 24 April. But even before events had really got started, things began to go wrong, a portent for the rest of the mission. The three C130s carrying the Delta Force and the Rangers had just touched down at Desert One when a passenger bus drove up the road towards them. It was stopped by the American infiltrators and found to contain thirty passengers who then had to be held prisoner for the duration of the operation.

Shortly afterwards, a petrol tanker came driving up the road, followed by a smaller truck. One of the Rangers, providing protection for the landing force, fired off a LAW (Light Anti-tank Weapon) anti-tank missile at the tanker. The tanker exploded in a fireball. Why the soldier decided to compromise the Americans' position like this has never been explained.

The driver of the tanker leapt out of his cab and ran for the smaller truck behind. Before the soldiers could do anything, the small truck turned around and headed off at speed in the opposite direction. It was more than certain that they had seen the soldiers and the planes, but it was too late for anything to be done about it. Despite the heightened risk, Beckwith decided to continue with Eagle Claw and it wasn't long before the final three C130s landed. Once Delta had been offloaded, the three aircraft that had brought them took off immediately to return to base. The other three had to wait for another thirty minutes until the helicopters arrived and refuelled. The waiting time was not wasted: camouflage was set up to cover kit and equipment and a SATCOM radio link was established.

Thirty minutes passed. The helicopters were badly late and daylight was approaching. When they finally did arrive, there were only six instead of eight, due to the effects of a bad sandstorm on the way. Beckwith considered that the mission was still viable: he could do it with six choppers – but only just. Then, as they were being loaded, another of the helicopters became unserviceable. Extremely disappointed, Beckwith now knew that he had to call off the mission.

The men of Delta Force prepared to get back into the C130s still on the ground. Before they did, however, one of the helicopters that had just taken off crashed into one of the Hercules planes, creating an enormous fireball as ammunition and rockets carried by the aircraft also went up. In the explosion, five USAF aircrew on the C130 and three Marines on the RH53 were killed.

In a state of near-shock, the rest of the men, including the surviving helicopter pilots, got onto the remaining C130s and returned to Masirah. The helicopters that were left behind were destroyed by an airstrike. Beckwith was devastated that his unit's first mission had had such an ignominious end. Of course, most of what happened was through no fault of Delta, but it gave the unit's detractors a chance to criticise. President Carter, though, still held them in high favour: a few days after their return to the US, he paid them a visit, praising their efforts. Since that time Delta has gone from strength to strength and the name of Charlie Beckwith (now deceased) is written proudly in the history books.

13. CAPTAIN PETER FRITZ

D uring the war in Rhodesia (now Zimbabwe) between 1966 and 1980, C Squadron (there is no C Squadron in the British SAS, this slot having been taken up by the Rhodesians), commanded for much of that time by Major Brian Robinson, played a major role in mounting cross-border operations in Zambia and Mozambique. They inflicted heavy losses on ZIPRA (Zimbabwe People's Revolutionary Army) and other enemy forces, and by June 1978, having expanded to three squadrons under the command of Lieutenant Colonel Garth Barrett, the unit was redesignated the Rhodesian 1st SAS Regiment.

During the first half of 1978, the rebel forces of ZIPRA met with severe opposition from the Rhodesian 1st SAS Regiment. A number of raids had forced the terrorists to retreat from their forward bases near the Zambesi River to positions deeper inside Zambia. It was discovered that ZIPRA were using Russian-supplied trucks to transport their troops in. Most nights these trucks would set off from the area of Kabanga and head south to cross the border into

Rhodesia, stopping off at the staging post of Simani on the way.

B Squadron was given the task of ambushing these trucks as they travelled between Kabanga and Simani. On the evening of 13 June, twelve men under the command of Captain Peter Fritz were dropped into an LZ (landing zone) just inside Zambia. Using the cover of the night, they advanced towards their target, only stopping to lie up just before dawn. The next day they set off again and reached the target area for the ambush in the early hours of 15 June. They carried out a brief reconnaissance of the area and it was decided that Squadron Sergeant Major Pete Cole and an NCO should mine the road with a single command-detonated mine, made even more deadly with an added thirteen kilograms of plastic explosive. The men then settled down into their ambush positions to wait for the enemy to appear.

They had a long wait. The next ZIPRA convoy did not show up until 11.15 hours on 24 June. Three trucks full of heavily armed ZIPRA terrorists drove down the road towards the patrol. The vehicles were moving slowly, following an advance party that was checking the road for mines. But, luckily for the patrol, they seemed to give up this practice just ten metres short of the ambush location. As the lead vehicle drove over the mine, Cole exploded it, destroying the truck completely. At the same time, the two remaining trucks came under heavy automatic gunfire from the rest of the ambush patrol. The relentless fire set the trucks ablaze and killed all aboard. When a final body count was done, it was calculated that 69 terrorists had been killed.

Their mission completed, the whole group was taken out of the area in three helicopters. Two of these returned to base in Rhodesia. The third flew on to the Simani Mine where another such ambush was planned on the road from the mine to Kabanga. This time the ambush party was much smaller and was led by Sergeant Phil Cripps. His group laid a mine in the road and left. Three days later, Alfred Mangena, a senior ZIPRA commander, decided to inspect the area and see what damage the first ambush had done. Upon returning to Kabanga, his Land Rover drove over Cripps's mine, activating it and killing him. The ZIPRA leader's death was a great blow for the terrorist organisation and therefore a major victory for the Rhodesian forces.

14. CORPORAL MICHAEL 'BRONCO' LANE AND SERGEANT JOHN 'BRUMMIE' STOKES

These two friends had climbed together for many years when they were selected, in 1976, to be part of a team put together by the Army Mountaineering Association to climb Mount Everest. The idea had been conceived five years earlier but it had taken time to get everyone fit enough and for the Government of Nepal to give their consent to such a venture. The team spent this time in preparation and in honing their climbing skills. One such undertaking was an attempt on the 25,850-feet-high Mount Nuptse, the lowest peak in the Everest triangle. The peak is difficult and on this occasion cost the lives of four of the original climbing party. This early disaster did little to inhibit the team's morale: all of them had been chosen not only for their climbing skills but also for their ability to work under the adverse conditions found on Everest. The team was led by Lieutenant Colonel Tony Streather and was part of a joint venture with the Royal Nepalese Army and a group of

Sherpas. The team consisted of 27 service personnel, with a high percentage from the Parachute Regiment and the SAS. These two regiments also formed the final ascent party in support of Stokes and Lane who had been chosen to be the summit pair due to their extreme fitness.

The combined endurance of Stokes and Lane had been naturally forged from ten years of climbing together, and it was this endurance that was needed to conquer Everest. The world's highest peak does not fall easy to humans. It requires a continuous supply of food and oxygen to be ferried up in support of the summit team and even then luck plays a big part. Battered by high winds and blinding snow, the mountain presents hidden dangers at every turn. At one base camp at around 22,000 feet, one of the party simply walked out and fell down a deep crevasse. Such was the treachery of the mountain. However, despite the continual hardships and growing dangers, by 14 May the support party and the summit team had climbed up to Camp 6 at 27,000 feet where Stokes and Lane were left alone to carry out their attempt the next day. Bad weather suddenly closed in, delaying their departure from Camp 6 for 36 hours. The pair patiently bided their time. Their patience was rewarded and finally they were able to tackle the summit. However, the weather was still not perfect and it took them from half-past six in the morning until three o'clock in the afternoon to cover the 1,400 feet to the top.

Standing triumphantly on the summit and looking down on the rest of the world, the two men quickly took some photos and decided it would be best to make the descent as soon as possible. The weather looked as if it would turn again at any minute and they wanted to make it back to camp before it got dark – at 6 p.m. Getting back down was less easy than they thought and visibility started to fail; they were running out of time to make it back to camp. By sheer coincidence, they stumbled across some oxygen bottles that they had cached on the way up. This helped to fix their location – about 1000 feet above Camp 6 – but darkness was now falling fast and they knew it would be sheer folly to try and carry on in the dark. The cold was intense and there was only one thing they could do to save themselves. Using the sparse equipment they carried and their bare hands, Stokes and Lane scooped out a hole in the snow, huddling together in it to conserve their body heat. The night seemed endless, and the cold slowly reduced their ability to talk or even to think. The one positive factor was the oxygen bottles that helped them to survive the long, freezing night. At some stage Stokes became completely blind, the result of removing his goggles earlier in order to see better in the darkness. When morning finally arrived both men were unable to walk, or even to move. They knew that their only chance of survival now lay with the support team at Camp 5 – 2,500 feet below them.

Luckily for them, the weather had now improved and the sun was shining. The alternative summit team reached their location at 9 a.m. and arranged for their rescue. Even then the ordeal was not over: it took four days for the party to reach base camp where a helicopter could fly in. Four days of enduring the extreme pain of frostbite and blackening toes and fingers. Both men were flown out of the base camp to the hospital at Kathmandu to be treated for the results of their unscheduled night on the bare mountain. Due to the effects of severe frostbite, Stokes had lost several toes, while Lane had to have several fingers of his right hand amputated.

In 1984, both Stokes and Lane returned to the mountain that had nearly claimed their lives. This time, the team they led was made up solely of SAS soldiers, drawn from the Regiment's various Mountain Troops. It was a well-planned expedition, with fit and experienced men, and the first part of the climb went extremely well. The summit pair had already reached 22,800 feet when tragedy occurred. On 3 April, just after dawn, falling ice set off an enormous avalanche. Base camp was directly in its path and men and tents were swept down the mountainside. When everything became still again, one man lay dead and several of the others were seriously injured.

15. LIEUTENANT COLONEL JOHNNY WATTS

Johnny Watts was the most unlikely-looking officer you could come across: he was scruffy and at times you would take him for one of the older troopers. That said, he was a superb leader of men, a brilliant commander who above all had the respect of his men. Watts had a quick, decisive mind, yet he would not commit the SAS without committing himself. His SAS career is second to none and even today there are few members who do not know his name.

As Commander of D Squadron in 1958, he and his men were transferred from Malaya to Oman and took part in the victorious Jebel Akhdar Campaign. During this time he took part in many solo reconnaissance missions so that a way could be found onto the Jebel. By 1964 he was commanding B Squadron in Borneo and by mid-1970 he was the Commander of 22 SAS.

Always on the lookout for work, it was Watts who took the regiment back into the Oman war. Before the SAS made their main assault on the rebel-held Jebel Massif, he was tasked with making an assessment of what an SAS presence could offer Oman. He first advised that the best course of action was to get the SAS and SAF (Sultan's Armed Forces) from their coastal enclaves and back onto the Jebel. The task as he saw it was not only to fight the Adoo rebels but also to win the support of the Jebel tribesmen and the coastal Omani people. Only then would they stand a good chance of defeating the enemy. His original plan, later to be changed, had five main points: To establish an intelligence operation by turning captured rebels into friendly forces. To set up an information network (Psy Ops) to inform the isolated peoples of Oman of the policies of their new Sultan. To provide medical and economic aid (two separate points). Finally, to raise an army from the local people who would fight for and be loyal to the new Sultan.

This 'Five Fronts' campaign, as it became known, was to prove that the future of a government and its people can be positively affected by careful planning and the presence of a few, select Special Forces. The local people responded favourably to the medical and economic aid that was offered, building a bond that was strengthened by the psychological operations and radio broadcasts. Through this plan, Watts was also responsible for the formation of the Firqats – units of local tribesmen trained to fight for their own country.

Operation Jaguar was launched to establish a firm base on the Jebel. It began in October 1971. Dispensation had been given by the senior Qadi (religious leader) to all Arabs fighting during the Ramadan period, which is normally a time of fasting. This was the start of the war proper: almost two full Squadrons of SAS, together with their Firqats, spearheaded the operation. Additionally, several companies of the SAF and various support units also took part. The whole force was personally led by Watts who was no stranger to the battlefront. Getting the men onto the Jebel was not as easy as one would anticipate, although a diversionary plan had been in place for several weeks. (Heavy patrolling had been initiated from Taqa and Mirbat and directed at the Wadi-Darbat. The Darbat had always been an Adoo stronghold and the intention was to make it look as if a full-scale attack were imminent.) Helicopter hours were limited and, although some could be used in the initial lift onto the Jebel, most would be required to ferry ammunition, water and rations in the early days of the operation. They would need to sustain the war effort until an airstrip could be built and secured that would allow the larger Skyvans in with resupplies.

The SAS units and Firqats from Mirbat and Sudh climbed the Jebel to the east at a feature known as Eagle's Nest, working their way westward during the day in order to divert the Adoo's attention. Meanwhile a full Squadron of SAS undertook a gruelling march up the Jebel to occupy an old airstrip at a place called Lympne. The experience still stands out in the minds of those men who did the march. The route was over very difficult terrain: the bergens each man carried contained enough ammunition and water to last for several days. But so severe was the march that upon arrival even the SAS were in no fit state to fight without a rest. Luckily the Adoo were occupied further to the west and although the SAS soldiers were totally exhausted they made their objective. Later that morning SOAF helicopters and Skyvans started bringing in the other SAS Squadron and Firqat of the KBW (Kalid Bin Walid).

Watts decided to move to a more defensible position. On the morning of the second day the SAS and Firqat units that had arrived by helicopter and were obviously fresher set off for a location known as Jibjat. Some two hours after dawn, with the FKW in the lead, the SAS topped a small rise near Jibjat and came face to face with a large Adoo group having breakfast. A firefight developed and the surprised Adoo started to break up and tried to disperse, but not before a full-frontal attack was jointly carried out by both Firqat and SAS. They overran the Adoo position and continued to clear the area to the south, whereupon any further advance was stopped by a large wadi.

There then continued a prolonged firefight that lasted until the SAS heavy-gun teams moved up. (GPMGs were adapted to the heavy support role and the human element consisted of a three-man team. One man would carry the whole GPMG unit, gun complete with tripod, while the other two would carry ammunition and act as gun-loader and spotter. In the early days of the war these gun groups proved decisive in the winning of the firefights, as initially the SOAF Strickmasters were not so quick on the scene.) All the second day, small battles could be heard flaring up at one location or the other. By day three, Watts had split his force into two main battle groups, which were dispatched to clear the Wadi Darbat and a ridge line known as the *gatn* (pronounced 'Cuttin' by everyone).

During one firefight around the *gatn* Watts, carrying two containers of ammunition, ran side by side with a heavy-machine-gun crew. Due to his years it was difficult for him to keep up with the younger and extremely fit SAS soldiers, who growled at him, 'If you can't keep up, Boss, get off the mountain.' The colonel's reply is not printable, but needless to say he did keep up throughout the entire day, fighting alongside his men as he supervised their actions. Such simple methods made Johnny Watts one of the most popular colonels the Regiment has ever had.

For several days the Adoo fought with everything they had, mistakenly thinking that this was nothing more than a short operation by the SAF who would shortly give up and leave. It was not to be so. The KBW, many of them back in their own territory, fought as well as any professional soldier, bounding forward, stride for stride with the SAS men. By 9 October the initiative was clearly on the side of the SAF and the Adoo broke up into smaller groups and disappeared in the small bush-covered wadis.

Meanwhile the eastern battle group, who had moved to a location called 'Pork Chop Hill,' began to have problems with their Firqat. It was not the first time the Firqat A'asifat had posed problems, wishing as they did to observe

Ramadan. Despite the Sultan's dispensation and calling of the Qadi, they were withdrawn to Jibjat for the month of Ramadan. A few days later, Watts descended on the Firqat's leaders and, expressing himself in no uncertain terms, left them in no doubt about how he viewed them.

As both sides in the war eased back a little, a main base was established at a place known as 'White City'. By this time the choppers were quickly using up their flying hours and desperately needed servicing. Likewise ammunition supplies were dwindling, especially mortar bombs, and water was at a premium. Under Watts's orders an airstrip was to be constructed at White City. This would allow the Skyvans – which had a much greater capacity than the helicopters – to alleviate the resupply problem.

As troops began arriving into the location the Firqat were send to picket the high ground while SAS men set to work constructing the airstrip. They worked all night, coming under fire from the enemy several times, but by dawn they were ready to receive the first aircraft. Again the battle flared up. Each time a Skyvan landed the Adoo were waiting; mortar bombs began to fall and small-arms fire was directed at several aircraft. To counter this, heavily armed dawn patrols were sent out to engage and distract the enemy while the aircraft unloaded. This period saw some of the heaviest fighting of the war.

Despite the problems with the other Firqats, the KBW in the western group continued to fight hard. When news arrived that a large contingent of Adoo had been observed in the Wadi Darbat, most of them suffering from the effects of recent battles, the KBW set about planning a raid. Bombardment by air or artillery had little effect and ammunition was in short supply, so eventually a strong patrol was sent against the Adoo-occupied village of Shahait. A fierce gun battle erupted that left two Adoo dead, but many others escaped before the SAS and Firqat could arrive. From a distance of three miles a large group of Adoo was spotted by an SAS trooper who pinpointed their position on his map. He plotted their location and called in an artillery barrage from gun-lines at Taqa. It was an unbelievable sight when the first spotting salvo landed smack in the middle of the Adoo, and the trooper could be heard screaming into the radio, 'On target – fire for effect – fire for effect.' Night and day the SAS units pushed forward. As one position was taken it was quickly handed over to the Sultan's Armed Forces (SAF) while the SAS and the Firqat units chased the enemy.

Those first weeks were by far the toughest and, as with all things new, it took time for the systems to fall into place and to establish effective control with the supporting units, such as the Sultan's Artillery, SOAF and some of the Firqats. It would be wrong not to stress the importance of the bond between the Firqat and the SAS, something that Watts impressed on all his men. The Firqat had been trained to act as a military body, though in reality they were far from being such. Yet they possessed a feeling for their own backyard that the SAS did not have. It was not uncommon for them to wander into battle with their rifles slung over their shoulder – then, quite suddenly, they would drop to the ground and start darting forward. It was a movement the SAS soldiers came to recognise: it meant 'Adoo'. In battle they were courageous, always dashing into the fight even if sometimes their firing became a little erratic. They were also honest and direct: if, for some reason, the accompanying SAS unit did not do as they requested they would soon make their point obvious. At the same time, when they were around the SAS units would be guaranteed a good night's sleep. As the war progressed, many of the Adoo who were captured or who surrendered would help swell the ranks of the local Firqat. Captured Adoo differed greatly. It was not uncommon to find, after the battle, dead or wounded Adoo dressed in a better uniform than that of the SAS. (Khaki shorts and shirt, ammunition belt, water and AK47, all topped off with a blue beret complete with red star, and for a finishing touch a copy of the *Thoughts of Chairman Mao* in his pocket.) While dead Adoo were often stripped of their weapons and ammunition, their bodies would be left unmolested for their comrades to retrieve later.

Skirmishes and battles would always be fought very close and frequently. Rarely an hour would go by without one of the three battle groups coming under fire. The routine was to advance to contact, hold the firefight, bring up gun groups and call in jets. Winning the firefight is the basis of most military strategy. Hit the enemy with a wall of accurate fire and he will be destroyed. Like David Stirling before him, Watts knew this and hence supplied his troops with three of the best infantry weapons ever: the AR15 rifle, the 81mm mortar and the GPMG.

In the face of such firepower the war developed into a steady round of stand-off raids by the Adoo. In reply strong patrols and ambushes were carried out by the SAS, Firqat and SAF operating from their established bases. However, it soon became obvious that to stop the enemy completely two things would be needed. Break the Adoo lines of communication and resupply, and then win the hearts and minds of the Jebeli people. The first was a matter of laying minefields and establishing firm defence lines in order to monitor the Adoo movements and respond accordingly. The second was a task at which the SAS are past masters: winning hearts and minds. Small aid stations were set up and manned by SAS medics. SAS Arabists would regularly talk to village leaders and their problems became the SAS's problems. Civil-aid teams soon moved into the liberated areas. Water was found and drilling teams brought it to the surface, in a land where water has an importance next to life itself – the expression on a Jebeli's face is one of pure wonder and delight when the cool clear liquid gushes from the ground. Above all, communications open up trade and commerce and nothing was more clear than this when at last a metalled road linked the Jebel with Salalah.

While the Oman war continued for several more years, in 1971 Johnny Watts was to relinquish command of the Regiment but went on to command the SAS Group and later the Sultan of Oman's Armed Forces.

Author's note: The war in Oman has been over for many years and today the Jebel is settled with towns and villages where people live without fear and go about their business in safety. Places like White City are no longer a dirt runway protected by a ring of barbed wire and SAS gun emplacements: they are real towns with schools and shops. When considering this, it would be fair to say that it was Watts's personal policy that snatched back the country from the grip of communism and helped make this kind of peace possible.

16. COLONEL IAN 'JOCK' LAPRAIK

Major Ian 'Jock' Lapraik had trained as a lawyer and in his youth had been a a runner of some international acclaim. Having joined the Cameron Highlanders in 1941, he served in Abyssinia and the Western Desert before taking over M Squadron, SBS. One of his first missions was to move the squadron from Palestine to the island of Simi. This was done on the night of 17 September 1943, the squadron having sailed their caiques via Kos and Leros.

As the squadron approached the island Lapraik sent Anders Lassen (see chapter 58) forward to recce in a canoe. Although the Italian garrison opened fire on both the canoe and the approaching caiques, Lassen's voice bellowing out in Danish subdued the foe. During this lull M Squadron was able to get ashore while Lassen took surrender of the 140-man garrison. From their base on Simi, Lapraik sent out patrols to establish what German presence occupied the other various islands. However, on 9 October the Germans made an attempt to recapture the island and attacked Simi. The Germans were ferried from Kos (which had been recaptured a few days before) by schooner. Some of the German soldiers made it ashore and attempted to take the high ground but were driven back by the SBS. It is reported that Lassen actually got the surrendered Italians to fight for the SBS by using his pistol as persuasion. When one of the caiques started firing at the schooner, the Germans retreated after taking some sixteen dead and many wounded.

The following day Luftwaffe bombers carried out a series of raids during which twenty Greek civilians and two SBS soldiers were killed. One of the bombs landed on Major Lapraik's headquarters and two men, Guardsman Thomas Bishop and Corporal Sidney Greaves MM, were buried under the rubble. As others fought to rescue them, it became apparent that Bishop could not be freed without further debris and rubble falling on Greaves. The only solution was for Bishop's foot to be amputated and to this he very bravely and selflessly agreed.

By the light of a candle, lying on his back and working with only the minimum of instruments an SBS medic, Sergeant Porter Darrell, carried out the operation under the guidance of an RAF medical officer, Flight Lieutenant Leslie Ferris, who could not perform the operation himself as he was suffering from an injured wrist. It took 27 hours, during which more air raids took place, to free Guardsman Bishop. Unfortunately, however, he died soon afterwards from pain and shock. Sadly, his death was in vain as Corporal Greaves was found to be dead on being pulled clear. Due to the continual bombing, M squadron was ordered to leave the island on 12 October.

On 20 November 1943 Lapraik led his men on another raid on Simi, this time against a German and Italian garrison that housed troops totalling some one hundred in all. Having landed, he and his men advanced into the town of Castello and reached the Governor's house. Entering the building, a troop commander, Lieutenant Bury, came upon the quarters of a light-machine-gun detachment whose members were swiftly dispatched when he threw a grenade into their room. Immediately afterwards, Sergeant 'Tanky' Geary, who had been covering the main entrance to the house, killed eight Germans who appeared outside on the quayside by the building. Bury shot another before detonating a twenty-five-pound explosive charge in the building next door that demolished it and part of the Governor's house. Having planted a booby trap in the street, which was set off soon afterwards by the enemy, the SBS withdrew.

On the night of 13 July 1944 Lapraik's men returned to Simi as part of a combined force, comprising some 220 men of M Squadron SBS and the Greek Sacred Squadron, that landed on the island unobserved by the enemy. At dawn on the following day the castle on Simi was subjected to heavy fire by machine-guns and mortars. The combined force attacked the enemy positions in the monastery and eventually forced their occupants down a promontory at one end of the island where they were subsequently persuaded to surrender.

Major Ian 'Jock' Lapraik was later seconded to the Raiding Forces Middle East, a force that, including the earlier SBS operations, made over 380 raids on 70 different islands. During his period of service in the Second World War he was wounded six times and captured three, but always managed to escape. He was made Honorary Colonel of the 21 SAS (V) between 1973–83. He died on 15 March 1985, aged 69.

17. STAFF SERGEANT SIMON 'LOFTY' LAYCOCK (PSEUDONYM)

Lofty Laycock joined the SAS in 1977, having previously served with the Parachute Regiment. Several tours in Northern Ireland soon indicated that Lofty had developed special skills when it came to dealing with the IRA so it was no surprise when he was chosen to lead one of the teams sent to Gibraltar to counter a terrorist threat.

From the mid-1970s onward the role of the SAS began to change, although the basic structure and strategy of the Regiment remained the same. One such change was the formation of the anti-terrorist unit that the SAS now maintains. Another development is its closer link with other security service agencies, MI5 and MI6 in particular. Through such alliances the operational remit of the SAS now has few bounds, especially when it comes to protecting the interests of Great Britain. Sometimes the British government will dispatch no more than a couple of SAS men to sort out a particular problem. However, when dealing with the IRA experience has shown that it is best to deploy a full team.

This was the case in 1987, when MI5 received information that a notorious member of the IRA, Sean Savage, was living in Spain with another IRA suspect, Daniel McCann. Savage was a known bomb-maker and it was thought the two men were planning bombing campaigns against British targets. MI5 kept the pair under surveillance for six months and their vigilance was rewarded when a further IRA member, Maraid Farrell, arrived at Malaga airport on 4 March 1988. She was met by Savage and McCann and together the three of them formed what MI5 considered to be an active IRA cell. Surveillance was stepped up, and several of their conversations were recorded. Through this it was discovered that they were planning to bomb the British garrison in Gibraltar by exploding a car bomb at a military ceremony.

The appropriate authorities were informed and the SAS was asked to send in a counter-terrorist team. Their task, code-named 'Operation Flavius', was to seize the active unit before it could cause any damage. Despite the surveillance, the IRA unit managed to escape from sight for a short while but the SAS were not too worried: they thought they knew what the terrorists were up to and what their next move would be. They believed that the unit would place a decoy car in Gibraltar, parking it at a strategic point along the route of the military parade and leaving it there. This decoy car would ensure that the car with the bomb actually in it would have a parking space on the day in question since the decoy vehicle could be moved to make way for it at the appropriate time. The most effective place – as far as the likely scale of devastation was concerned – for the bomb to be detonated was the plaza, since this was where most of the troops and the public would be gathered together in one place at one time. The SAS decided to keep watch on this area.

At 2 p.m. on 5 March 1988, they were proved right when Sean Savage was seen parking a white Renault 5. It looked as though he was setting up the bomb-triggering device. At approximately the same time, British Intelligence was alerted that McCann and Farrell had crossed Gibraltar's border with Spain and were heading into town. Once Savage had finished with the car, he left the plaza, leaving it clear for the SAS to go and check it out. An explosives expert gave the car a good looking-over, but could find no obvious signs of a bomb. Nevertheless, it could not be ruled out that the car might contain some sort of explosive device, for example Semtex, which is easy to hide. The local police chief, Joseph Canepa, agreed that the IRA operation looked as if it was going ahead and passed all authority over to the SAS team. It was now urgent that the IRA unit should be apprehended and, if possible, captured alive. However, because there were so many lives at risk if things went wrong, the SAS also knew that they would have to shoot to kill, if there was no other option.

Dressed casually but armed with concealed 9mm Browning High Power automatic pistols, the SAS soldiers got into position. They were able to keep in contact through small radios hidden about their persons. Keeping in the background, they watched as Savage met up with McCann and Farrell and made their way back to the Spanish border. However, suddenly everything changed as Savage, for no reason that was apparent, turned and started to head back into town. The SAS team of four were forced to split into two two-man groups to keep up with this new twist.

More trouble followed. A local policeman out in his car was recalled to base just as he was driving past McCann and Farrell. This action spooked the two terrorists and they turned around, looking nervous. McCann immediately saw one of the SAS soldiers behind him, only ten metres away. That soldier was Lofty Laycock. Lofty started to issue a challenge and McCann began to move his arm across his body. It looked to the soldier as if the terrorist was about to detonate the bomb remotely. Not taking any risks, Lofty immediately shot McCann in the back. Farrell grabbed for her bag, as if about to go for a weapon, and was also shot by both soldiers.

Hearing the shots, Savage turned back and immediately came face to face with the other two soldiers. They shouted a warning but Savage ignored them and went for what was assumed to be a weapon. Once again the SAS men opened fire, killing Savage instantly.

At the time, it had seemed like a straightforward case of having to kill in order to prevent a greater loss of life. But later, after the scene and the bodies had been examined, things became more complicated. All three terrorists were found to have been unarmed and there was no explosive device in the Renault 5. However, another car with a bomb inside *was* discovered later in Malaga, proving that the cell had indeed intended to carry out some atrocity. The whole event suddenly became very public and controversial with accusations from 'witnesses' being given front-page treatment in the papers. There were allegations that the SAS had shot the terrorists at point-blank range while they were surrendering with their hands in the air. The true facts, however, came out at the inquest in September 1988. With a majority verdict, the SAS soldiers were cleared of unlawful killing and it was hoped that the whole affair had come to an end.

It was not to be. The relatives of the three dead terrorists were still convinced that the SAS had operated a shoot-to-kill policy and took them to court. Eventually the European Commission of Human Rights in Strasbourg concluded, by eleven votes to six, that, given the circumstances, the SAS had not used unnecessary force. Even this was not the end of the case, however, as the matter was then referred to the European Court of Human Rights. As a result, despite the earlier rulings, the British government was forced to compensate the terrorists' relatives for the deaths of the IRA cell members.

18. CAPTAIN JOHN HAMILTON

During the Falklands War in 1982, one SAS officer stood out not so much for his name as for his deeds. This young man was Captain John Hamilton, troop commander of D Squadron's Mountain Troop. His time in the SAS was short since, having passed selection in January 1981, he was sadly killed in June the following year. In this short time he displayed a talent that few, especially by SAS standards, have for daring and leadership.

One of his first tasks was to take his troop onto the Fortuna Glacier on the island of South Georgia. Once there, they were to set up observation posts around the town of Leith to help the retaking of the island by British forces. The troop was ferried to the glacier by Wessex helicopters from HMS *Antrim* and HMS *Tidespring*. Even as they were dropped onto the icy surface of the glacier with their equipment it was obvious that the weather was unfavourable. Conditions on the glacier were bad and deteriorated as night fell: blizzards swept the camp, destroying one of the two tents and exposing all inside to the dangers of hypothermia and frostbite. Realising that the situation had become untenable and even life-threatening, Hamilton requested an evacuation.

The following morning, a radar-equipped Wessex helicopter, leading two others, attempted a rescue. The conditions were still bad but all three helicopters managed to locate the men and touch down on the ice. Once the helicopters were loaded up, they took off again. Then disaster struck – one of the helicopters crashed into the glacier. Luckily only one man was slightly injured, but the helicopter itself was a write-off. The other two Wessexes returned and dumped fuel and equipment so that they would be able to take everyone from the stricken aircraft. As they did this, the weather started to worsen again, causing another helicopter to crash into an ice ridge. Again, amazingly, there were no casualties. The remaining helicopter, nicknamed 'Humphrey', had no choice but to fly back to the *Antrim*. However, later in the day it returned to the glacier to pick up the rest of the men. The pilot was Lieutenant Commander Ian Stanley RN, who knew that by carrying so many men the helicopter was dangerously overloaded. Nevertheless, he flew it skilfully back to the ship where it eventually crash-landed on the deck. Because of his professionalism and courage, Stanley was later awarded the DSO.

For Hamilton the war continued at a fast pace, and a few days later he led his troop into Grytviken to witness the surrender of the Argentine forces. But, always on the hunt for work, Hamilton threw his troop into operation after operation.

One such task was the raid on Pebble Island. Here, in the north of West Falkland, there lay a small Argentine-controlled airstrip. This base housed a number of ground attack aircraft that had been inflicting casualties on and causing other problems for the British forces. Fearing the base could become a threat to the main troop-landings at San Carlos Water, the SAS were given the task of assaulting the airstrip, destroying all the aircraft and, if necessary, killing all the ground crew and supporting garrison. Three ships – HMS *Hermes*, HMS *Broadsword* and HMS *Glamorgan* – were to provide fire support by supplying an on-shore bombardment.

On the night of 14 May 1982, 45 men of D Squadron were dropped by helicopter about six kilometres from their target, the airstrip. Their weaponry was impressive, including LAW anti-tank rockets and 81mm mortars. It was planned that the men from Mountain Troop, under Hamilton, would lead the attack while the other two troops formed a back-up force.

HMS *Glamorgan* started off the offensive by laying down a heavy bombardment on the airfield. Then the SAS opened up with 81mm mortars, M203 grenade launchers, 66mm LAWs and small-arms fire. The intense barrage forced the Argentines to take cover as Mountain Troop invaded the airfield and began to fix explosive charges onto the planes. Once their job was complete, they withdrew. Although the men came under return fire from the Argentines, most of it was inaccurate and no one was hit. There was one SAS casualty, though: one man was slightly injured by an exploding mine.

The men were extracted back to the *Hermes* where the operation was applauded as a success. All the aircraft, including six Pucaras, four Turbo-Mentors and a Skyvan Transport, were destroyed and the airfield put out of use. A great amount of enemy ammunition had also gone up in the explosions.

While 3 Para and 45 Commando pushed forward, the SAS commander, Mike Rose, proposed that D Squadron should be allowed to take and occupy Mount Kent. The fact that it lay some forty miles behind the Argentine lines at the time seemed of little importance. In fact, G Squadron had inserted an OP (observation post) in the area on 1 May. This patrol of four men had lain hidden, living in extreme cold and suffering great hardship not only from the weather but also from the constant tension of the risk of detection by the enemy. In the end Brigadier Thompson gave Rose the go-ahead to seize the position. A small patrol was inserted to recce the area and reported that the SAS could move in whenever it wanted to. Unfortunately, on the eve of the mission the ship *Atlantic Conveyor* was hit and sunk by an Argentine Exocet, resulting in the loss of several vital helicopters. While this made resupply to the SAS extremely difficult, Rose decided to push ahead. The taking and holding of Mount Kent would put the British forces within striking distance of Port Stanley.

The insertion of D Squadron onto Mount Kent signalled the start of several skirmishes between the SAS and the Argentine Special Forces. However, this was very much a one-sided affair as many of the Argentine patrols simply fell into well-laid ambushes. Many of these encounters were the work of John Hamilton and his troop, who continually roamed the heights laying waste to any enemy patrol they came across. By 28 May 42 Commando had arrived to reinforce the position and by 31 May the British had themselves a firm base from which to assault Port Stanley.

In early June, towards the end of the war, D Squadron had taken over some of the hazardous duties of close observation from G Squadron. Hamilton was leading a patrol close to Port Howard, on West Falkland and, having established a secure hide, moved forward for better observation. The position he chose for himself and the signaller was just 2,500 metres from the Argentines and so they were able to radio back precise details. On 10 June Hamilton suddenly realised that he and his signaller had been spotted and surrounded by the enemy. Deciding to make a fight of it, Hamilton gave covering fire while the signaller tried to retreat to a better position. During the firefight, Hamilton was hit in the back but still continued firing his weapon. However, it wasn't long before the sheer number of Argentine soldiers overwhelmed his position and he was killed. His signaller continued to fight until he ran out of ammunition at which time he was captured. He was not treated badly and as the war came to an end he was repatriated, having been found by the Royal Marines.

Captain John Hamilton was highly praised by the SAS for his bravery and selfless actions and strangely enough also by the Argentinean Commander. He was posthumously awarded the Military Cross.

19. SERGEANT LAWRIE FRASER – AUSTRALIAN SAS REGIMENT

During the Vietnam War, Sergeant Lawrie Fraser was in command of a patrol from C Troop, 1 Squadron SASR during its tour of duty from March 1967 to February 1968. Although Fraser was only 29 years old at the time, he was well experienced in jungle fighting. Having joined the army in 1956, he had served in Malaya and later, having joined the SAS, went on to patrol in Sarawak.

On the evening of 3 May 1967, a helicopter dropped his patrol into an LZ (landing zone) five kilometres north-east of Nui Thi Vai, in the western part of the Phouc Tuy Province. The helicopter had dropped the patrol in a small open area covered with metre-high grass. This grassy area was no larger than a hundred metres square and surrounded by thick jungle, but almost immediately Fraser found some tracks. Within minutes the patrol came under fire. It was answered with suppressive fire from the air – the helicopter light-fire team was still covering their insertion. Fraser realised that their position was now hopeless due to their discovery by the enemy and immediately recalled the helicopter that had dropped the patrol to come and take them out again.

On the afternoon of 18 May, the patrol was in action once again; this time their mission was to carry out an ambush north-west of Binh Ba. Once more they were inserted by helicopter into an LZ where everything seemed quiet enough, so they set off for their objective. Not far along the route, while crossing a track, they saw a Vietcong (VC). Private Jim Harvey immediately fired off a 40mm grenade and the VC was killed. Suddenly a heavy machine-gun manned by a group of VC opened up on the patrol and Harvey was wounded. Taking Harvey with them, the rest of the patrol tried to get back to the LZ under the cover of smoke, putting through an urgent request on the radio for an extraction. With the VC attempting a flanking movement to cut them off, it was a race as to who would get there first. Fraser's patrol won. Once again, a helicopter light-fire team laid down suppressive fire, although this time the firefight was much fiercer than at Nui Thi Vai. Eventually, under heavy enemy salvos but without any further casualties, the patrol was extracted.

Emergency extractions were not always necessary, however. On 7 June, Fraser's patrol was dropped off at an LZ in an area of primary jungle seven kilometres north-east of Nui Dat. This time the insertion was completed without any dramas. Two days later the patrol had laid an ambush of Claymore mines on a track frequently used by the VC. Sure enough, at 14.45 hours six enemy walked into the ambush and one, later revealed to be a VC tax collector with a large sum of money on him, was killed. Their mission a success, Fraser's patrol was extracted and returned safely to Nui Dat.

20. MAJOR IAN FENWICK

During the early summer of 1944 it was planned that D Squadron, 1 SAS, commanded by Major Ian Fenwick, should be infiltrated into France to organise the local Maquis (the Resistance) into a fighting force, blow the railway lines and generally cause as much chaos for the Germans as possible. It was to be known as 'Operation Gain'. On the night of 13 June 1944, the advance party, under the command of Captain Jock Riding, dropped into the area of the Forest of Fontainebleau, just south of Paris. This advance party had the job of finding a base suitable for the use of Fenwick and his men when they landed three nights later. Another party of men, led by Lieutenant Watson, also landed that night; they were tasked with sabotaging some railway lines before linking up with the main party.

As planned, Fenwick's men landed three nights later, making their way to the location selected as a base by Riding and the advance party. It was in some woods to the west of Pithiviers that at first seemed well suited to their needs. It soon became clear that Maquis security was less than satisfactory but men from the SAS squadron still managed to mount foot patrols and blow up local railway lines. As well as soldiers, Fenwick had had a number of jeeps and their drivers dropped into the area, making their team mobile. As soon as they felt their work in the area was done, the main party moved base to the Forest of Orleans, further south. Riding and his men stayed behind at the old camp.

On 4 July, reinforcements, under Captain Garston, were dropped into the area. This time the Germans had had word of what was going on and were waiting for them as they landed. Three men managed to escape but nine were captured and taken to Paris. Of the nine, two – Lieutenant Weihe and Corporal Lutton – were taken to hospital with wounds. Lutton died the next day. The other seven were held captive until 8 August when they were taken into some woods near Beauvais and shot. Of the three who escaped, two – Jones and Vaculik – incredibly managed to make their way eventually back to Allied lines.

The fate of the reinforcement party had been a great blow to Operation Gain, but it didn't stop Fenwick and his men. A train at Beaune was destroyed and the Malesherbes-to-Corbeil line was raided by Watson. However, things did not always go so smoothly. Fenwick and a group of his men planned to sabotage a shed full of locomotives at Beligarde, on information given to them by the Maquis. Upon arriving there, they found themselves surrounded by Germans. They had been betrayed. In the fierce firefight that followed, all the SAS soldiers managed to escape, reaching their jeeps safely.

Maquis treachery was something that Fenwick soon had to contend with every day. To maintain security, he and his men changed bases frequently. Fenwick had decided to disperse his force for added security and so scattered his patrols. One small unit under Lieutenant Leslie Bateman was dispatched to link up with a large group of several hundred Maquis at Thimory, under the command of a 'Captain Albert' who was preparing for an attack on Orleans. Shortly after their arrival, however, the Maquis base was attacked by a large enemy force equipped with armoured vehicles and flame-throwers. The resistance fighters scattered and the SAS patrol, who were travelling in civilian cars, came under heavy fire as they made their escape. The vehicle carrying Lieutenant Bateman, Corporal Wilson, Lance Corporal Essex and a shot-down US Air Force officer who had earlier been sheltered by the Maquis was hit. Bateman was wounded but succeeded in leaving the car and gaining the cover of the woods, unlike the American who was killed as he attempted to crawl under the vehicle. Corporal Wilson received a head wound and was initially knocked unconscious; on coming round inside the car, however, he drew his Colt .45 automatic pistol and opened fire on four Germans as they approached, killing or wounding three of them. He was subsequently taken prisoner and after interrogation was sent to a hospital in Orleans where he was released by American forces who arrived in the city two days later. Lieutenant Bateman, meanwhile, had met two of his patrol who had also been wounded in the ambush. The three men remained in hiding until they linked up with the Maquis and eventually made their way to an area in the forest where they met their commanding officer, Lieutenant Colonel Paddy Mayne.

At the beginning of August Major Ian Fenwick's orders changed. No longer were he and his men to engage in offensive action against the Germans. Instead, High Command wished them to concentrate on gathering intelligence. The reason for this was that an airborne drop was planned for the Orleans Gap, so the Germans needed to be lulled into a false sense of security. Nevertheless, the betrayals continued. On the afternoon of 6 August, the base in the Forest of New Orleans was attacked by the Germans. On being told of this, Fenwick decided that he had had enough. He jumped into his jeep with four others and drove off, determined to find out why the attack had happened. Just before the village of Chambon, the jeep was flagged down by a woman who warned them that the Germans were waiting for them in the village itself. Fenwick, now in a foul temper, ignored her advice and decided to drive into Chambon at high speed. As they reached the village, they were met by a storm of bullets. Three of the soldiers, including Fenwick, were killed. The fourth, a corporal by the name of Duffy, was wounded and taken to hospital. From there he managed to escape and eventually reached American lines. The Americans were so impressed by his bravery that he was later decorated with the Purple Heart.

Through the treachery of those they'd come to help, D Squadron was decimated. Paddy Mayne, driving all the way from the 'Houndsworth' base, ordered the men remaining to carry on collecting intelligence but to keep a low profile. The intelligence was still necessary for the forthcoming airborne drop. This they did but they were still not out of danger. On 10 August another of their bases was raided by the Germans, indicating that the Maquis could still not be trusted. Apart from the raid, further betrayals meant that two more SAS soldiers were captured and executed. D Squadron's ordeal came to an end when American soldiers reached their position in mid-August. Operation Gain was at an end. D Squadron was particularly active under Fenwick, doing great damage to the German war effort and supplying vital information. But his daring had a terrible price.

21. SQUADRON SERGEANT MAJOR LAWRENCE 'LOFTY' GALLAGHER

Nicknamed 'Lofty' because of his height and physical strength, Lawrence Gallagher joined the SAS in January 1968 from 9 Field Squadron Engineers. He started as a member of D Squadron's Boat Troop but later managed to reach the rank of WOII (Warrant Officer II) and was awarded the BEM (British Empire Medal). Respected both as a soldier and on the sports field, Lofty managed to notch up many achievements, among them raising the British flag on South Georgia after its recapture from the Argentines.

As the first attempt to land on the Fortuna Glacier on the island of South Georgia had ended in failure, it was decided to try again. This time the SAS, along with the SBS, went in by boat rather than by helicopter. Even this proved to be difficult – some boats developed engine trouble, missed the island altogether and had to be rescued. Eventually, though, they succeeded and managed to carry out what they were tasked with: setting up OPs (observation posts) to gather intelligence about Argentine strengths and positions on the island. According to one of the SBS OPs, the main Argentine force, a group of about a hundred Marines and the crew of the submarine *Santa Fe*, was stationed at Grytviken.

On 25 April, a helicopter pilot, returning to HMS *Antrim*, reported the submarine leaving port and on the surface. Immediately it was attacked by helicopters from HMS *Endurance* and the frigate HMS *Brilliant*, using depth charges. The submarine was badly damaged and only just managed to limp back to Grytviken, its appearance alerting the alarmed Argentines to the fact that British forces were not very far away and on the attack. In fact, British forces were closer than they imagined: taking advantage of the enemy's confusion, a joint force made up of SAS, SBS and Royal Marines assaulted the base. They were inserted by helicopter three kilometres away and slowly made their advance towards the port. When they reached the top of Brown Mountain, they looked down to see white flags being flown from every building in the port. Despite an order to stop and hold their ground, elements of the SAS continued forward while the others covered them from Brown Mountain. Cedric Delves, the SAS commander, arrived in the Argentine position (having walked through a minefield) only to be greeted with a flurry of white flags. The Argentines had surrendered and the assault force had not even had to fire a shot. Lofty Gallagher walked into the base at last light. Around his waist was a Union Jack that he had carried all the way from England. In the time-honoured tradition, the flag was immediately raised by Lofty, giving the British forces their first victory of the Falklands War. By the next morning, a small Argentine detachment at the old whaling station of Leith had also surrendered. South Georgia was back in British hands. Tragically, Lofty Gallagher was killed, along with many others, in a helicopter accident during a cross-decking operation towards the end of the Falklands War.

22. SERGEANT BARRY 'TEX' GLOVER – AUSTRALIAN SAS REGIMENT

On 21 June 1967, during the conflict in Vietnam, an SASR patrol was inserted at 18.05 hours into an area five kilometres north-east of Thua Tich in the Phuoc Tùy Province. The patrol, part of 1 Squadron, was commanded by Sergeant Barry Glover.

The drop at the LZ was uneventful and the patrol moved forward into the thick undergrowth. However a short way from the LZ the patrol came across a Vietcong (VC) camp from which they could hear voices. As they had not been seen by the enemy 'Tex' Glover decided to swing around the VC camp and move north. Once at a safe distance and having established a lying-up position (LUP), they would be able to radio HQ for back-up and wipe out the camp. They had not gone far when suddenly three VC appeared out of the jungle, causing one of the patrol to open fire, killing two of the Vietcong. Knowing that their shots would have been heard, the patrol quickly moved out from the position. The patrol tried to distance itself but it wasn't long before the rear man, Corporal Steve Bloomfield, reported that the enemy were getting closer.

Glover decided that if they kept retreating the enemy would soon have the advantage. He placed his men into a temporary defensive position and the patrol waited in ambush for the VC to advance. They didn't have long to wait. About twenty VC approached the patrol's position and a fierce firefight began. During the battle some of the VC were killed and the patrol managed to disengage and move off. Unseen, they managed to make it to the LUP. The VC did not give up easily, however, and mortared the area throughout the night. The bombardment was so relentless that Glover was not able to request an extraction until midday on 22 June.

The helicopters that arrived to take them out came under heavy fire from VC positions. Even the suppressive fire from the helicopter gunships could not silence them. Despite the danger, the helicopters stayed on site, dropping down lines in order to winch the patrol members up through the jungle canopy from a height of some 129 feet. Those patrol members still on the ground provided covering fire until everyone was safely extracted. Once aboard the helicopter, the men were able to add their weapons to the aircraft's own, raining down a hail of bullets on the VC. Amazingly, both patrol and rescue helicopters emerged from the battle unscathed and returned to the 1 Squadron base at Nui Dat. It was later estimated that Tex Glover's patrol had faced a VC force of company strength.

23. LIEUTENANT COLONEL JOHNNY COOPER

A most outstanding member of the SAS, contributing greatly to its history, Cooper was an original member of L Detachment during the Second World War and went on to a distinguished career within the SAS. He joined the unit via a spell with the Scots Guards, in which David Stirling himself was a junior officer, and No. 8 Guards Commando. Arriving in North Africa in February 1941, Cooper spent time with Layforce before volunteering to serve in Stirling's new SAS command. Cooper was trained as a navigator and went on many of the SAS's desert missions, usually serving as Stirling's driver. He played such a role during the attack on Benina, the location of a major German aircraft-repair base and the target of three attacks by L Detachment SAS.

In 1943, Cooper was sent to an Officer Cadet Training School and at the end of that year flew back to Britain where he was closely involved in the creation and training of the SAS Brigade in preparation for the liberation of Europe. Cooper took command of a troop in A Squadron 1 SAS and became involved in 'Operation Houndsworth'. A Squadron 1 SAS was tasked with establishing a base in the densely wooded area to the west of Dijon. The commander, Major Bill Fraser, was under orders to sabotage German communications and railway lines as well as to give help to the local Maquis units. On the night of 5 June, an advance party that included Johnny Cooper and Reg Seekings was dropped 'blind' in terrible weather. Cooper hit a stone wall on landing and knocked himself unconscious but later recovered to play his part.

Contact was established with the local Maquis and a landing strip was prepared so that supplies and reinforcements could be brought in. Soon the Houndsworth base was up and running, with 18 officers, 126 other ranks and 9 jeeps. The SAS men carried out their disruptive and destructive missions around Dijon for the next three months, continually cutting the railway lines. Soon the German troops (many of whom were actually Russians fighting for the Germans) realised that they were dealing with a large resistance force and moved to eliminate it. They were garrisoned at Chateau Chinon nearby and wasted no time in beginning a campaign of intimidation in the local villages. People assumed to be Maquis sympathisers were kidnapped and taken by force to the Chateau Chinon where they were tortured and executed. Their houses were burned to the ground.

The actions of the enemy did nothing to intimidate the Houndsworth force, however. Captain Alec Muirhead and his troop, together with a number of Maquis, picked a site from which to ambush the enemy as they took their hostages back to the chateau. With forest on one side and open fields on the other, it seemed ideal: an opportunity not to be missed. Johnny Cooper, who took part in the ambush, later gave an account of what happened: 'The first three-tonner, crammed with soldiers, drew level with the wood pile and over came two plastic bombs. One hit the bonnet and the other the rear of the vehicle. Pandemonium among the occupants. Many were killed by fire from the Maquis as they fled across the road towards the open fields. Our Brens opened up with devastating effect and many of the Russians retreated back to the ditch, which was within Reg's sights. It was a massacre. Three trucks were set on fire, the hostages were released unharmed from two civilian cars, but the German light vehicle bringing up the rear managed to turn round and take off.'

The Germans, infuriated by the attack, retaliated by executing thirteen villagers from Montsauche before burning the place to the ground. Nevertheless, Houndsworth continued, notching up success after success. On one such occasion the SAS launched a mortar attack on a synthetic-petrol manufacturing plant near Autun. The result was said to have been spectacular. By September, the men of A Squadron were withdrawn for a well-deserved break and were replaced by C Squadron. By the time they left, 'Houndsworth' had harassed the enemy at every opportunity – 22 railway lines had been cut, 200 Germans killed or wounded and 30 targets bombed.

By 8 April, Captain Johnny Cooper led a section of one of the 1 SAS troops that would confront a variety of enemy units, including *Fallschirmjager* of the German 1st Parachute Army, Hitler Youth and *Volkssturm* home-defence units. Although the war was almost over they experienced hard fighting during the advance into central Germany. On one occasion, while reconnoitring an area of woodland in advance of an armoured-car squadron of the Inns of Court Regiment, they were ambushed by enemy troops who were also supported by three armoured vehicles. Three of Cooper's men were killed and five more wounded, the latter including Lieutenant Ian Wellsted.

Shortly after the end of the war Cooper accompanied most of the brigade to Norway to assist in the repatriation of German troops. Cooper was demobilised in January

1947, though he joined the Territorial Army as a lieutenant a year later. At the beginning of 1951 he rejoined the regular Army and was posted to Malaya to serve with 22 SAS. Here he commanded A Squadron during 'Operation Ginger', which was designed to flush the terrorists from the south of Ipoh. His men finally found and killed Ah Poy, a communist terrorist district-committee secretary in Malaya, in 1954. During his time in Malaya Cooper held many positions within the regiment: commander of C, B and A Squadrons, officer in charge of transport, operations officer, recruiting officer, finally rising to the rank of major. Another of his contributions was the introduction of a technique for parachuting into the jungle. The idea was to land on the high jungle canopy, which would entangle with the parachute canopy, whereupon the men could release themselves from their parachute harness and abseil down to the ground. This technique became known as 'tree-jumping'. The first true operation to utilise it took place in February 1959 when 54 men 'tree-jumped' into the Malayan jungle to assist troops on the ground. Hailed as a success, the technique became accepted as a standard tactic. However, it soon became apparent that it was more dangerous than it had first appeared – three men had lost their lives tree-jumping in 'Operation Stone' alone, and by the end of the Malayan campaign the practice was discontinued, its demise accelerated by the increasing use of helicopters for jungle missions. Cooper himself was badly injured while tree-jumping into the jungle.

In January 1959, while still commanding A Squadron, he was suddenly withdrawn from Malaya and transferred to Oman. There, A Squadron played a diversionary role during the attempt to reach the summit of Jebel Akhdar. Unfortunately, two men died and a third was seriously injured when a stray bullet struck a grenade in one of their bergens. Mopping-up operations followed before Cooper returned to the UK in December 1959. At the beginning of the following year Cooper left 22 SAS to take up the post of company commander of the Omani Northern Frontier Regiment, afterwards becoming second-in-command of the Muscat Regiment. However, Cooper was soon to be once again involved with the SAS.

Now a Lieutenant Colonel, Johnny Cooper led two covert operations in the Yemen involving men from the SAS. These missions were to gather intelligence on Egypt's involvement in the conflict as well as their order of battle, to give assistance to loyal forces of the deposed Imam and to provide medical services to the local tribespeople. On 26 September 1962 the ruler of North Yemen, Imam Mohammed al-Badr, was ousted by a military coup instigated by Colonel Abdullah Sallal. Sallal declared the Yemen an Arab Republic and President Nasser, the then ruler of Egypt, gave him his full backing. Badr retreated to the mountains to assemble an army. The British and French, envisaging the spread of Arab nationalism in the Gulf, planned to infiltrate North Yemen to check the scale of Egyptian involvement before they were willing to accept this new regime. Cooper, second-in-command of the Omani Muscat Regiment, was chosen to lead this mission and in June 1963 the French/SAS eight-man team met up with royalist forces near Sana. The group included three members of 22 SAS – Sergeant Dorman, Corporal Chigley and Trooper Richardson – who trained the royalist tribesmen, supplied them with weapons and gathered intelligence that confirmed Sallal's reliance on Egyptian aid.

After three months the group was ordered to leave the country but Cooper returned to assimilate more intelligence and to arrange further air drops to the royalists. All in all, the Israeli Air Force completed nine air drops totally unbeknown to the Arab nationalists. Cooper continued to work alone in this way for a further eleven months, although he was joined by two SAS men, Cyril Weavers and David Ailey, before the air drops. Cooper spent a total of three years working in North Yemen, gathering information on Egyptian forces and training royalist soldiers.

24. MAJOR MIKE KEALY

Mike Kealy was best known for his outstanding conduct at the Battle of Mirbat in Oman in 1972 (the full story of which is told in the next chapter). On that occasion, under his command, his men fought off overwhelming odds, a feat that earned him the DSO. He left the SAS for a while but returned in early February 1979, at the age of 33.

Now a major, Kealy felt the need to prove himself again and decided to attempt an endurance march on the Brecon Beacons during the SAS selection course. He wanted to show that he could still manage the distance in the allotted amount of time. He started off in terrible weather conditions – driving sleet, rain and wind. The higher the selection students climbed the more intense became the conditions and soon many were walking through thick, wind-driven snow. Unfortunately, Mike Kealy was not carrying the issue waterproofs, preferring instead to make up his bergen weight with bricks. From the start his outer clothing got wet; nevertheless, he continued to march up the mountain. As he encountered the higher altitude where the rain turned to snow, his clothing began to freeze. This combination of the wet, the wind and the cold, lowered Kealy's body temperature to a point where he was dangerously close to being overcome by hypothermia.

Kealy had set off at a quick pace, passing many of the students who had left before him. However, he could not maintain the pace and soon several students whom he had passed earlier caught up with him. Two of the students talked to Kealy, telling him of their intention to get off the mountain to lower and more sheltered ground. (Many of the students, realising that the weather conditions were life-threatening, got off the mountain. Despite the protective clothing issued, a lot of them were suffering from the first signs of hypothermia.) Other selection candidates encountered Kealy who by this time was lurching around in the snow. They tried to help him with spare clothing, but Kealy insisted that he was all right and for a while he staggered on behind.

At around 10 a.m., two more students found Kealy. He was sitting down, covered with snow and unconscious. Searching for a pulse, the students detected a weak sign of life and hurried to get Kealy into a sleeping bag and form a snow shelter around him. One man went off to raise the alarm, while the other tried desperately to keep Kealy warm. Although the police were informed at 1.55 p.m. they did not rediscover the body until 4.30 a.m. the following day, by which time Kealy was dead. The delayed rescue attempt was mainly due to the atrocious weather and the fact that several other students were missing at the same time. However, there was some criticism, mainly about the SAS keeping the search-and-rescue under their control and not involving the civilian Mountain Rescue teams who knew the Brecon Beacons extremely well.

25. CORPORAL LABALABA

In September 1952, D Company of the 1st Fijian Infantry took part in Operation Hive together with two squadrons of the SAS. By the early 1960s a number of Fijians had joined the British Army, many of them making their way into the SAS where they achieved great status with their peers. Of the several Fijians who served in the regiment one man, Labalaba, stood out. To describe this man is difficult. He was always friendly, a man of strength, and liked by everyone. In the early days he would dress as an Arab and patrol the back streets of Aden as part of the 'Keeni-Meeni' operations. However, his greatest achievement was as one of the men who defended the town of Mirbat against the Adoo in Oman.

At 5 a.m., on 19 July 1972, 250 rebel Adoo tribesmen initiated an attack on the port of Mirbat in the Dhofar province of southern Oman. The sheer size of the assault should have spelled success for the Adoo – but they hadn't counted on there being two SAS Squadrons in the area at the time who were conducting an end-of-tour handover, or on the determination of the eleven SAS men stationed in Mirbat.

Just before first light, the Adoo crept up the slopes of the Jebel Ali, a small hill a kilometre to the north of Mirbat. At the top of the hill there was a small picket manned by a section of DG (Dhofar Gendarmerie). The Adoo knew that this important defensive feature had to be taken first if they were to make a move on the town below. Quietly, the rebels crept among the sleeping men and slit their throats. It wasn't long, though, before the alarm was raised and a firefight broke out, the Adoo and the DG shooting at each other with pistols, rifles and suchlike weaponry.

Down below, in the town, a house was occupied by an SAS BATT (British Army Training Team). The sound of gunfire coming from the Jebel alerted them to the attack. The commander of the BATT, Captain Mike Kealy, seeing that the DG position on the Jebel Ali was being overwhelmed, ordered that an 81mm gun should be used in support. The signaller immediately got onto the SAS Headquarters in Um al Quarif to let them know the situation, and Corporal Labalaba ran 500 metres to the old fort where he manned an old Second World War 25-pounder gun. The rest of the team got into position behind the sandbagged emplacements and waited.

As the light improved, Kealy could just about see the silhouette of the fort and the gun emplacement. The battle on the Jebel Ali had grown quiet. Kealy could now see figures approaching the perimeter fence of the town out of the morning mist from the direction of the Jebel Ali. Suddenly there was the sound of small-arms fire as rebel guns were directed at the town. The Adoo were now intent on taking the town, attacking in wave after wave. Immediately, the SAS opened up from their machine-gun bunkers and the 81mm gun also joined the battle. Over in the gun pit by the DG fort, Labalaba fired the huge 25-pounder continuously, sending shell after shell to blast the enemy. Both sides were determined to win, and it seemed that neither was going to give any ground.

Suddenly a short message came over on the Tokki (a small commercial walkie-talkie used by the SAS in the Oman War). It was Labalaba, saying that he'd been hit on the chin. Labalaba was known as a man of great strength and stamina who never made a fuss unnecessarily. Therefore to receive such a message was worrying – he must have been badly injured. Captain Kealy sent Takavesi, Labalaba's countryman, to his aid. While the others gave covering fire, Takavesi ran through a hail of tracer bullets and exploding shells, all of which he managed to avoid, before throwing himself head first into the pit.

Labalaba was still firing the big gun on his own. He did not mention his injury but pointed instead to the unopened ammunition boxes. Takavesi understood immediately. It was vital that the gun kept firing, especially since most of the Adoo fire was now aimed at it. Desperate to get some more aid, Takavesi decided to run to the fort to get help from the Omani gunner. Once more dodging bullets as they cut the air around him, he reached the front door of the fort and banged on it for all he was worth. Eventually the door opened to reveal the face of the Omani gunner. Takavesi grabbed hold of him and they raced back to the gun pit. While Takavesi settled down behind the sandbagged emplacement and fired his rifle the Omani gunner fed the gun. The enemy fire intensified and suddenly the Omani gunner fell back, having taken a bullet in the stomach.

The Adoo now threatened three stretches of the perimeter fence. Behind the first wave, more enemy reinforcements could be seen. They had also started trying to breach the fence, throwing themselves onto the razor wire. The main thrust of their attack seemed to be in front of the fort, where rockets were now slamming into the walls, bringing down great chunks of ancient masonry. Kealy suddenly realised that the situation had got worse: the Adoo had now managed to breach the perimeter fence and were advancing on the fort and its gun position in large numbers. The big gun was levelled at the closing attackers, firing point-blank into their ranks. Suddenly the men in the BATT house heard Takavesi cry out over the radio 'I'm hit!' Falling back against the sandbags in the pit, he took hold of his SLR (self-loading rifle) and managed to keep firing, despite being in incredible pain. Labalaba, seeing the desperate situation, went to grab a small 60mm gun that lay nearby, but before he could reach it, a bullet hit him in the neck, killing him instantly.

Unable to get any reply from the gun pit, Kealy knew the two soldiers must be in a bad way. Together with an SAS medic, Trooper Tobin, he decided to risk going forward to the gun pit to see if they could give any assistance. First, though, he radioed through to Um al Quarif, requesting urgent air cover and a helicopter to take out the injured men and bring in more ammunition – they were using theirs up at a worrying rate. As luck would have it, the newly arrived G Squadron were at the headquarters, already dressed and equipped for the firing range. Upon hearing about the BATT team's predicament, G Squadron's commander, Captain Alastair Morrison, briefed his men and within five minutes they had collected a formidable selection of weapons including eight GPMGs and several grenade launchers. To supplement this impressive array, the reinforcements were also taking over 25,000 rounds of ammunition with them. Without a doubt, the Adoo were in for a bad time.

Back at Mirbat, the battle continued mercilessly. Kealy and Tobin made their way through the firestorm, trying to reach the gun pit. As they neared it, the number of bullets heading their way increased and they were forced to dive for cover. Tobin reached the pit first and dived in. Kealy, seeing that there wasn't enough room, threw himself head first into the sandbagged ammunition bay, tripping over the dead body of a gendarme on the way.

Tobin, now in the pit, made a quick assessment of the injuries of the earlier arrivals and set his priorities. Takavesi sat held up by the sandbags, but still able to fire his SLR. The Omani gunner lay at the rear of the gun clutching his stomach: he was alive but seriously wounded. Labalaba lay face down on the ground, unmoving and silent. Tobin immediately tended to the Omani gunner, setting up a drip. He could see that Takavesi had been badly hit in the back and was losing blood, but at least he was still conscious and fighting, able to cover the left side of the fort with his weapon.

Kealy could see that the Adoo were now making a concentrated effort to overrun the gun and had reached the fort wall. They were throwing grenades, several of which bounced close to the lip of the pit before exploding. Suddenly an Adoo appeared next to the gun pit. Kealy immediately turned his gun on him and shot him dead. In the pit itself, Tobin reached across to check Labalaba but the gaping wound in his neck made it obvious he was beyond all help. Tobin began to move away again when he was hit in the face by a bullet and fell beside Labalaba. It now seemed there was no hope for the gun pit or those left alive in it.

Without warning there was a huge explosion nearby. At last the SOAF (Sultan of Oman's Air Force) jets had arrived with the much-needed air cover. The pilots did not have an easy job – it was monsoon weather, with very low cloud cover, and so they had to work their aircraft dangerously low to the ground. With their heavy cannons blazing, they drove the Adoo back into a wadi beyond the perimeter fence. Having so many enemy grouped in one place was a heaven-sent opportunity; on the next pass, one of the planes dropped a 500-pound bomb onto the position.

Meanwhile, G Squadron were already making good headway. Packed into helicopters, they covered the thirty miles to Mirbat in ten minutes. Because of the low cloud, they had to be dropped just south of the town to make their way in on foot. Straightaway they had their first contact, with an Adoo patrol that was covering the rear. It was only small, made up of one older soldier and three youths, but they holed themselves up in a nearby cave and refused to surrender. Not having time for negotiations, the SAS let rip with several LAW rockets and GPMGs, eliminating the opposition in no time.

With the pressure now off, Kealy was able to crawl his way to the gun pit. The Omani gunner was still alive and Takavesi, although weak, managed a smile. Tobin, too, was still alive but his injuries were appalling. The helicopters were now arriving on the scene, despite taking hits from the rebel guns. Reinforcements took over the defence of Mirbat, while the wounded were evacuated as soon as possible. Tobin (who died from his injuries shortly after) and the Omani gunner were the first to go, stretchered to the choppers. Takavesi, on the other hand, even though he had sustained a wound that would have killed most men, insisted on walking to the chopper without help. The BATT house had managed to capture three Adoo prisoners and these too were sent back to the base on the choppers for interrogation.

Finally, Kealy and the rest of his men were relieved by the incoming G Squadron. Captain Alastair Morrison made sure that Mirbat's defences were repaired and then went about collecting the Adoo dead and injured. Once all the bodies had been collected, it was confirmed that 38 Adoo had been killed in the battle. It had been a close thing and the Adoo would most certainly have succeeded in their attack had not a second SAS Squadron, by sheer coincidence, been only thirty miles away at the time. The SOAF pilots had played their part well, too; their flying in the adverse weather conditions was nothing short of courageous and skilful. The attack on Mirbat was the last major assault by the Adoo forces in the Omani war. Many of those who fought at Mirbat have registered their distress that Labalaba only received a Mention-in-Dispatches when his actions deserved a much higher award.

Author's note: I am led to believe that a life-sized painting of Labalaba hangs in the government building in Fiji. If this is so, then I am glad that one of Fiji's bravest sons has at last been recognised.

26. PETER McALEESE (VARIOUS RANKS IN VARIOUS ARMIES)

One of the most colourful characters ever to come out of the Regiment, Pete McAleese started his military life in the Parachute Regiment in 1960 and a year later volunteered for service with 22nd SAS. Being successful in selection, he joined D Squadron and took part in operations in Aden and Borneo. He left the army in 1969 for life as a civilian but obviously found no satisfaction because in 1975 he was back on the battlefield again. This time he was fighting as a mercenary in Angola, helping the FNLA (National Front for the Liberation of Angola) guerrillas in their war against the Cuban-backed MPLA (People's Movement for the Liberation of Angola) government forces. His mercenary career lasted about a year and again he returned to England. It wasn't long before Africa called him back and he joined C Squadron Rhodesian SAS, serving with them until 1980. After Rhodesia fell into the hands of Robert Mugabe's regime, McAleese travelled to South Africa, joining the 44th Parachute Brigade. Achieving the rank of Warrant Officer, he was soon to see action in Angola once more, this time fighting against SWAPO (South West Africa People's Organisation) guerrillas.

In 1986 he retired, going back to England. Not a person to be settled in one place, McAleese returned yet again to Africa, this time working for a security company in Uganda. After that job ended, he found employment in South America and Colombia where he was tasked with leading an attack on a Communist base in the jungle. This particular operation was called off when in 1988 he was asked to carry out another operation by his employers – to assassinate Pablo Escobar, the leader of the Cali drug cartel. (It has never been established who his paymasters were at the time or if this mission was genuine.) Through his extensive contacts, McAleese formed a force of twelve men and trained them for the mission. All seemed to be going well when disaster struck at the last minute. One of the helicopters carrying the men to the target crashed into a mountainside in mist. The operation was aborted and McAleese returned to Britain. He now works in the security industry.

Author's note: At around the time McAleese was in Colombia the British and American governments were sending in Special Forces. The powers that be had decided that the SAS would help train the Colombian anti-narcotics police. This would allow the Colombians to carry out their own special operations within a jungle environment. As a direct result of this training one of the police units was able to track and kill Gonzalo Rodriguez Gacha (known in the drugs world as 'El Mexicano'). There had been some speculation, although without foundation, that McAleese had been training Gacha's bodyguard. Whatever really happened, it has to be said that McAleese remains one of the most daring and adventurous soldiers the SAS has ever produced.

27. CORPORAL MICHAEL 'MAC' McAULIFFE

'Mac' McAuliffe became part of G Squadron's Mountain Troop after joining the SAS in 1966. He had previously served with the Guards Independent Parachute Company. McAuliffe was a skilled climber and in 1969 was one of the first men to climb the treacherous 'Old Man of Hoy'. As a new member of the Squadron, Mac was posted to Aden. This was at a time when the area was becoming unstable and the British were finally ready to withdraw. Once the withdrawal had been announced, things got really bad, and the rebels started attacking any British targets they could find.

One December morning in 1967, the town of Crater (so named because it sat in the base of an extinct volcano) went ballistic. The rebellious locals killed almost every white man, woman and child that they could find: rumours of terrible atrocities quickly spread. At the time I was sitting in Ballycastle House, near Khormaksar airport, which served as the SAS operational headquarters. Mac had been lying on his bed when the order came to move. Like the rest of the troop Mac grabbed his belt kit, shouldered his rucksack and grabbed his L42 sniper rifle. A helicopter was waiting outside on the pad. Here a small group had assembled while the squadron Boss was making his selection. Taking one look at the L42 sniper rifle in Mac's hand, he said, 'You're on the chopper, all Crater is hostile.'

Minutes later Mac and five others were on Jebel Shamsan, a high mountain that looked down over the town of Crater. As the noise of the chopper faded away, Jock Logan, who was senior, gave everyone the full picture. It would seem that the rebels really were slaughtering all the whites, and the SAS men's task was to shoot anyone roaming the streets with a weapon. That included the local town police, who had sided with the rebels. The patrol had six members, all troopers, and made its way to a good defensive position overlooking the town. Three of them were armed with sniper rifles and, as things turned out, this was the ideal weapon for the situation since most targets were between 300 and 600 metres distant.

Over the years most SAS soldiers become used to death, but in those days Mac was a novice and totally unprepared for what he saw. The bodies of butchered men, women and children had been laid out neatly in the street, deliberately, so that any traffic could run over them.

The patrol settled down and started selecting targets. At one stage several dissidents climbed a short way up the hill to raise a rebel flag. Mac was on his feet and, despite orders from Jock not to, he ran to the flag and tore it down. Then the shooting started, but some ten minutes into the exchange of fire nothing moved on the streets. Next day, Lieutenant Colonel Mitchell ('Mad Mitch'), against the advice of the High Commissioner, bravely led the boys of the Argyll and Sutherland Highlanders into Crater and retook the town. Rumour has it that the local police had cleaned up the bodies and placed them all in tea chests before handing them back to the British – but this was never confirmed.

Mac later saw action in Oman, being shot in the arm in January 1975 during the battle for the Shershitti Caves. He was acting as MFC (Mortar Fire Control) to a battery of mortars after taking over from the previous MFC who had been shot a couple of hours earlier.

Two months after the Shershitti incident Mac, along with eight other members of Mountain Troop, established a defensive position in the centre of a horseshoe-shaped ridge that became known as Point 825. The SAS unit shared the position with a company of Baluchi soldiers serving under British seconded officers. At one stage, the British major commanding the unit took his company out on patrol forward of Point 825 and, having spotted several enemy, called for mortar fire. The gun pit was next to the SAS main bunker whose occupants were not involved with the patrol but who watched with interest. However, the major's fire directions were grossly inaccurate, resulting in the death of a Baluchi soldier. As it later transpired, the brother of the dead soldier had also been killed in a similar situation for which the major had been responsible only two months before.

That evening, dressed in full combat kit and heavily armed, the Baluchi company rebelled against the officer, calling for his death. Two other British officers in charge of some tanks were disarmed by the Baluchis and forbidden to intervene.

At this stage, four of the SAS group under Mac McAuliffe quickly slipped away and headed for the high ground where several heavy machine-guns had been placed for defence. These were quickly turned around to cover the eighty or so Baluchis. Matt, the sergeant in charge of the SAS unit, went with one other to speak to the Baluchi leader in order to calm the situation down. However, the Baluchis demanded blood and for a while it looked like a widespread mutiny would develop. Matt was well experienced and knew that if one shot was fired all hell would break loose, leaving behind a lot of dead bodies. At that point he sent a signal to Mac who fired a long burst over the heads of the Baluchis.

On seeing the heavy machine-guns turned against them the Baluchis calmed down and a deal was struck. The hapless major was made to run the gauntlet from the tent where he was cowering to a Land Rover some one hundred metres away. It was not a pretty sight but far preferable to getting killed. The major eventually drove off into the darkness.

That should have been the end of the incident, as the Baluchis were quite prepared to accept the remaining two British officers and work under their command. However, a few days later the two seconded officers called for a helicopter in order to carry out a recce from Point 825. Shortly after it took off it was hit by enemy fire and crashed, killing all three on board. The incident took place just two miles from Point 825 and it was SAS soldiers who were tasked with recovering the bodies. This they did.

Some time later Mac McAuliffe was driving a Land Rover from Ravens' Roost to Point 825 when his vehicle hit a landmine. It was Sod's Law that he was driving the only vehicle with a front windscreen. Unfortunately he hit this as he was thrown forward by the explosion. The blast caused massive damage to the front of his skull, but he lived. Unhappily, his injuries were so bad that he had to be invalided out of the SAS. His condition deteriorated and Mac died at home several years later. Much has been made about his death in the book *The Feathermen* by Sir Ranulph Fiennes, but the mysterious circumstances described therein are all fiction.

28. CAPTAIN RICHARD WESTMACOTT

Captain Richard Westmacott was a tough, well-respected officer. Although from a distinguished naval family, he served with the Grenadier Guards before joining the SAS as a member of G Squadron. He had boyish looks, fair curly hair and a love of poetry that somehow never quite fitted in with what he did for a career.

Despite his boyish looks he was very much the man of action and when he discovered that his sister, who resided in London, was having a little trouble with two male flatmates who were outstaying their welcome he did something about it. Together with an SAS colleague, he called at the flat on the pretext of visiting his sister but with the actual intention of staying overnight to remove the two freeloaders. The result was quite dramatic: the two SAS men frogmarched the no-longer-welcome flatmates barefooted in the rain to the nearest Tube station while uttering threats to ensure they never would return. Few saw this tough side of Westmacott and he was given little chance to exploit his talents for eviction further since shortly after this incident his squadron was posted to Northern Ireland.

While Westmacott was working in Belfast, keeping some terrorist weapons under observation, a slight problem arose. The weapons had been moved and their new whereabouts were unknown. Eventually, the location of the cache was narrowed down to three houses in a terrace on the Antrim Road. Intelligence confirmed that one of the houses had been used by the IRA before, so it was considered that this house, number 369, should be targeted again. On the afternoon of 2 May 1980, two cars drew up outside the house while another vehicle, with three SAS men inside, secured the rear of the premises. Because the operation had to have the vital element of surprise, no cordons had been set up prior to the raid and no military activity of any kind had taken place.

The assault teams burst straight into the house and up the stairs when they heard automatic gunfire. Unbeknown to them, the IRA had set up an American M60 in the upstairs window of the house next door. The commander of the SAS team, Captain Westmacott, was still sitting in the rear seat of one of the cars, waiting for the rest of his men to get out, when he was hit by shots from the M60 and died instantly.

Realising their mistake, the SAS teams immediately switched their attention to the adjoining house, number 371. The covering SAS team arrested two men as they tried to get out through the rear door. However, by this time the gunfire had brought both the RUC and the Army to investigate what was happening and the SAS were forced to back off after it was claimed that the IRA hit men had a woman hostage. The terrorists would not surrender at first for fear of being shot dead by the SAS so a Catholic priest was called in as a witness in order that the IRA men should be allowed to surrender safely. The four captured terrorists had been on the run from Crumlin Road jail in Belfast, having escaped some days earlier. Several weapons were also retrieved.

For his services Captain Richard Westmacott was awarded the posthumous Military Cross and his death climaxed the chapter of bad luck in Ireland for the Regiment. Two days later, the SAS would very much redeem itself in its successful assault on the terrorists who had taken over the Iranian Embassy in London.

29. TROOPER IAN 'JOCK' THOMSON AND SERGEANT EDDIE 'GEORDIE' LILLICOE

Sergeant Lillicoe and Trooper Thomson were two soldiers from D Squadron 22 SAS that, while carrying out a cross-border operation during the Borneo campaign, ran into an Indonesian ambush.

Geordie Lillicoe was a very experienced jungle soldier who was involved in many of the 'Claret' cross-border raids in Borneo. On 26 February 1966, Sergeant Lillicoe led his patrol into the area of an old Indonesian camp that was situated close to the border. The patrol moved very slowly and with caution for they had purposely intruded into Indonesia. The camp had been found the day before and appeared as though it had not been used for some time. However, a cursory search the previous evening had been curtailed due to the gathering dusk. What little information they had gleaned was of great interest. There were bamboo beds that the SAS refer to as 'bashas': they have no canopies, these being provided by a military poncho. The camp's military nature was confirmed by labels on rusted tins that indicated Indonesian Army rations.

The patrol, which numbered some eight men, had withdrawn for the night on the slopes of Gunong Rawan, where they 'bashered up' for the night. That evening, Lillicoe reviewed the orders given him by his Squadron commander, Major Roger Woodiwiss, in the light of this unexpected discovery. His main task was to watch the River Sekayan, three miles over the border, which was known to be the enemy's main line of communication. Since the SAS were operating in Indonesia, they did not wish to have their presence detected. And another reason for avoiding contact with the enemy was that this was, in part, a training patrol, planned by Woodiwiss for the benefit of several recruits to D Squadron, whose third tour in Borneo was only just beginning. Lillicoe's problem lay not so much with his orders but in having to visit the same place twice, for that would contravene Standard Operating Procedures (SOPs). However, few had learned to master the jungle like Lillicoe and his prime directive was to gather information.

Next morning Lillicoe decided the camp was worth a second look, but he chose to split his forces. His reasons for doing so were based on clear military thinking. The patrol was large enough and he would in any case leave the four new recruits in the relative safety of the overnight camp, which would also serve as the Emergency Rendezvous (ERV). They would act as a rearguard and protect the bergens that Lillicoe decided to leave behind. Dropping their heavy packs would give the other men greater mobility, and in a firefight the SAS soldier is better off with just his belt-kit and rifle.

They made good time, quickly covering the 1,500 yards from the ERV to the camp. When Thomson, on point, reached the outskirts he stopped, motioning discreetly for the others to do likewise. They waited, listening to the jungle, and all seemed quiet. Nothing looked suspicious, and Thomson turned his head slowly to get the go-ahead from Lillicoe. A perceptible nod told Thomson to continue. Ducking under some bamboo that lay across the track he emerged on the other side. There was an Indonesian soldier with a light automatic no more than twelve yards away to his right. The patrol had walked directly into a well-prepared ambush.

Almost immediately the soldier fired. At this signal several more guns opened up on the SAS patrol. Thomson was hit in the first burst, taking a bullet in his left thigh that shattered the bone. However, the impact knocked him off the track where he landed in thick bamboo. Here Jock found himself confronting another Indonesian soldier. He was so close that he could see the tiger's-head shoulder flash of the Indonesian's unit. The soldier was very young and extremely scared: he seemed to be having trouble with his rifle. Jock, who had recovered from the initial shock, found his Armalite rifle that he had dropped when he'd been hit and shot the soldier. He then crawled out of the immediate danger zone. The sight of bright blood pumping from his wound made him want to stop, but he knew that if he did not clear the Indonesian ambush area a second and third bullet would find him. So, with the lifeblood pouring from him, he crawled into the thick bush. Although not out of immediate danger, Thomson felt it was safe enough to dress his wound and stop the bleeding. His shattered femur was giving him excruciating pain so Thomson injected himself with morphine. (Every member of the SAS carries two syringes that are operated by squeezing the flexible container.) While he did this the gunfire died down to a few sporadic shots. Even so, he felt it necessary to stay alert by constantly surveying the tactical situation.

Lillicoe was a short way off and was lying quite still, with blood all over him. As patrol commander, he had been immediately behind Thomson and had also been hit by the initial bursts of Indonesian gunfire. As Thomson was thrown to the left of the bamboo clump, Lillicoe had leaped to the right, firing forward as he did so. Almost immediately he was knocked off his feet. Hit in the legs, he was unable to move and was forced to return fire while sitting in the centre of the track.

Despite their injuries, both men continued to lay down suppressive fire while the remaining members of the patrol 'bugged out'. Then, as quickly as it had started, the firing stopped. Lillicoe and Thomson sat waiting before struggling to remove themselves from the immediate ambush zone. Then Thomson saw a figure stand up and move out into the open. It was an Indonesian soldier coming out to check the killing area. It was a serious error of judgement – Thomson and Lillicoe fired together. Once more the area fell quiet. This time Lillicoe and Thomson exchanged words, telling each other of their injuries. At this time Jock Thomson came forward to give Lillicoe covering fire. As Thomson had managed to get to his feet Lillicoe thought the trooper could walk and ordered him to get the rest of the patrol. Thomson shouted that he had been hit too but would try and make it back up the ridge where he could RV (rendezvous) with the rest of the patrol.

After Thomson had gone some yards he fired several bursts into the area where the Indonesians had been waiting in ambush. This fresh gunfire from an elevated position led the enemy to believe that reinforcements had entered the area and for a while they withdrew. The other members of the SAS patrol had decided that the best course of action was to move to the nearest infantry post, close by, and lead back a stronger party to search the area. This they did, starting back towards the scene of the contact late the same day.

At the earliest opportunity Thomson applied a fresh field dressing to his wound and injected himself with more morphine. Then, very slowly, he continued crawling his way towards the ridgeline above him. Darkness fell and gave him some protection. To provide additional camouflage he settled down in the mud of a pig-hole to wait out the night. By morning of the second day Thomson had managed to cover half the distance back to the infantry camp, firing single shots to attract the attention of any search party. He finally managed to make it back to the RV point where he was discovered by a Gurkha patrol who had been sent to look for the wounded men. He was extremely weak from loss of blood and required immediate medical attention.

Geordie Lillicoe managed to conceal himself in the nearby bamboo and, like Thomson, dressed his wound and gave himself morphine. His left leg felt numb and detached: there was no sensation in it. He could feel his right leg, although it would not support him. Everywhere there was too much blood. The bullet had entered his left leg a little below the thigh and exited by blowing a huge hole through his backside. Additionally, the nerve had been severed – thus there was little pain and, luckily, the main artery was undamaged. Bandaging the entry point was easy but trying to stem the bleeding from his buttock proved an ordeal.

These wounds to Lillicoe's legs made it almost impossible for him to move and he was soon passing in and out of consciousness. Hiding under the trunk of a fallen tree, he, like Thomson, waited out the night. He had lost a tremendous amount of blood and after a while he fell unconscious. It was daylight when he recovered and he heard Indonesian soldiers all around him. One of the enemy had climbed a tree about forty yards away and remained there for about half an hour in full view as he looked around. By this time Lillicoe could hear a helicopter searching for him but the proximity of the enemy deterred him from deploying his Sarbe rescue beacon. It was only when he was absolutely certain he would not be detected that he risked using his survival radio, calling in a helicopter that managed to winch him out.

Both Thomson and Lillicoe survived and recovered sufficiently to continue service in the SAS. Geordie Lillicoe is also one of the longest-serving members of 22 SAS and is very much respected for his devotion to military training, especially in SAS techniques. He was awarded the Military Medal.

30. MAJOR DARE NEWELL

Major Newell saw action with the SOE (Special Operations Executive) in the Second World War and was also part of Force 136 in Malaya in 1945. A veteran jungle fighter, his skills were welcomed when he joined the Malayan Scouts in the 1950s. It is fair to say that the professionalism that Dare Newell brought to the Malayan Scouts helped pave the way for the modern SAS. He worked alongside Mike Calvert to give the force a greater professionalism, a task in which they succeeded.

The Malayan Scouts were formed as a counter-insurgency unit to fight the communist guerrillas in Malaya, the original recruits of A Squadron coming from local volunteers, some of them with SOE experience in the Second World War. The men of A Squadron were trained at Johore to live and fight in the jungle in groups of three or four. Their main task was to track and ambush guerrilla forces and to direct air strikes.

Almost immediately the Malayan Scouts were called upon to tackle the problem of open rebel insurgency in Ipoh. Despite a distinct lack of discipline, caused mainly by inadequate training methods, they successfully subdued much of the guerrilla activity. A Squadron was soon joined by B Squadron, made up of men from a temporary unit called M Squadron. This squadron, consisting of members of 21 SAS and other Second World War special-forces reservists, had originally been intended to serve in Korea. Political considerations demanded instead that they should be stationed in Singapore. From there they were dispatched to Malaya. Unlike their counterparts in A Squadron, the men of B Squadron displayed more discipline and professionalism. C Squadron was added after Calvert visited Rhodesia and raised some more volunteers there.

In 1951, Calvert was replaced by Lieutenant Colonel John Sloane who tasked his senior officers, John Woodhouse and Dare Newell, with instilling a greater sense of discipline and professionalism into the scouts. By 1952, the Scouts were proving to be very successful in their operations and the way was now open for the formation of 22 SAS.

In February 1952 an operation, comprising 22 SAS, a troop of Royal Marine Commandos and elements of the Police Field Force (PFF), was mounted into the Belum Valley of northern Malaya. This isolated valley is near the border with Thailand and, at the time, was the headquarters of the Communist Terrorist (CT) organisation that numbered around one hundred. The Commandos and the PFF approached the area on foot, moving along steep mountain tracks, climbing slippery muddy slopes and crossing rivers. B Squadron, numbering 54 in total, was inserted into the area by parachute, this being the first occasion on which the SAS used operationally the technique of parachuting into trees. There were only three casualties and none of the injuries proved to be serious. The operation itself, however, proved inconclusive.

Dare Newell later became the Regimental Adjutant of the SAS and Secretary of the SAS Regimental Association. He is best remembered for his devotion to the Regiment, defending it from political attacks from Whitehall. Awarded the OBE for his services, he died in 1989, aged 71.

31. SERGEANT BARRY BLYTH (PSEUDONYM)

Barry Blyth joined A Squadron in 1968, having served with the Green Jackets. He was a professional SAS soldier and one of the many who had distinguished themselves during the Falklands War.

By December 1993, Blyth's squadron was once more in Northern Ireland. This time his troop were providing protection for an RUC man who was under serious threat of assassination. By methods that cannot be revealed, it was learned that the weapons intended for the murder attempt were hidden under a large thorn bush in a field near Coalisland, County Tyrone. Although the field was separated from the country lane alongside by a thick hedgerow, there was a gateway that allowed easy access. In the major operation that followed, the SAS provided surveillance on the weapons cache while members of 14 Intelligence and Surveillance Group kept a close watch on the IRA suspects. In addition, a Special Branch surveillance team was to provide the Quick Reaction Force, and, as this was an IRA-friendly area, a platoon from the Devon and Dorsets was called in to supply a cordon once the action had taken place.

Barry Blyth and his partner had established an OP in a ditch about twenty metres away from the weapons cache. Two further OPs were placed at either end of the road to supply an early warning and vehicle stops. The Special Branch surveillance team was positioned, on standby, at nearby Lurgan. Several days of waiting followed, until at last the news was received that the intended assassination was due to take place on the next Sunday evening. This was welcome information to the men sitting in the ditches: being December it was cold and wet and they were only allowed cold food lest the steam rising from any hot meals gave away their positions.

On the Sunday afternoon in question, at about 3.30 p.m., one of the vehicle stops reported a car heading down the lane that ran alongside the field. Sure enough, it stopped beside the gateway and two men got out, leaving the driver in the vehicle. Climbing over the gate, the men made directly to where the weapons were stored. The first terrorist to reach the spot, Colm McGirr, kneeled down by the bush, pulled out a weapon and passed it to the second man, Brian Campbell. Campbell turned and started to make his way back to the car with the weapon. At this stage Barry Blyth stood up in the OP and issued a challenge. McGirr, still kneeling by the bush, turned, a weapon in his hand pointing straight at the soldiers. Blyth fired and shot McGirr dead instantly. Campbell ignored the warnings and made a run for the gate, still holding the gun. Blyth fired again, hitting him twice, once in the chest and once in the neck. Campbell fell, mortally wounded.

The driver of the terrorist vehicle heard the shots and realised that they had walked into a trap. Revving the engine, he drove off at high speed. The gunfire had also alerted the vehicle stop further down the road. The SAS men at this stop jumped out and pumped four high-velocity rounds straight into the car. The bullets found their mark, hitting the driver several times, including once in the head. It did not stop him and he drove off towards a small housing estate a couple of miles away. At this point the surveillance team were called in and went after the car. By the time it was finally located the driver had been spirited away by Republican sympathisers and had been taken over the border to a hospital in the south for treatment.

After the area had been secured, an SAS medic gave Campbell emergency treatment, inserting an airway and dressing the wound in his lung. It was all in vain, however, as he died ten minutes later. Of course, the IRA used the incident to stir up trouble and give the SAS a bad press, most of it based around a report from an ambulance driver on the scene. However, as far as the SAS were concerned, it had been a good job. The only fault was that the driver had got through the vehicle stop. The SAS soldier responsible was taken to task by his commanding officers and was later RTU'd (returned to unit).

32. SERGEANT SIDNEY 'SID' DAVIDSON

Sid Davidson joined the SAS in 1973. He served with both B and D Squadrons, working in both Amphibious and Mountain Troops. Sid was a real cool soldier, professional and ambitious. He was also a good man to have around when the going got tough. I first met Sid in Northern Ireland when his squadron were doing their tour of duty. A job came up that required the SAS's attention.

A farmer had been cutting grass and had discovered a wire running across the field. This information had worked its way through the informer system before finally finishing up on the desk of Special Branch. They in turn requested that the SAS have a look, confirming the information one way or the other. The area was put out of bounds to all other security forces and a search was carried out. Sid, who at the time was only a corporal, led the patrol and managed to find the wire – together with a large culvert bomb at one end and a firing position at the other.

It was not advisable to keep the area out of bounds for too long as the local military and police would get suspicious. Before you knew it your secret information would be common knowledge. To rectify the situation, Sid was instructed to return to the culvert the following night: this time he would take an ATO (Ammunition Technical Officer). The ATO would disarm the bomb, thus making it safe to lift the out-of-bounds traffic order. At the same time he would fix the detonator in such a way that if the IRA tested the integrity of the wire it would prove active. This all sounds very simple, but approaching several hundred-weight of home-made high explosive can turn the strongest stomach to jelly.

It was gone midnight when Sid and his men did the drop-off. Three cars passed the crossroads from different directions during an hour. Each group had been given a different task. One would go uphill and make sure someone was actually sitting at the firing point while the ATO carried out his work. Another would look for a hide from where they could observe the firing-point position in order to establish an OP. While this was being done Sid and two others led the ATO towards the small culvert that ran beneath the road.

About fifty metres away from the culvert Sid instructed the two patrol members to stay put while he and the ATO went forward. Before moving off the ATO placed a blanket around his shoulders and wore it like a Batman cape falling from his neck down to his ankles.

Closer to the site Sid instructed the ATO to wait while he did a quick recce of the bomb itself. The ground was wet so Sid chose a route that would leave no footprints. He eventually located the bomb and managed to isolate the milk churn into which a wire was running. (It was not uncommon for the IRA to use milk churns packed with explosive, as the churn shape helps 'tamp' the explosive during detonation.)

Sid retraced his steps before bringing the ATO back to the bomb. Sid indicated the milk churn and stood to one side while the ATO flipped the blanket over his head. This served to hide the light from the small torch he needed in order to disarm the device. After several minutes of struggling with the milk-churn cap it came off with an audible 'pop', releasing with it the stench of fertiliser and diesel oil. The ATO quickly pulled on the wire, removing a wet and sticky blob: the detonator. Working methodically, the ATO cut the wire and attached a small electrical device that would indicate the wire's integrity if tested but would not detonate the bomb. To save having to return to the site the ATO decided to check his handiwork. As he did so he gave a little gasp. Sid asked what was wrong, to which the ATO replied that the bomb was going intermittently live.

Many ATOs have died in Northern Ireland and it is a profession much respected by all the armed services. The men who volunteer for such duty deserve the greatest respect. This particular ATO had been working in Northern Ireland for several years and had a gut feeling about the work he did. He asked Sid to step forwards a pace and then to step back again. Sid did as instructed. As he stepped back the small diode which the ATO had put in the place of the detonator lit up. The IRA had very cleverly attached two metal lids together, separated only by a thin sheet of rubber foam. The metal lids had been punctured with a large nail, creating a series of sharp teeth on each rim. When anyone stepped onto the lids the serrated edges would cut through the rubber and make contact. As luck would have it, the booby trap had not been activated until after the detonator had been removed.

Sid and his team completed the operation before returning to barracks, whereupon they went straight to the bar (at six o'clock in the morning) where Sid and the ATO got drunk.

Author's note: I was in the bar that morning and listened to Sid's story. Both he and the ATO were still sweating profusely, shuddering each time they thought about the possible consequences. Sid went on to serve with the SAS in the Falklands and was one of the soldiers who took part in the South Georgia operation, surviving two helicopter crashes. However, he did not survive the third and died in the helicopter that was cross-decking SAS personnel some weeks later.

33. LIEUTENANT RICH STANNARD

Joshua Nkomo was the leader of the ZAPU/ZIPRA guerrillas, one of the rebel forces fighting for independence in white-ruled Rhodesia. In April 1979, the 1st SAS Regiment were given the task of assassinating the rebel leader and attacking a ZIPRA headquarters building known as the 'Liberation Centre'. On the evening of 12 April, 42 officers and men of C Squadron, as well as seven heavily armed Land Rovers, crossed Lake Kariba on a ferry and landed in neighbouring Zambia. They were commanded by Major Mike Dodson, the second-in-command of 1st SAS.

In Zambia, the SAS men mounted up in their vehicles and headed straight for Lusaka. The following morning, in the early hours, they reached the city. Lieutenant Rich Stannard took two of the vehicles away from the main force, heading towards the Liberation Centre. The main force continued towards Nkomo's house. By 02.55 hours, the main assault team, under the command of Captain Martin Pearse, was preparing to enter the rear of the building when they were spotted by a sentry who opened fire. Despite having been sighted and shot at, the team still managed to cut through the wire of the perimeter fence to approach the house. On the way in, encountering more gunfire, one man was wounded. The ZIPRA guard force was now alerted to the attack and began to fight back, but they were soon all dead, mown down by the twin machine-guns on the team's Land Rover. With the opposition neutralised, Captain Pearse and two of his men made their way through the house, clearing all floors. Nkomo was nowhere to be seen.

The noise of the gunfire alerted Lieutenant Rich Stannard that the attack on the house was under way. It was the signal to launch his assault on the Liberation Centre. The Centre was a large building, important in that it housed the senior members of ZIPRA as well as offices and a large armoury. A one-kilogram bunker bomb was thrown through the window of the operations room by Sergeant Billy Gardner, the explosion and subsequent blaze destroying the room completely. With the machine-guns of both vehicles erupting into life, the Land Rovers drove through the open gates of the building's compound. The gunners laid down savage covering fire while the remainder of Stannard's force laid explosive charges wherever they could: the armoury, the offices and even thirty or so vehicles parked outside were all targeted. The job took twenty minutes to complete and when it was done Stannard and his men quickly withdrew and joined up with the main force who were waiting for them. It was not long before they heard explosions as the charges detonated. The Liberation Centre and all of its contents was destroyed.

By now, Lusaka was in pandemonium and the SAS forces withdrew quickly to Lake Kariba. Once the ferry appeared, the men and their vehicles crossed back over, safely, into Rhodesia. Later it was found out that Nkomo had not been at his home that night because he had been forewarned of the attack by British intelligence, who had an agent inside

Combined Operations Headquarters. Despite the failed assassination attempt, the successful attack on the ZIPRA headquarters meant that any rebel invasion attempt was foiled and the Rhodesian elections went ahead as planned.

34. SERGEANT JOHN SIMMS (PSEUDONYM)

A uthor's note: This next story is a dark secret within the SAS and I have heard several different versions. Nevertheless, the version below is the one most commonly accepted as the truth and corroborates what John Simms told me while on a train journey from Hereford to London. He is not a man to tell lies.

John Simms joined the SAS in 1976 and was posted to D Squadron. He became a very confident soldier and a proficient demolitionist. In May 1982, during the Falklands War, he and three others were sent on a one-way mission to Chile. Their task was to act as an advanced recce for a much larger force that would eventually attack a mainland Argentine airfield. The British were fighting the war on a very long supply line and the sinking of British ships, especially HMS *Sheffield*, persuaded the powers that be to remove any further threat of Exocet missile attacks. The Americans were against such a mission, fearing that any such action would drag other Latin American countries into the conflict and thus escalate the war. However, the risk of alienating the other South American countries did not count for much against the risk of Britain losing the war. If the French-built Super Etendard war planes kept on delivering the surface-skimming Exocets, Britain's sea power would be destroyed.

It was rumoured but not confirmed that the number of Exocets remaining in Argentina at this time did not exceed eight. The same French source also happened to name the airfield concerned – Rio Gallegos. It was this precise information that led to the SAS operation. So it was that John Simms found himself sitting in a Royal Navy Sea King helicopter that had been stripped of all unnecessary items. In addition, it had been fuelled to maximum capacity, thus making it possible to reach the Chilean coastline. The helicopter, piloted by a crew of three, flew the long and arduous journey before finally landing the SAS reconnaissance unit just thirty miles from the airfield. Due to bad weather the pilots were forced to land the helicopter on the Chilean coast near Punta Arenas.

The SAS signaller made contact with the UK via the portable SATCOM equipment. While this was being done John Simms fitted a magnesium bomb to the helicopter. The chopper's crew were told to make their way to the British embassy in Chile and say that they had got lost during bad weather and had crashed on the shore. The SAS continued on their mission.

Some thirty-six hours later, it is reported, the aircraft controller on Ascension Island was watching the activity around the two remaining C130s, which were being made ready for take-off. He also noticed a large column of men making their way to the rear of the aircraft and estimated their numbers to be around seventy. The embarking soldiers were heavily equipped: armed with grenade-launchers and anti-aircraft missiles, they were clearly heading for action. The controller found this extremely odd since none of the soldiers were wearing parachutes. There was nowhere for aircraft as large as C130s to land on the Falklands except Stanley – which was still occupied by thousands of Argentines.

What the air-traffic controller had witnessed was the start of a full SAS Squadron attack on the airfield of Rio Gallegos at the southern tip of the Argentine mainland. The SAS were to fly almost five thousand miles, keeping very low to avoid enemy radar. Up-to-date information would be supplied by the advanced recce team and relayed to the attacking troops. They were to land on the enemy airfield and destroy the Exocets and as many enemy aircraft as possible. Once the mayhem was over, the SAS men were to head for the border of neutral Chile, some fifty miles away.

Unfortunately, the helicopter was discovered and news of the presence of the British aircraft in Chile was broadcast around the world. It didn't take the brains of an Einstein to realise that this was possibly the precursor of a raid against Argentina. Even with extra fuel on board the helicopter, the flight duration alone made it a one-way mission. It was decided to abort the whole operation. The two C130s, which by now were almost halfway to their target, were ordered to return to Ascension Island. The SAS advance party slipped quietly out of Argentina and a few days later had rejoined the task force. Had the raid been allowed to continue, the lives and equipment lost aboard the *Atlantic Conveyor* might well have been saved. She was hit by an Exocet a few days later.

35. SERGEANT MICHAEL REEVES

Sergeant Michael Reeves was an SAS free-fall instructor who, in his spare time, also taught students at a civilian club to which he belonged (a common weekend activity for SAS free-fallers). On 17 September 1967 he was preparing to take another group of students on an extended static-line jump. With this sort of jump, the student exits the aircraft and the static line ensures that the canopy opens automatically after a short delay yet still gives the parachutist time to adopt the free-fall position. On this day everything proceeded as normal, with several students making a clean exit. Suddenly one of the students jumped and there was a sharp and distinct tug on the aircraft. Reeves realised that something was wrong. Looking out of the open doorway he could see that the man's static line had failed to release, leaving him dangling underneath the aircraft.

Reeves quickly sat the remaining students down and got the pilot to increase his altitude from their current level of 2,500 feet to 5,000 feet. He then waited until the aircraft had circled back over the drop zone. Once the required height had been reached, Reeves, strapped into his own free-fall parachute, clambered out of the aircraft and slowly made his way down the line. The slipstream buffeted him against the side of the aircraft and the weight of two men being dragged along made the aircraft very unstable. However, the pilot kept it flying until Reeeves managed to reach the student. He wrapped his legs tightly around the man and released them both from the aircraft by cutting through the static line. As they plummeted towards the ground, Reeves activated the man's reserve 'chute and waited until the canopy had opened fully. Then, satisfied that his student was safe, he let go, falling away and making sure he had put distance between himself and the other man before opening his own parachute. It was just in time. His canopy deployed only as he was about to hit the ground. Seconds later the student landed safely nearby, surviving a situation that could have easily claimed his life. Reeves was awarded the George Medal for his brave and selfless act.

36. LIEUTENANT COLONEL MIKE ROSE

Captain Michael Rose got through SAS selection successfully in 1967 and was posted as troop commander of 24 Troop (Freefall). His attitude and professionalism caused him to be liked and respected by his men. However, at times he could also display a more playful attitude. He was made Squadron Commander in 1975, serving with the Squadron in Armagh, Northern Ireland. He had a knack of being able to communicate with the men: it was nothing for him to suddenly decide to go out on patrol, leaving the corporal or sergeant in charge. He would listen, he would laugh, he would make suggestions, but he would never interfere. Later on, during the war that threatened to erupt between Belize and Guatemala, he flew out with the Squadron, having received orders to observe any Guatemalan troop movements crossing the border. With the promise of action pending, Rose inserted several strong fighting patrols. But the arrival of six heavily armed Harriers zipping up and down the border was enough to curtail any real action and the Guatemalan threat fizzled out. Although British gunboat diplomacy had worked, and Belize had returned to normal, the SAS patrols remained in the jungle for several weeks under Rose's command, carrying out a hearts-and-minds campaign before quitting Belize and finally returning home to the UK.

Mike Rose when he took over as commander of 22 SAS was promoted to colonel. Shortly after the Argentines invaded the Falkland Islands Rose was convinced that the SAS could play an important role in the war. Realising that, unless he intervened, the Regiment could well end up with a back seat, he contacted Brigadier Julian Thompson, the Commander of 3 Commando Brigade, and persuaded him to use the SAS as part of the Landing Task Force Group.

SAS soldiers were deployed in many operations in the Falklands War and Rose himself wasn't content to stay in the background. Towards the end of the war, Rose used psychological warfare on the Argentines, broadcasting morale-lowering propaganda with the aid of a Spanish-speaking interpreter. It seemed to have an effect because on 14 June Rose flew into Port Stanley for talks with the Argentine Generals who now realised that their cause was lost. The Argentines capitulated soon after and Rose, along with Brigadier Peter de la Billiere, was there to accept their surrender. Rumours abound that Rose did, in fact, offer the commander of the Argentine troops, Major General Mario Menendez, a demonstration of the firepower possessed by the Harrier jets as the Argentine troops gathered around Stanley. He is also said to have 'confiscated' a valuable statue of a horse given to Menendez by the Argentine government as a token of thanks for his capture of the islands.

After the Falklands, Rose's career went from strength to strength as he went on to become a Brigade Commander in Northern Ireland, Director of Infantry at Warminster and Director of Special Forces. He came to the forefront of public notice, though, when he was appointed the Commander of UN forces in Bosnia on 24 January 1994. It was a daunting task as those who had taken on the role before him had not come out of it very well: the first commander, Canadian General Lewis Mackenzie, through his actions, had earned himself the title of 'Serb-lover'; the French General Philippe Morillon's efforts had proved inadequate and the Belgian Lieutenant General Francis Briquemont asked to leave the post six months before he was due to go. Without a doubt this new role would be the most challenging yet, but challenges were what motivated Rose to be at his best.

Six days before he took over the role, six children had been killed by a mortar shell in Sarajevo. Rose knew that he couldn't waste any more time and immediately set to organising all that had to be done to bring the warring factions, and especially the Serbs, under control. First of all, all information had to go directly to him: he wanted to know everything that was happening. He made it clear that aid convoys should be allowed free passage through any area – previously they had had to negotiate their way. A few days later, when an aid convoy travelled through a hostile area, it was targeted by sniper fire. The British soldiers accompanying the convoy immediately fired back on their attackers, sending a very clear message that Rose and the men under him were prepared to give as good as they got, if not better.

This aggressive attitude might have worked and persuaded the Serbs to back off but Rose soon found himself up against more than a foreign army. The weak attitude of the UN and NATO's seeming inability to know what to do next undermined everything Rose tried to achieve. The Serbs knew how to play on the politics within the UN and often made agreements that were later broken, told lies and generally did everything they could to play for time. Then, while the senior UN diplomats argued the rights and wrongs amongst themselves, the Serbs would go and take more land, killing and evicting its Muslim population.

Rose tried everything he could to stop the Serbs' little game but, without the backing of the politicians, his hands were tied. He was not allowed to use the force he needed to protect the innocent civilians and the almost casual decisions taken by those who had not experienced the situation on the ground angered him greatly. In March the Serbs carried on their quest for 'ethnically pure' lands by shelling the eastern enclave of Gorazde. Rose decided to play his trump card and requested authority to bring in the SAS. Permission was given and the soldiers were brought in to act in a close-reconnaissance role against enemy positions around Gorazde. Their covert observations gave Rose detailed assessments of both Serb and Muslim positions.

Some SAS men became trapped in a bunker after being deserted by Muslim soldiers. The Serbs, seeking revenge for air strikes on some of their positions, began to shell the bunker. Rose, concerned for his men, tried everything to stop the attack and requested air support. The UN Special Envoy at the time, Yasushi Akashi, refused him but did manage to arrange a temporary ceasefire so that the wounded could be evacuated. One of the SAS men, Corporal Rennie, had been hit in the head and killed but the other soldiers weren't as badly wounded and managed to escape.

The SAS stayed in their role as observers throughout the war and also acted to laser-mark targets that required an air strike. There was a rumour that two members of the Regiment were seen by the enemy and shot at, leaving one man dead and the other badly wounded.

Mike Rose's greatest asset was his quick mind and his ability to initiate swift action. He was often found roaming the operations room, frustrated at not being able to accompany his men as they flew off on missions, especially during the Falklands War. It was, therefore, some small compensation that he was able to negotiate a ceasefire and surrender from the Argentine military. He is possibly one of the greatest soldiers of this century.

37. STAFF SERGEANT DAVE NADEN

S taff Sergeant David Naden joined the SAS after serving in the Royal Signals; on passing selection he was posted to Boat Troop. The conflict in Northern Ireland has meant the SAS has had to work closely with the RUC, especially with its SB (Special Branch). When the Regiment was first deployed to the Province there was more than a little tension between the SAS and SB. But over the years and via the attachment of men such as Dave Naden a spirit of close cooperation has developed that has reaped many operational dividends. This liaison was introduced so that the SAS could work directly with their SB counterparts, with one man being posted to each of the three main TCG (Tactical Control Group) headquarters in Northern Ireland. These liaison officers would sift through intelligence as it arrived at the various TCGs and with the blessing of SB were able to mount operations with SAS manpower provided from the Province, or if necessary directly from Hereford.

The actual role of Dave Naden and his colleagues is still secret but, needless to say, it was fraught with danger on a daily basis. Often working alone, Dave would drive an undercover car through the streets of Londonderry, drink in the local bars and establish the truth behind snippets of information. On one occasion he and a senior SB officer went for a drink and while they were talking the policeman happened to mention that a local farmer had seen some unusual activity in one of his fields. Both Dave Naden and the SB man decided to verify the information by carrying out an impromptu recce. Having crossed several fields they came upon a deep drainage ditch running alongside a hedgerow. After following this for some distance they discovered a large plastic dustbin buried into the side of the ditch. Using a small torch, Dave investigated, lifting a small flap that had been cut in the bin lid. The bin was packed with weapons and various waterproofed parcels that they concluded must contain ammunition or explosive. One parcel, which was sealed with red insulating tape, sat in the centre and Dave tried to remove it. It took three attempts: each time he got the parcel to the small opening it was pulled back from his reach. Upon further investigation Dave realised that this particular parcel was attached to an explosive device at the back of the bin by a length of string. The fright of almost blowing themselves up sent them swiftly back to the bar. This was just one small incident that Dave experienced, but suffice to say that events like this were very much everyday occurrences.

Dave Naden died on 7 June 1978 while travelling alone from Portadown to Londonderry when his car left the road at Shanalongford Bridge. As a mark of respect the RUC Special Branch attended the funeral in very large numbers and continued the wake for several days after.

38. SERGEANT TOM BROWN (PSEUDONYM)

This is a difficult one to write as I have no idea where Tom is at this time. Many will know his real name and recognise the man in question. Few, however, will know him for the man he really was. Though I find it difficult to describe him as a hero, without doubt he is worth writing about.

Tom came to the SAS around 1970 and finished up as a member of Mountain Troop. When he was a new recruit to the SAS the first thing you noticed was how prone to accidents this guy was. At every turn he would knock over a cup of tea or bump into someone, to the point where many of us were convinced that he was doing it deliberately. He never volunteered, never shone at any SAS skill, but as time went on one aspect of his character did reveal itself: Tommy's reliability in battle. A more cool and rock-steady soldier could not be found and in later operations this became his hallmark.

One such example of Tommy's steadfastness happened when the SAS received the information from Special Branch that the IRA were planning to firebomb the post office depot in Belfast. The SAS were tasked to work out a plan to stop the terrorists. The SAS knew from which side the IRA would approach but they did not know when. For the first week the observation was carried out in a car, with the main intervention team sitting waiting in a nearby van. But it was impossible to use such a tactic for long and accordingly several observation posts (OPs) were set up. The main OP was located in a house from where a clear view of the small alley that ran along the side of the post office compound could be had. This compound was surrounded by high fencing and housed the bulk of the post office utility vehicles.

During the hours of darkness, several cut-off groups were placed strategically around the compound, with two men hidden in a large bush. On the night the IRA chose to bomb the post office depot this particular place of concealment was given to Tom and John. Tom was senior and as such would initiate any action. This was just as well for, while Tom was a good man to have by your side, John was much younger and not quite as unflappable. In fact, he was downright dangerous. (Even the SAS get a few scoundrels.)

Up in the observation house, the man on watch was becoming bored. After several days of sitting and watching with nothing happening, the operation was beginning to get beyond a joke. For a while the SAS thought that the RUC Special Branch was winding them up, despite their reassurance that the job would eventually come off. Suddenly the house OP noticed two figures acting suspiciously in the alley below, close to the compound wall. Before he could raise the alarm, one of the figures swung his arm upwards, hurling the first bomb over the compound fence. Reaching for the radio, the OP operator shouted, 'GO, GO, GO!' and the SAS sprang into action.

With Tom leading, the two men leaped from their hiding place in the bush and ran the few paces into the alley.

Suddenly several figures were illuminated in the beam from the light attached to Tom's MP5. Tom saw three figures in the alleyway, two of whom were about to throw satchel bombs over the fence. In such circumstances the rules of the yellow card allow for soldiers to open fire without uttering a challenge. Tom fired two short bursts – both men fell dead. The third made to escape, running back the way he'd come, but another short burst from Tom's weapon brought him down too. This was all very neat and would have been fine, except that John, armed with an automatic SLR, decided to confirm the kills. In a hail of heavy-calibre rounds he proceeded to fire at the bodies. While this was happening two more men entered the alleyway from the bottom end. Not knowing whether they were more terrorists, Tom called out a challenge. One of the men immediately dropped to the ground and placed his hands on his head as instructed, the other made a break for it. Tom fired a short three-round burst and the man fell, dead.

In the aftermath of the incident the three IRA bombers were identified and it was revealed that the two men who came along later were civilians who had just been returning from the pub and had stumbled into the firefight by accident. It was a tragedy that the dead man, a Protestant by the name of William Hanna, had run away after the challenge had been issued. If he had stayed still, he would have been alive today. Of course, the legal eagles got involved and each man's weapon was taken away for forensic tests. As required, everyone gave their story and it all seemed simple enough until it came to John's account.

'Well, I saw Tom move and I backed him up,' John said. 'He slotted two but the third made a run for it. As Tom fired, I stepped to one side and shouted to the boys in the bottom cut-off: "Keep your head down, Bobby." Then I let rip with a thirty-round mag.'

Of course, this casual statement about the cavalier use of such firepower caused looks of horror from the military lawyer, much to the amusement of everyone else present.

John's story was duly corrected and no court case was brought against him and Tom. Such was the way in the bad days of Northern Ireland.

Author's note: Tom went on from strength to strength, serving in the SAS until the early 1990s. Like so many of his peers, he has now dropped off the face of the planet. No doubt he is either doing security work somewhere or is shacked up with a barmaid. That was another side of Tom's life.

39. SERGEANT TERRY WILLIAMS (PSEUDONYM)

On Friday, 8 May 1987, Terry Williams was in charge of the main intervention group during a successful SAS operation that took place in Loughall, Northern Ireland. The operation was planned to stop an IRA attack similar to that which had happened a year before. Then an RUC station at the Birches, County Armagh had been attacked by the IRA using a stolen mechanical digger packed with explosives. The station had been badly damaged. Now, according to intelligence, another digger had been stolen in East Tyrone, and it was assumed that the IRA were planning to carry out a copycat attack. After a concerted search, the digger was located on a farm about fifteen kilometres away and a weapons and explosives cache, thought to be intended for use in the attack, was also discovered. Additional surveillance was carried out by Special Branch who confirmed that the target was to be the Loughall RUC Station. Special Branch found out the date and time by using a telephone tap.

Loughall police station stood next to the main road, its main single building running parallel to the security fence. It was manned only part-time. The two IRA terrorists suspected of masterminding the attack were well known to the security services: Patrick Kelly and Jim Lynagh, the commander of the East Tyrone active service unit. When a Toyota van was stolen in Dungannon by two masked men, Jim Lynagh was seen close by. This made the security services think that the van might also be used in the attack. Soon after, the OP set up to watch the digger reported that it had been moved from the farm and was most likely on its way to Loughall.

The SAS, their numbers temporarily boosted by a back-up force from Hereford, prepared themselves for the attack and got into their ambush positions. Most of the SAS men took up position on the side of the road opposite the station, concealed behind a fence and a row of fir trees. All possible escape routes were also covered by heavily armed stops. The only place the men were not positioned was the police station itself.

At last, just after 7 p.m., the blue Toyota van was seen heading towards the station with several people inside. However it drove straight past, obviously doing a quick recce. A short while later, it returned again from the direction of Portadown and this time it was followed by the JCB. The digger was being driven by Declan Arthurs. He was accompanied in the cab by two others: Michael Gormley and Gerald O'Callaghan. All three men were armed, hooded and dressed in blue boiler suits. It was noted that the bucket of the JCB contained a metal drum, most likely packed full of explosives. It had been partly concealed under some rubble. The blue van cleared the way for the JCB which then crashed through the gate of the station, closing in on the building itself.

At that point two things happened: firstly, one of the men riding shotgun on the digger ignited the bomb's fuse before all three evacuated the vehicle and ran away as fast as they could. Secondly, the blue van stopped a short way down the fence, and several hooded men jumped out and started to fire their weapons at the police station.

The SAS jumped into action almost as swiftly, opening up with their own weapons. The rate of fire was ferocious and by the time it ended all eight of the IRA unit had been hit. During the battle, to add to the chaos, the bomb exploded, destroying over half the police station and showering rubble over a large area. As the SAS began to check over the bodies, a white car was seen approaching the site. Inside were two men, dressed in blue boiler suits similar to those worn by the terrorists. As they came across the ambush, they must have decided that they did not like what they saw and started to reverse. Thinking that they too were part of the terrorist unit, one of the SAS stops fired on the retreating vehicle, killing one of the men inside and wounding the other. Later on it was discovered that the dead man in the white car, Antony Hughes, had nothing at all to do with the IRA and had just been wearing the wrong clothes and had been in the wrong place at the wrong time.

The SAS rapidly got the situation under control for the noise of the gunfight and the explosion was beginning to draw a crowd. The scene of the aftermath was one of incredible destruction: the half-demolished building, the twisted remains of the JCB, the bullet holes peppering the van and the number of bodies lying around must have looked like a war zone to the onlookers. The IRA lost two complete active-cell units in the attack, a serious blow for their morale but a great success for the SAS in their fight against terrorism. The family of Antony Hughes was compensated for his loss and the case was not taken any further as far as the security services were concerned. The IRA, shaken that their plans had been discovered before the operation, became convinced that they had a traitor in their midst and went quiet for a short while as they tried to find out who it was.

Soon, however, the terrorists were back to their old tricks. Not long after Loughall, the IRA detonated a huge bomb at Enniskillen on Remembrance Day. Eleven people were killed and more than sixty injured by the blast.

40. LIEUTENANT COLONEL BRIAN FRANKS

After serving with both the Phantoms and the Commandos, Franks became a key figure in the early days of the SAS. He became the Second-in-Command of the Special Raiding Squadron, seeing service in Italy, before becoming the Commander of 2 SAS after its original commander, Lieutenant Colonel William Stirling, resigned. He was in charge of Operations Loyton and Archway, both covert missions behind enemy lines.

Operation Loyton was carried out by 91 men of 2 SAS in the Vosges, eastern France. The mission was detailed to collect intelligence about German rail and road movements, to strike at enemy installations and to cooperate with the local Maquis (which was problematic at the best of times). The advance party, together with a Phantom patrol and Jedburgh team, were dropped on the evening on 12 August 1944, with subsequent drops taking place in the days that followed. Unfortunately, the Germans had placed large numbers of troops on the crests of the Vosges and the east bank of the River Moselle. The SAS party thus dropped into a veritable nest of vipers. (To make matters worse the Gestapo were also in the area, at Nancy and Strasbourg, and both locations had anti-partisan units.) The SAS men had to contend with large numbers of enemy troops and with traitors within the Maquis. There were also a number of reprisals against local villages in response to SAS successes. The male population of Moussey, for example, was rounded up and packed off to concentration camps. Of the 210 men between the ages of 16 and 60 who were taken, only 70 returned. Franks brought the operation to an end on 9 October, by which time two SAS soldiers had been killed and 31 captured (all of whom were shot by the Gestapo). The lack of supplies and erratic resupply drops had brought the mission to an end.

For Operation Archway, Brian Franks used a composite force (christened 'Frankforce') comprising elements of A and D Squadrons 1 SAS, under the command of Major Harry Poat, and A Squadron 2 SAS commanded by Major Peter Power. Power would subsequently be joined in the operation by another 2 SAS squadron under Major Grant Hibbert. In total Frankforce numbered 430 all-ranks, mounted in 75 armed jeeps, some carrying 3-inch mortars, and a number of 15-cwt and 3-ton trucks which transported the administrative 'tail'. The 1 SAS element was divided into three large troops commanded respectively by Majors Bill Fraser, Alec Muirhead and John Tonkin. A Squadron 2 SAS was organised into two troops under the command of Captains Mackie and Miller.

Frankforce left England on 18 March 1945 and, having landed at Ostend, made its way to a concentration area west of the Rhine. On 25 March, its two squadrons crossed the Rhine in Buffalo tracked amphibious vehicles and thereafter pushed forward through the area held by 6th Airborne Division to take up its main role of reconnaissance. Thereafter it operated under the command of 6th Airborne Division, 11th Armoured Division and 15th (Scottish) Division.

Confronted by a variety of enemy units, including *Fallschirmjäger* of the German 1st Parachute Army, Hitler Youth and Volkssturm home-defence units, Frankforce experienced hard fighting during the advance into Germany. On 8 April, a section of one of the 1 SAS troops, commanded by Captain Johnny Cooper, was ambushed by enemy troops supported by three armoured vehicles while reconnoitring an area of woodland in advance of an armoured-car squadron of the Inns of Court Regiment. Three men were killed and five wounded, the wounded including Lieutenant Ian Wellsted.

A week later, on 14/15 April, 1 SAS elements of Frankforce arrived at Belsen concentration camp where they found some 50,000 to 60,000 inmates living in conditions so appalling as to be beyond description. Four days later, several patrols were deployed in support of the Field Security Police, who were hunting down known Nazi war criminals. They carried out a number of arrests.

Frankforce rejoined the advance through Germany. At the crossing of the River Elbe at the end of April, it was joined by Major Grant Hibbert's squadron of 2 SAS which had earlier been deployed on Operation Keystone, involving the capture of bridges north of Arnhem, that had subsequently been cancelled. Thereafter, it continued its advance through Germany, heading through Schleswig-Holstein and eventually reaching Kiel on the Baltic coast. Shortly afterwards, it was withdrawn to Belgium and on 10 May departed for England. Its losses during Operation Archway had been light: seven killed and twenty-two wounded.

Once the war ended, Brian Franks was tasked with the job of hunting down those Nazis who had been responsible for the murder of captured SAS soldiers, a task he undertook with fervour and great success. He served with the SAS until its disbanding at the end of hostilities. As a man of some vision he later became the driving force behind the SAS Association, so forming a link that helped former SAS members stay together. He also played an important role in re-establishing the SAS as a territorial unit and in 1947 he became the first commander of 21 SAS. He remained Colonel Commandant of the SAS until 1980. Sadly, he died in 1982.

41. GENERAL SIR PETER DE LA BILLIÈRE

General de la Billière is a man who epitomises the perfect SAS soldier. Born in 1934 and educated at Harrow, he originally joined the King's Shropshire Light Infantry in 1952 and served with the Durham Light Infantry. He arrived to join the SAS in 1955, as a captain, and was posted to Malaya as a troop commander with D Squadron.

One of his first claims to fame came when he parachuted into the Telok Anson swamp and spent twenty days there in February 1958, making a significant contribution to the capture of the notorious terrorist Ah Hoi. Ah Hoi was nicknamed 'Baby Killer' after murdering the pregnant wife of a man suspected of being an informer for the security force. This brutal act was carried out as a warning to all local people in the area of Kuala Tengi and Kuala Selangor. Ah Hoi was reported to be in hiding in the Telok Anson swamp, which covers an area of some 180 square miles in the state of Selangor. B Squadron 22 SAS, commanded by Major Harry Thompson MC (6 Troop was commanded by Captain Peter de la Billière), was given the task of dealing with him.

In February 1958 a force of 37 men from the squadron was dropped by parachute into the area. Unfortunately one man, Trooper Jerry Mulcahy, broke his back after his parachute canopy failed to snag in the trees and he had to be evacuated by helicopter. Thereafter the search began, with 6 Troop following the line of the Sungei Tengi.

As the troop progressed upriver, it came across a number of abandoned terrorist camps. After seven days, just as dusk was falling, a troop commanded by Sergeant 'Bosun' Sandilands was informed by an aboriginal that he had seen two CT (communist terrorists), a man and a woman, by the river. Accompanied by Corporal Finn, Sergeant Sandilands moved up and shortly afterwards spotted the two terrorists. Working their way to within fifty yards, Sandilands and Finn opened fire, killing the man but missing the woman who disappeared into the jungle. The troop followed up and soon afterwards found two camps that showed signs of hasty abandonment.

A cordon of troops and police was established around the area while B Squadron closed in on its quarry. Two days later a female terrorist, named Ah Niet, approached a police post with a message from Ah Hoi offering to surrender in exchange for a sum of money for himself and each of his men, as well as an amnesty for all previously captured terrorists languishing in prison. Not surprisingly, this offer was refused and Ah Niet was despatched back to the jungle with a message that made it clear to Ah Hoi that he should surrender within twenty-four hours or face being hunted down and killed. That evening, Ah Hoi and some of his men appeared and surrendered. The remainder gave themselves up forty-eight hours later. Ah Hoi himself was subsequently dispatched to exile in China.

Between December 1958 and January 1959, de la Billière also took part in the victorious assault on the Jebel Akhdar in Oman and was awarded the Military Medal for his actions. Staying in the Middle East, he spent the winter of 1963–64 on attachment with the Federal Regular Army in

Aden. Later in 1964 he was promoted to major and given command of A Squadron in the Radfan. He devised and established a Close-Quarter Battle course for the soldiers engaged in the 'Keeni-Meeni' operations in the colony, as part of his continuing efforts in developing anti-terrorism strategy and tactics.

In 1965 de la Billière and A Squadron were dispatched to Borneo. Here he undertook a thorough reorganisation of the SAS in an attempt to make the unit more efficient, most notably by improving transport to ensure that supplies were successfully delivered to the jungle patrols. Together with A Squadron, de la Billière undertook a three-week sweep of the area between the Bemban and Sempayang rivers, working together with the Gurkhas on the cross-border 'Claret' raids. In addition, he undertook a series of lone reconnaissance expeditions into the jungle. In 1966 he was awarded another Military Medal for his services.

By the time of the war in Oman, de la Billière was second-in-command to Johnny Watts, the two of them making a formidable team. It was not unusual for either man to take part personally in the many battles, and when there was no fighting they would prop up morale by going around the various locations and chatting at length to individual soldiers. On several occasions de la Billière would take out a toilet roll and write down on it a message or request, or simply pass on a message he had taken from individual soldiers' friends in other SAS positions.

From 1972–74 de la Billière held the position of Commander of 22 SAS, before becoming Director of the SAS and Commander of the SAS Group in 1978, by which time he had a Distinguished Service Order to add to his Military Medals. He was the primary force behind the transformation of the Regiment into a crack counter-terrorist unit, and played a critical command role in the Iranian Embassy siege in 1980.

By the time the Falklands War began in 1982, de la Billière had been promoted to Brigadier and was instrumental in the decision to include the SAS in the Task Force, convinced, rightly so, that they were ideally suited for the campaign.

In October 1990 de la Billière commanded forty-five thousand men and women of the British forces during the Gulf War, as part of the United Nations contingent sent against Iraq. By now fluent in Arabic, and with fifteen years' experience of the Arabian Gulf, he earned himself enormous respect, both for his diplomacy and his ability to work closely and effectively with both his Arabic allies and General Norman Schwarzkopf, Commander of the Allied Ground Forces. It was de la Billière who convinced Schwarzkopf to employ the SAS in operations behind enemy lines, and the outstanding success of the ground offensive in February 1991 was largely due to this partnership. When he returned to the UK, de la Billière was awarded the KBE and CBE and promoted to full General. He retired from active service in June 1992.

42. STAFF SERGEANT MEL JONES (PSEUDONYM)

I write this next section tongue-in-cheek as I have no idea how Mel will take this. For that reason I have not given his true second name or rank. Mel is no longer with the SAS but there are few SAS soldiers, past and present, who will not recognise this character. He was, and still is, a man whose military talents and skills are recognised and appreciated. Go to any military exhibition in the world and you are sure to see Mel or at the very least a photograph of him. Military skills apart, Mel's other deeds are legendary.

Mel had joined the SAS from the Parachute Regiment, arriving in Hereford in 1965. I first met this character when he and his long-time buddy 'Frenchy' Williams were demonstrating various parachute techniques by jumping off the top of a building – needless to say, they were drunk. When he was being an SAS soldier there was none better. Mel was keen, adaptable and extremely professional. However, when he was off duty he could be a nightmare, as many of his poor victims discovered.

In the early 1960s the SAS barracks at Bradbury Lines consisted of old wooden huts that had been built as temporary accommodation during the Second World War. Each of these 'Spiders' had six long rooms with a row of beds down each side, to accommodate around sixteen soldiers. One of Mel's favourite tricks was to glue a drawing pin on the end of a light switch onto which he would put a small amount of excrement. He would then lie on his bed with the lights out and wait. Around eleven o'clock the rest of the lads would return from the local pubs and switch on the lights. Their finger would hit the switch, there would be a scream – then a sucking sound as the individual tried to stem the flow of blood from the injured finger. While this was happening there would be a low snigger coming from Mel's bed.

On one particular occasion Mel had been chosen to be the Sergeant-instructor on a training job in Africa. The officer in charge was young and new to the SAS, but instead of taking advice from Mel and bowing to his years of experience he followed his own path. This confrontation was soon settled in Mel's favour by the colonel, who had flown out to Africa to visit the team. Everyone sang Mel's praises: his work and that of the team had been outstanding. As so often on these occasions, the SAS were invited to the local Government House for a celebratory gathering where gifts in the form of watches are normally bestowed on the training team by the participating country. In this instance the function took place around the swimming pool and gardens of the British Consulate. All SAS soldiers on such training jobs are prepared for these functions and normally pack a lightweight suit. In Mel's case this suit was made of white cotton fabric.

With a job well done it was time to relax so Mel, like the other guests, had several drinks. He had been talking to the colonel, reiterating his view about what should be done with the errant young officer, when nature called. Instead of entering the building to relieve himself in the toilets, Mel just walked calmly into the garden and squatted down behind a large bush. Halfway through 'number twos' the daughter of the British Commissioner happened to walk by and saw Mel. Quick as a flash Mel pulled up his trousers and headed back to the party. As he started to mingle once more a startled colonel suddenly noticed a large brown stain forming on the rear of Mel's white suit. In his rush to the toilets Mel fell into the pool. Thus the stain grew even larger, added to which everyone had heard the splash and was looking.

Author's note: I find it strange that Mel's military deeds have gone unpublished, for he was an outstanding member of the SAS. While the above stories are intended to be light-hearted, his participation in worldwide SAS operations would fill several books.

43. CAPTAIN DAVE DOBSON

Captain Dave Dobson was one of the most outstanding officers of the Rhodesian SAS, taking part in almost all of the actions during the conflict between government forces and terrorist guerrillas. In March 1977 the Rhodesian military decided to deal with a strong ZANLA (Zimbabwe African National Liberation Army) garrison, numbering some one hundred terrorists, based one kilometre south of the town of Chioco in the northern Mozambique province of Tete. A and B Troops of C Squadron Rhodesian SAS, numbering twenty-two all-ranks in total, were given the task of carrying out a raid on the terrorist camp.

At dusk on 22 March the assault force, under Captain Dave Dobson, was inserted by helicopter in two lifts from a forward base at Mtoko. Having been dropped approximately seventeen kilometres west of their objectives, Captain Dobson and his men moved off to an LUP in some thick undergrowth about a kilometre away, where they lay up until the moon rose. Marching through the rest of the night, they halted just before dawn and lay up until dusk on the following evening.

At 23.00 hours on 23 March the force moved up to its objective. In the distance, coming from the direction of Chioco, they could hear music and singing which indicated that a major celebration was being held in the town. Captain Dodson sited a three-man 60mm-light-mortar team, whose task was to shell Chioco and its police station to prevent any attempt at reinforcement from the town during the attack on the camp. The camp itself consisted of a parade ground bordered by barrack blocks on three sides, with the guardroom positioned nearest the town on the northern side. Between the buildings and the wire perimeter lay a series of defensive bunkers.

The groups moved to within five hundred metres of the camp, setting up a mortar position. As the four assault groups moved past the mortar position, they dropped off their packs and quantities of mortar bombs before moving up to a three-strand perimeter wire fence and taking up their positions. Just before first light Captain Dobson's and Sergeant Iain Bowen's groups slid under the wire and positioned ten claymore mines along the back walls of two barrack blocks on the western side of the parade ground. At the same time, Corporal Nick Breytenbach was siting eight more claymores at the northern corner of the camp.

The attack was launched at first light. Corporal Breytenbach's claymores were exploded first, followed a split second later by those of Sergeant Bowen. At the same time, Corporal Frank Booth tossed two fragmentation grenades into a bunker holding a number of terrorists. The four assault groups then began their advance through the camp, firing at everything that moved. Having cleared the barrack buildings, they turned their attention to the terrorists' defensive positions, which comprised a network of trenches leading from inside the camp to outside the wire fence. The assault group threw grenades and 'bunker bombs' – one-kilogram explosive charges fitted with four-second fuses – into the trenches as the terrorists attempted to escape unseen from the camp. Some of those who succeeded in doing so encountered a stop group, positioned to the north of the camp, who picked off them off. Meanwhile the 60mm-mortar team was bombarding Chioco from where FRELIMO (Front for the Liberation of Mozambique) troops and ZANLA terrorists were firing at the SAS.

Sergeant Andy Chait's assault group approached the camp from the south. Crossing a gully via a makeshift bridge, he and his men moved through a field of maize until they came under fire from terrorists in a trench to their front. These were engaged with AK-47s, fragmentation grenades and an accurately thrown white-phosphorus grenade that exploded in the trench. Those terrorists not incapacitated by the burning phosphorus were dispatched as they fled. While clearing the trench, Sergeant Chait and his men came under fire from a light machine gun and shortly afterwards Chait was seriously wounded in the thigh, suffering a ruptured femoral artery. Enemy fire, including shelling by some 75mm recoilless rifles sited in bunkers nearby, prevented the SAS medics from carrying out emergency treatment until they had moved him to cover behind some buildings. A medevac (medical evacuation) helicopter was called and this arrived a few minutes later. Unfortunately, the medics' efforts were in vain because Sergeant Chait died during the flight to Salisbury.

Shortly afterwards, the SAS withdrew, leaving a scene of destruction with at least 38 ZANLA terrorists dead and a large number wounded. They made their way for a few kilometres to an LZ from which they were extracted by helicopter under cover of four RRAF Hunters, which had been poised to carry out a strike in the event of interference by FRELIMO. The operation had been entirely successful and the enemy abandoned their camp.

44. CORPORAL JOE COLEMAN

I did promise that not all the characters in this book would be heroes in the literal sense and it is certainly difficult to call Joe Coleman a hero. However, anyone who knew him will tell you that these stories are true and, once again, you will not find them in any other SAS books.

Joe came to the SAS from the Scots Guards in 1968 and settled into Freefall Troop. Before his story can be told one has to understand a little about his character. Joe Coleman was a scruffy individual, but he had a heart of gold and he did the most stupid things one could ever imagine.

On one occasion in the late 1960s Joe's squadron was halfway through a four-month tour at the British base in Sharjah. Also sharing the barracks on a two-year posting were the Scots Guards, and at the time they had organised a friendly boxing match with the RAF contingent. Unfortunately, the Scots Guards were short of a middleweight and the commanding officer, Colonel DeClee, asked if any members of the SAS would like to participate on their behalf. The SAS are normally discouraged from taking part in any military competitions, but on this occasion Joe Coleman agreed. We all thought this a bit of a laugh and went along to support Joe. (One thing I forgot to mention: Joe had false teeth.)

Joe entered the ring looking really savage, pulling on the ropes and spitting out his teeth before dancing around like Mohammed Ali. His behaviour was so bad that he received a caution from the referee. When the two fighters came together to bang gloves Joe almost knocked his RAF opponent over, for which he received a second warning. At the bell, Joe left his corner, ran across the ring and hit his rival just once, knocking him unconscious. However, Joe was disqualified for ungentlemanly behaviour – although for us his legend had just started.

As well as being scruffy, Joe never had any money. He had married an older woman with several children and most of his pay went on their upkeep. However, this did not stop Joe getting drunk, particularly when there was a special occasion. Like the time when he was in Oman and stationed in the village of Mirbat (prior to the battle). The town had come under fire and Joe manned the mortar. Several bombs had landed close to him, hitting several men, but Joe remained untouched. He was lucky like that. Another SAS soldier at the scene described Joe running straight into the impact zone of an exploding bomb – only to emerge from the dust and smoke with a smile on his face, clutching a half-empty bottle of whisky.

Between tours of Oman Joe's squadron went to the Far East where Freefall Troop were to give a demonstration for several high-ranking officers. Joe, as previously mentioned, was never too fussy with his kit and this extended to the parachute he would use for the demonstration. A handle that, when pulled, releases the canopy is formed in the shape of a 'D'. This handle has a small hole in it, allowing a thin cable to be securely attached. In Joe's case the attachment had come off. Joe's answer to this was to have a local welder seal the cable through the handle with a small knob of solder. Later that afternoon, in front of a full VIP stand, the Free Fallers jumped.

All went well until the parachutes started to open – it was clear that one had malfunctioned. Yes, it was Joe's. As usual, he had given the handle a sharp tug but instead of releasing the parachute he had simply removed the blob of solder. Joe's version of events was as follows: on seeing the disengaged handle he ripped away the cable housing and gripped it with his teeth, thus releasing the parachute. To those on the ground it seemed as if he was a dead man, but with just two hundred feet to go the chute blossomed into life. At the presentation, Joe stood in line with his colleagues, still holding the detached handle and smiling a toothless grin. (He had lost his false teeth.)

By this stage Joe had decided he needed a drink and took off in search of the nearest bar. Unfortunately for someone, this happened to be the Australian Sergeants' Mess. Some hours later we learned that Joe had been in a fight with several Aussies and had had to be forcibly removed from the mess. Not content with this, Joe had picked up a gigantic concrete flowerpot, balanced it above his head and 'ram-raided' a large window in the mess. Fortunately, most of the occupants saw the hellish fiend staggering towards the window and had time to get out of the way. Joe was put in jail.

In the early hours of the following morning, while a group of us were drinking in the overcrowded streets of Singapore (it was wild in those days), a drunken figure staggered through the sea of faces: it was Joe. We tried to hide but it was too late – he had seen us. The reunion was painful as he hugged us all, swearing undying friendship while beseeching us for more drink. In this particular street there happened to be a large number of 'Kie-Ties' (men dressed as women) and one sat on Joe's lap. What happened next is unprintable. Needless to say, it was the only time we'd ever known Joe Coleman to be silent. The trouble was that we and all those around us could see what the Kie-Tie was doing. Joe was oblivious to our embarrassment, and just sat there with a toothless smile.

Several years went by and Joe was back in Oman and, as always, short of cash. On this occasion he had been gambling with some civilian workers at an outpost north of the enemy-held territory. To offset his losses, Joe decided to steal a Land Rover and dispose of it in Salala. He chose a white one and drove it cross-country, sleeping overnight in enemy-held territory, before finally arriving at the town of Salala. At the nearby SAS base in Um al Quarif he enlisted the aid of the two REME (Royal Electrical and Mechanical Engineers) mechanics who sold the vehicle to an Arab in the local market. I had just come off the jebel for a few days' R&R when Joe entered the bedroom flashing a large wad of money and offering to buy everyone drinks.

That was when Joe's luck ran out. The only Land Rover in the whole of Oman that was wanted by the police was the one Joe had stolen. Apparently the civilian he had stolen it from was wanted for gun-running. Joe and the two REME guys were arrested and sent back to the UK where they received a prison sentence. Joe was kicked out of the SAS, and his wife left him for a younger man (again). I have not seen Joe Coleman since, but I did hear that he was happy working in a children's home. Whatever he's doing, I wish him good luck.

45. LANCE CORPORAL A. KENT

D ue to the nature of the Regiment, it can be years before you finally meet some members of other SAS Squadrons. So I have no idea when Trooper Kent joined the SAS but I can vouch for this story, which was told to me by an SAS soldier who served with Kent in Oman.

From time to time the SAS mounted specific operations with the Sultan's Armed forces (SAF). On one occasion information was received that a group of Adoo were lying in wait for a resupply that was coming by camel train from Aden. This camel train had to penetrate and pass through the defences of the Hornbeam Line (an artificial barrier made from barbed wire).

The operation took place near the Wadi Sha'ath to the east of the Hornbeam Line. A group of four SAS men was attached to a company of the Northern Frontier Regiment. The NFR company was split into two, with one half moving out at night to lie in ambush while the other stayed in reserve, providing mortar cover and back-up firepower. At dawn the next day there was no sign of the Adoo or of the supply train. By way of having a second cast, the ambush party, together with the four SAS men, moved their position. As they crossed a low ridge, they came under machine-gun fire from their front. Kent, who in addition to his large rucksack was carrying a General Purpose Machine Gun (GPMG), went swiftly into action.

The firefight grew more intense as more guns on both sides began to join in. Mortar bombs started to whistle down as the second half-company rallied in support. Since during most battles in Oman the enemy would 'shoot and scoot' if they were in small numbers, any sustained fire normally meant that they were in strength and had heavy weapons with them. Kent continued to fire while the company commander (on loan to SAF from the British Army) fed the gun and spotted for him. Suddenly Kent slumped forward and lay motionless, his head against the butt of the gun. The officer tried hard to render medical aid but Kent's large rucksack, which he was still wearing, made assistance difficult. However, the small amount of blood coming from a wound on his face led the officer to believe that he was only unconscious.

At that moment two other SAS men, Corporal Wildman and Trooper McLaren, arrived with two Omani soldiers and made an effort to get Kent away. By this time the Adoo fire had intensified: Wildman took a bullet in the thigh and both Omanis were hit, one seriously. Neither the SAS or SAF would leave their wounded, but by now four of the original six in the small position had been hit so it was decided to pull back a few metres to better cover and use the rest of the company to consolidate their defences. By this time the Adoo were trying hard to encircle the SAF unit and the exact location of friendly forces was getting confused. What was certain, judging by the amount of firepower in use, was that the Adoo had certainly received their supplies, including fresh manpower.

The second half of the company was some two kilometres away and out of radio contact but luckily their British officer had already decided to join the fight. Additionally two Strikemasters appeared in the skies above and helped keep the Adoo at bay by dropping 500 lb bombs. The Strikemasters seemed to have stunned the enemy as well as the SAS and SAF and the encircling movement was stopped at about the same time as the rest of the company arrived. Unknown to all but the SAS Kent had been carrying a new type of radio set and Corporal Wildman now specified that the radio must be retrieved at all costs. As the second half of the company arrived they were deployed forward in order to recover the bodies and their kit. Even with the added manpower, getting the bodies and equipment required several mad dashes into the open and exposure to Adoo fire. Eventually, after some six hours, the battle ebbed and the helicopters managed to get in to evacuate the dead and wounded.

It was discovered that Kent had not been shot in the head. The face wound had come from the rear sight of the GPMG as he slumped on top of it. He had been shot in the heart through the right side of his body. The Adoo had got close to the bodies of Kent and the two Omanis but had left them unmolested. But they had cut off Kent's epaulettes, presumably under the impression that they had killed an officer.

46. SERGEANT FRANK CASHMORE – AUSTRALIAN SAS REGIMENT

In early 1968, aerial reconnaissance of the northern borders of Phuoc Tuy Province in Vietnam revealed the tracks of a tractor and trailer on a route known as the Firestone Trail. At the point of discovery the route crossed an area of open grassland known as LZ Dampier. The theft of a tractor had previously been reported by the owner of the nearby Courtenay rubber plantation and it was suspected that the Vietcong (VC) were using the vehicle to move weapons and stores.

The Commander of 1st Australian Task Force, Brigadier Ron Hughes, gave 2 Squadron SASR the task of destroying the tractor and disrupting the VC supply route. The squadron commander, Major Brian Wade, in turn allocated the mission to Sergeant Frank Cashmore and his patrol. It was decided to carry out a demolitions ambush on the track using four 6.8kg beehive charges and four American claymore mines. Beehive charges are shaped and designed for cutting metal, while claymore mines are normally sited to target ground troops, scything them down with thousands of small ball bearings. All were to be detonated by a special electrical pressure switch.

On the morning of 17 March, Sergeant Cashmore and the other five members of his patrol were brought in by helicopter. Unfortunately, Private Dave Elliott injured his leg as the patrol jumped from the aircraft, which was hovering about a metre from the ground. The injury was serious and Elliott was unable to continue, so the helicopter was recalled and he was evacuated. Sergeant Cashmore led his patrol to an LUP (laying-up position) some two hundred metres away before heading north-west for the Firestone Trail and the ambush site. At about mid-afternoon the patrol lay up and Sergeant Cashmore and Corporal Danny Wright moved forward to reconnoitre the Firestone Trail, which they came across some two hundred metres west of LZ Dampier. Cashmore selected a spot on a bend in the track for the siting of the charges that would be buried in the track and for the claymores that would be sited to deal with the VC escorting the tractor. After nightfall, the patrol moved nearer to the track and sat in wait. At 2320 hours they observed the tractor and trailer moving west along the track towards them. At 0145 hours, the vehicle returned eastwards. From this Cashmore was able to determine the exact spot he would use to ambush the tractor. This observation having been completed, the patrol withdrew to its LUP.

At 1920 hours on the following night, the patrol moved once more to the Firestone Trail. While Privates Kim McAlear and Adrian Blacker moved off as sentries in opposite directions along the track, the demolitions team, Corporals Danny Wright and Dave Scheele, commenced digging the holes for the beehive charges. This proved to be no easy task as the soil was heavily compacted. Meanwhile, Sergeant Cashmore sited the four claymores to cover the entire area used by the Vietcong advance and rear guards as well as the tractor and trailer. Once the positioning of the charges and mines was completed, he recalled the two sentries. However, this proved difficult as it was found that the patrol's URC 241 radios, with which McAlear and Blacker were equipped, would not work to his own URC 243 set beyond a range of 100 metres.

The two sentries had just returned to the ambush site when the patrol heard the sound of the tractor to the east. Rapidly connecting the claymores and paying out the firing cable, they withdrew to a bomb crater some fifty metres away where they took cover and waited. Corporal Danny Wright prepared the claymore firing unit and shortly afterwards the tractor and its escort arrived in the killing zone, although the long grass hid them from the patrol's view. After a while they became concerned that the tractors wheels had missed the pressure switch. Sergeant Cashmore stood up in the crater to check on the vehicle's location. As he did so, there was a massive explosion as the beehive charges detonated, followed by another as Corporal Danny Wright detonated the claymores.

Complete withdrawal from the area was impossible due to the bright moonlight and thick jungle so, having left the bomb crater, the patrol crawled a further fifty metres away from the ambush area to some bushes where they took cover. At dawn the patrol moved carefully towards LZ Dampier, obeying orders to avoid contact with the enemy, and surveyed the area: the only evidence of enemy activity was a single heavily bandaged Vietcong staggering across the open ground. After a while, seeing no further sign of the enemy, Sergeant Cashmore radioed the 2 Squadron base at Nui Dat and requested extraction which took place shortly afterwards. That afternoon, the entire area was bombed with napalm by South Vietnamese Air Force Skyraiders. The mission had been a complete success as the tractor and trailer had been totally destroyed and, according to information supplied subsequently by a Vietcong defector, twenty-one VC had been killed.

47. LANCE CORPORAL ANTHONY 'TONY' FLEMING

Author's note: As with so many stories in this book, one individual has been chosen to represent the valour of the participating group. The courage of all those mentioned below, especially Sergeant 'Rover' Walker and Corporal Danny Bell, is clearly defined by their actions and defiance when facing the enemy.

The Zakhir Tree was a prominent landmark that stood on the edge of the Shershitti escarpment in southern Oman. It was proposed that the SAF, supported by the Firqat and SAS, should establish a base north of the Zakhir Tree at a place called Defa. Defa had been used during the Shershitti operation and much of the fortification remained. By 15 September 1975 the base held a company of SAF, a troop of Saladin armoured cars and several 25-pounder guns. The SAS had a whole troop in the location but, due to Ramadan, the Firqat were very thin on the ground.

There was only one problem with Defa: during the Shershitti operation the enemy had pounded the position with Soviet Katyusha rockets. Now they began to rain down once more, this time from somewhere near the Zakhir Tree. As the monsoon provided a thick mist, especially in the morning, the SAS decided to silence the rocket fire by sending in a heavy patrol backed by SAF and the armoured cars.

On the early morning of 19 September thirteen SAS men and two Firqats, under the command of Captain Charles Delius, slipped out of Defa, making their way towards the Zakhir Tree. Due to darkness and mist the patrol found themselves on a small spur to the west of the landmark. Delius decided to remain at the position with six men while Sergeant 'Rover' Walker took the other six down the spur for a recce. They dropped lower into the wadi, but as the dawn grew brighter and the mist became patchy, it was obvious that their tactical position was not good. Walker, a highly experienced SAS soldier, moved his men and dispatched Corporal Bell and one of the Firqat to proceed across the wadi bed and up the other side in search of the Zakhir Tree in order to fix their position. Bell moved cautiously until the mist cleared and he was able to observe the landmark and take a bearing. However, as he and the Firqat moved back to rejoin the patrol they came across several sets of freshly made footprints. Moreover, there was a very strong smell of meat hanging in the damp air.

While Walker waited for Bell to return he observed a man walking through the mist, heading roughly towards Delius's position, and quickly sent a message. Delius was still on the radio when three enemy soldiers appeared directly to their front and a rapid exchange of fire broke out. All three enemy were cut down by the SAS. One of the enemy had time to fire back. One of the bullets found its mark, hitting L/Corporal Geordie Small in the thigh and severing the femoral artery. The patrol medic quickly bandaged the wound and Small was moved to higher ground. Contact was made with the SAF at Defa and an armoured car was sent to pick up the casualty. Sadly, no one realised how bad the internal damage was and Geordie Small died while the medivac helicopter was flying him to the FST (Field Surgical Team).

On hearing the shots, Walker ordered his men to make their way up the wadi, heading north for the high ground. They had just started to climb when a burst of fire signalled an all-out contact. The men dropped and wriggled forward, using the scanty mist as cover. But the volume of fire was so close that it seemed as if the enemy were right on top of them. Suddenly L/Corporal Tony Fleming was hit badly in the back. At first Walker thought he was dead, only to see his eyes open. Dragging Fleming between them, the patrol forced itself forward, but such was the severity of the enemy fire that they eventually decided to stay put and defend themselves as best they could. Walker explained his only option to Delius: they must stand and fight and wait to be relieved. Delius immediately called for mortar fire but, due to the mist and the fact that he did not know Walker's exact position, adjustment control was difficult.

Walker's men huddled together, with those able to do so shooting at anything that moved while the medics attended the wounded. The mist cleared briefly and one of the patrol shouted with relief: a line of well-dressed military figures was advancing towards them in open order – the SAF had arrived. Or so they thought. Walker got to his feet and shouted, indicating their position, at which moment the soldiers opened fire. Walker was hit and he went down on his knees. Another bullet hit him and he fell to the ground. He tried to rise, and as he did so a third round hit him. The enemy advanced to within twenty metres and grenade-throwing range. Still the SAS held their ground, but by now they had been forced to switch to single shots as ammunition ran low. Walker, who by this time had been given morphine, shouted for Bell to take over the patrol, when suddenly an armoured car appeared coming down the slope; the enemy started to disengage.

By 9 a.m. the battle was over. Captain Delius rejoined his men, only to find that every man in Walker's patrol had been wounded. Fleming and Walker were the worst hit and Delius ordered that they should be placed on one of the armoured cars and carried to safety.

Author's note: As with most battles, word quickly spread to the SAS base at Hereford and from there to the sub-units operating around the world. What makes this particular story so good was the comments made by Fleming as they bounced along on the back of the armoured car returning to Defa. Danny Bell was cradling Fleming's head when Fleming whispered, 'Danny, I'm going off.'

'No,' replied Bell, 'hang on in there – think of those you love!'

Fleming smiled. 'No, Danny, I'm falling off the armoured car.'

Tony Fleming bravely fought the disability his wounds had caused. He died in 1994.

48. SECOND LIEUTENANT BILL HINDSON – AUSTRALIAN SAS REGIMENT

On 9 August 1967, Second Lieutenant Bill Hindson's five-man patrol was inserted at around midday into thick jungle in an area four kilometres south-east of Thua Tich, in the north-eastern part of Phuoc Tuy Province, to carry out a reconnaissance mission. From the very start of the operation it became apparent that there were a number of Vietcong (VC) in the area, at times as close as fifteen metres. On the following day four VC were sighted and a number of shots were heard. At 1015 hours on 11 August a large force of 63 VC, preceded by two scouts, moved carefully down the track near the patrol's position. At 1255 hours the patrol moved out, having passed the information about the enemy force over its radio, and started to cross the track. As the lead scout, Lance Corporal Alan Roser, stepped on to it a VC appeared some twenty metres away. Roser targeted him and then switched his aim to a light machine-gun that opened fire on the patrol. Second

Lieutenant Hindson also engaged the enemy, standing his ground instead of adopting the normal 'shoot-and-scoot' contact drill.

During the firefight, however, the patrol signaller, Private Noel de Grussa, was seriously wounded in the left thigh and rendered unable to walk. Under covering fire from Hindson the patrol withdrew, carrying de Grussa to a spot where the medic, Private Gerry Israel, was able to apply emergency medical treatment to his wound. Carrying de Grussa, the patrol then moved off again while Hindson covered their rear. Shortly afterwards, he activated his URC 10 radio beacon and the signal was picked up by an airborne forward air-controller in the area. Within 45 minutes US Air Force A1 Skyraiders and F100 Super Sabres were overhead, carrying out air strikes on the Vietcong who were approaching the patrol's location. Helicopters of 9 Squadron RAAF also arrived, accompanied by helicopter gunships that laid down suppressive fire while the patrol was winched up through the jungle canopy. The enemy were so close that they were engaged by the door gunner of the winching helicopter and by Second Lieutenant Hindson as he ascended. Nevertheless, the extraction was successful and the patrol arrived back at 1 Squadron's base at 1440 hours.

49. SOLDIER I

Author's note: I could give you this soldier's name as he finished with the SAS some years ago, but that would be a little unfair. Needless to say, he was a real character while serving with the Regiment and his exploits are well documented in one of his own books. His exploits, especially during the Iranian Embassy siege, are a single detail in a larger picture.

One of Soldier I's earliest exploits was to get caught and arrested for fighting in Hong Kong. He had been sent there as part of a team that was to teach unarmed combat to the three battalions of Gurkha troops based in Hong Kong and to some other official bodies. One night, after rugby practice, he and two friends from the Hong Kong police force, Buffalo and Clint, decided to head downtown for a drink and a bit of fun. After several drinks and the subsequent build-up of aggro that developed when chatting up a couple of women, a fight ensued. With the odds stacked against him and his friends, Snapper – such was his nickname – produced a knuckleduster and proceeded to lay out his foe in regular SAS style. The police arrived and arrested Snapper, taking him for a delinquent tourist since devices like knuckledusters were classed as dangerous weapons.

Although Snapper was in Hong Kong training a section of the police, among others, he did not want to jeopardise his own security or that of the Regiment, so he said nothing. A few hours later he was dragged in front of a judge. The sentence was simple: ten days in jail – or ten lashes and go free. Snapper was already late reporting back to the barracks and while he could explain away a few hours' delay, several days in jail were out of the question. Having opted for corporal punishment, Snapper was led downstairs to a windowless cell, the centre of which was taken up by a table covered with several straps. There were two guards with Snapper and two more Chinese in white coats stood watching from the sidelines, while in the corner stood the largest Chinese man Snapper had ever seen: he was selecting a whip from a rack.

What the hell, thought Snapper, it's only ten lashes, I'll be out of here in a few minutes. With that he allowed himself to be examined. Then, his trousers down around his ankles, he was bent over the table and strapped to it face down. He could only hear the footfalls of the giant as he ran forward with the whip – then he felt the contact. In his own words, 'It felt like someone had stuck an electric wire up my arse.' Snapper held it together for the first few lashes, then he let it all go. As a result of the whipping he was hospitalised and sent to Cyprus. Once he was better he was RTU'd from the Regiment – but not for long.

Snapper returned to the SAS and continued to soldier on in great style. He was one of those who climbed the jebel massif during Operation Jaguar, a nightmare ordeal that left most men unfit to fight. Later, in the same theatre of war, he helped defend the town of Mirbat as the Adoo made one final attempt to re-establish themselves. Then, in April

1980, his image was broadcast over the world's television sets as he and three others clambered through the window of the Iranian Embassy during the famous siege.

It all started when a group of terrorists arrived in London, looking for accommodation. Almost inevitably, they finished up in the Earls Court area, first port of call for many foreigners. However, as for so many members of the visiting Muslim community, the pubs and clubs of the district proved to be a temptation too good to miss. This round of drinking and womanising escalated to the point where the group were forced to leave their accommodation and seek fresh lodgings. Eventually, the whole crew finished up in 105 Lexham Gardens, where they remained until their departure on the morning of Wednesday, 30 April. By 11.20, having mysteriously collected several weapons, including two machine-guns and a quantity of grenades, the group stood outside 16 Princes Gate.

At 11.25 a.m., on the tree-lined avenue of Princes Gate in London's Kensington district, six armed gunmen took over No. 16 – the Iranian Embassy. It was thought that the terrorists were opposed to the regime of Ayatollah Khomeini and were seeking the liberation of Khuzestan from Iran. When they took over the embassy, they gained 26 hostages, including the British policeman who had been on duty at the entrance. This was something that might have gone unnoticed but for the fact that minutes later a burst of machine-gun fire could be heard. The police were on the scene immediately, their speed of response thanks to the captured policeman, Trevor Lock, who had managed to alert his headquarters before being taken by the terrorists. Armed D11 marksmen soon surrounded the building and the negotiating plans for sieges were put into operation.

The anti-terrorist team in Hereford were at this time practising in the killing house, but things were soon to change. By 11.47 a.m., Dusty Grey, an ex-D Squadron SAS man who now worked with the Metropolitan Police, was talking to the commanding officer in Hereford. His information contained the briefest details, but it was enough to alert the regiment. Several minutes later, the duty signaller activated the 'call-in' bleepers carried by every member of the anti-terrorist team. Although the SAS had prior warning, there could be no move before official sanction from the Home Secretary, who at the request of the police would contact the Ministry of Defence. Despite this red tape, it made sense for the SAS to think ahead and time could be saved by positioning the anti-terrorist team closer to the scene.

Around midnight on the first day, most of the anti-terrorist team had made their way to Regent's Park Barracks, which had been selected as a holding area. From here various items of information could be assembled and assessed. A scale model of No. 16 Princes Gate was ordered to be constructed. This task fell to two Pioneers, drafted in from the nearby Guards unit. Additionally, an intelligence cell was set up to gather and collate every snippet of information that would aid any assault.

By this time the terrorist leader, Oan, had secured his 26 hostages and issued his demands. These included the autonomy and recognition of the Khuzestan people, and the release of ninety-one Khuzestani prisoners. The line taken by the terrorists was hard, but despite several threats to blow up the embassy and kill the hostages, by Thursday, 1 May they had released a sick woman. Later that same day Oan had managed to get a telephone call through to Sadegh Ghotzbadeh, Iran's Foreign Minister. The conversation did not go well: Oan was accused of being an American agent, and Ghotzbadeh maintained that the Iranian hostages held in the embassy would consider it an honour to die for their country and the Iranian revolutionary movement.

This lack of cooperation almost forced the terrorist to seek a mediator who was more sympathetic. But it also meant that the Iranian government did not give a damn if their embassy staff were killed or not. Another problem for the terrorists had also come up. Inside the embassy Chris

Cramer, a BBC sound man, had become sick with acute stomach pains. His partner, BBC sound recordist Sim Harris, pleaded with Oan to call for a doctor immediately. This was done, but the police refused to comply, and in the end Cramer was released, whereupon he stumbled out of the embassy door and into a waiting ambulance.

Later that night, under the cover of darkness, three Avis rental vans pulled up in a small side street by Princes Gate. Men carrying holdalls quickly made their way into No. 14, just two doors down from the embassy. Within minutes they had laid out their equipment and made ready for an IA (immediate action). At first the plan for this was very simple: if the terrorists started shooting, they would run to the front door of No. 16 and smash their way in – slow, primitive, but better than nothing until a more clearly defined plan could be drawn up.

By 6 o'clock on the morning of Saturday, 2 May, the situation inside No. 16 was becoming very agitated. Oan used the phone that had been set up between the embassy and No. 25 Princes Gate – The Royal School of Needlework, no less – which now housed Alpha Control and the police negotiator. Oan's main criticism was that there had been no broadcasts about the siege in the media, so how could his cause be heard? He slammed the phone down in a rage. By late afternoon on the same day Oan was allowed to make a statement that was to be broadcast on the next news slot. In return for this two more hostages were released, one of whom was a pregnant woman. The trouble was that Oan would not release the hostages before the statement was read out, while the police wanted the hostages first. In the end a compromise was reached and the broadcast went out on the evening nine o'clock news.

Two hours later eight members of the SAS team had climbed onto the rear roof of No. 14 and were making their way through a jungle of television antennae to No. 16. Two of the men made their way directly to a skylight and, after some time, managed to get it open. It opened directly into a small bathroom on the top floor of the Iranian embassy and would provide an excellent entry point. Meanwhile, other members of the team secured abseil ropes to the several chimneys and made ready for a quick descent to the lower floors where they could smash in through the windows. Oddly enough, an enterprising television director had managed to get a camera into a bedroom window overlooking the back of the embassy: during the assault he filmed the whole action.

By 9 a.m. on Sunday things seemed to be heading for a peaceful settlement. Oan had agreed to reduce his demands and at the same time Arab ambassadors had attended a Cobra Committee meeting in Whitehall. This had been chaired by Willie Whitelaw, the Home Secretary, who was, to all intents and purposes, in charge of the whole operation. For the SAS anti-terrorist team things had become much more stable. By now access had been obtained into No. 14 and efforts were being made to penetrate the wall. To aid this, various sound distractions supplied by the Gas Board working in the vicinity masked the noise of the drilling. On the far side No. 17, the Ethiopian Embassy, had also cooperated. The basic plan had been formulated. This was to attack each floor simultaneously and to establish areas of demarcation in order to avoid overshoot. Mock-ups of the floor layouts were constructed from timber and hessian sheeting and were assembled at Regent's Park Barracks.

The police, who had adopted a softly-softly negotiating approach, managed to drag the siege out for several days – time that was desperately needed for the SAS to carry out covert recces, study plans, build models and, more importantly, locate the hostages and terrorists within the embassy building. A major break was talking to the hostage Chris Cramer, the BBC sound engineer who had fallen ill with a stomach disorder, and whom, as an act of faith, the gunmen had allowed to be released. This was a big mistake on the part of the terrorists: in his debrief to the SAS Cramer was able to give them precise and detailed information about the situation inside the embassy.

By the sixth day of the siege, 5 May, the terrorists were growing frustrated and the situation inside the embassy had begun to deteriorate. All morning threats were made about executing hostages, and at 1.31 p.m. three shots were heard. At 6.50 p.m. more shots were heard, and the body of the embassy press officer was thrown out. Immediately the police appeared to capitulate, stalling for time, while SAS plans to storm the embassy were brought forward. At this stage the police negotiator worked hard to convince the terrorist leader not to shoot any further hostages, saying that a bus would be with them shortly to take them to the airport from where they could fly to the Middle East. As the telephone conversation was taking place, the SAS took up their start positions.

A handwritten note effectively passed control from the police to the SAS. Shortly after, while a negotiator from Alpha Control talked to Oan, the SAS moved in. Oan heard the first crashes and complained that the embassy was being attacked. (This conversation was recorded, and one can clearly hear the stun grenades going off – Oan's conversation is cut short by a long burst of machine-gun fire.) For the assault team the waiting was over and the words guaranteed to set their adrenalin pumping were given: 'Go. Go. Go.' At 7.23 p.m. eight men abseiled down to the first-floor balcony, their ropes secured from the embassy roof.

The attack came from three directions, with the main assault from the rear. Frame charges were fitted quickly to the windows (by now this type of explosive had been perfected) and detonated. Stun grenades were thrown in advance of the attack team and the SAS went into action. The building was cleared systematically from the top down, room by room. The telex room on the second floor, which held the male hostages and three of the terrorists, was of utmost priority. Realising that an attack was in progress, the terrorists shot and killed one hostage and wounded two others before the lead SAS team broke into the room. Immediately they shot two gunmen who were visible. The third hid among the hostages and was not discovered until later.

As rooms were cleared, hostages were literally thrown from one SAS soldier to another, down the stairs and out into the back garden. At this stage they were all laid face down on the ground while a search was conducted for the missing terrorist.

Breaking the siege took just seventeen minutes. The SAS took no casualties, other than one man who got caught up in his abseil and was badly burned. Soon after the problem was handed back to the police. Meanwhile the boys vacated No. 14 and went back to the barracks in time to watch themselves on television. Still dressed in assault gear and clutching cans of Foster's lager (someone was on the ball) they crowded around, eager to see themselves in action. Halfway through, Prime Minister Margaret Thatcher, who had left a dinner date, arrived to thank the boys personally. She circulated, as one man put it, 'Like a triumphant Caesar returning to the Senate', her face glowing with pride and admiration for her Imperial Guard. Then, as the TV news started to show the full event, she sat down on the floor amid her warriors. There could have been no greater approbation from one's leader.

In total, there were 26 hostages taken in the Embassy when the siege started. Of these, five were released before the SAS assault. Two of the remaining hostages died, but the other nineteen survived. Of the six terrorists, only one survived.

50. SERGEANT ANDY BAXTER

A ndy Baxter was a first-rate soldier who joined the SAS in 1969, having been a boy soldier (making RSM) before serving with the Guards Independent Parachute Company. On passing selection he was posted to G Squadron's Mountain Troop where, over the next few years, he proved himself to be an excellent climber. As a corporal in Northern Ireland Andy always pushed for work, volunteering for a place on most of the operations.

One of the most memorable tasks Andy Baxter ever undertook was the observation of a church in Castleford (*name changed*). I was his Troop Sergeant at the time so I will relate the story to you from my own experience.

It had been a funny week. Nothing was going our way: the 'Paddy factor' was definitely against us. For example, as the current operational SAS unit in Northern Ireland we were at the beck and call of Special Branch. Not that we minded – any work was better than sitting on your backside, watching endless videos and waiting for something to happen. For the past two weeks we had been given several tasks by Special Branch and we had made a cock-up of two of them. In fairness, it wasn't all our fault: if Special Branch had just given us a little more information we would have approached the operations concerned differently.

Anyway, we were given another chance when Chief Inspector Bob Giles telephoned me, wishing to brief me on a new situation. I drove with Andy Baxter to Gough Barracks in Armagh. This was where Special Branch ruled the domain of intelligence. The trouble was that they kept most of it to themselves. Although the SAS got on well with the police it was not always a partnership based on trust.

Our job was to recce a Catholic church in Castleford. The essence of the information was that there was an IRA meeting taking place in a small building at the rear of the church grounds. The word was that Special Branch would like the SAS to have a look at the building, and that any photographs or documents of interest found should be copied. As Andy had come with me for the briefing I decided that both he and I should do the initial recce (Andy was a lock-picking specialist). We were driven to the town by two other SAS personnel who would stay mobile in the area and act as back-up.

At around 1 a.m. on a wet and windy morning, Andy and I were dropped off by a gateway at the edge of the town. We quickly made our way to the rear of the church, which was bounded on three sides by a twelve-foot wall and on the other by an iron railing on the road-side front. Approaching from the rear, we quickly climbed the wall and dropped into the shadows at the rear of the church. The meeting house lay ten metres to our right. In comparison with the church it was small, little more than a two-storey building built into the rear corner of the wall. From where we stood we saw it had one window and a single door to the bottom floor.

We approached the door – it was locked. Andy produced a set of picks and made short work of the padlock. Inside the ground floor we made a quick search. There was nothing of interest and much of the space was taken up by church props and junk. A small set of stairs led to the second floor. We climbed up only to find it barred by a door secured with a padlock. Once more Andy made short work of the lock. The upper floor had two windows, allowing the room to be illuminated dimly by the street lighting. It contained several lockers filled with paperwork and books; in the centre stood a large table and several chairs.

We carried out a methodical search of the room and the cupboards but found little of interest – certainly no reference to the IRA. It was then that we discovered a small trapdoor leading to the loft. I estimated that this could be reached by placing a chair on the table and was well worth a look. Checking the hatchway for any booby traps, I opened the flap and climbed inside. Securing the hatch behind me, I switched on my torch. What confronted me was a whole mess of large plastic bags, most of which contained bomb-making equipment. A more detailed investigation revealed several pounds of Semtex plastic explosive and twenty ready-to-go cassette incendiaries. Leaning back through the hatch I passed the information to Andy who in turn relayed the find directly back to our control desk. A find such as this would need an observation unit placed on it as soon as possible. Photographs were taken before Andy and I made our exit, leaving the building exactly as we had found it.

Upon our return to base Andy wrote out a report while I developed the photographs. By nine o'clock next morning the information had been delivered into the hands of Special Branch. Then, for some unexplained reason, the situation changed. MI5 became involved, and the target was electronically tagged. Andy and I had the pleasure of taking the MI5 operative into the building. Problem was, he was so fat that he demolished half the rear wall climbing over. He could not pick the lock and was hell-bent on calling for an expert. Andy had the lock open in seconds. For the time being the SAS were out of the picture other than to act as back-up.

Some three weeks later I got a call from Special Branch requesting that we remove the whole explosives find from the church and bury it in a hide we were to dig. The hide was to look like an IRA job and be at least half a mile from the church. Like the good soldiers we were, we did what we were told. Next day Andy stood on the site while the men of the local UDR (Ulster Defence Regiment) searched the area. As one of the soldiers came close to Andy he said, 'It's your lucky day, mate, it's under my feet.' Next day the papers told of a major explosives find by the UDR. This made the army look good and no doubt someone got a medal for it. In truth, the real reasons for the deception were simple. It told the IRA who had put the explosives in the church that they were being watched. And, of course, the consequences of finding explosives in a Catholic church would scarcely have been politically acceptable.

Author's note: Some years later Andy, having completed the Mountain Guides course in Germany, proved to be an excellent climbing instructor. My fondest memory of him was when the troop went to southern Germany for two weeks' climbing. He was really happy in a mountainous environment, so it was no surprise that he became a member of the second SAS team attempting to climb Mount Everest. During the ascent an avalanche swept the entire party down the mountainside. Another member of Mountain Troop, Tony Swierzy, was killed, and although Andy Baxter survived and returned to Hereford he died of a brain tumour on 12 August 1985. He was just thirty years old.

51. CAPTAIN ROBIN EDWARDS

During the Aden conflict of 1963–67, rebel forces backed by the Yemenis and Egyptians waged a guerrilla war on the British and Federal forces. The object of the British advance into the Radfan was to pacify the rebels and discourage them from, in particular, mining the Dhala road. The force under orders for this task consisted of 45 Commando Royal Marines, B Company, 3rd Battalion, the Parachute Regiment, and A Squadron, 22 SAS.

The SAS contingent arrived in the Aden protectorate in 1964 and were originally deployed immediately to the area of the Radfan mountains, then the heart of rebel territory. The whole area was about four hundred square miles and lay to the east of the Dhala Road, a British engineering project aimed at improving internal communications in the country. However, the rebels didn't necessarily see it that way and made the continuation of the project a risky business. The British thought that if they could advance into Radfan and win over the rebel tribes, they might be able to stop them from mining the road and shooting at the British engineers.

The first task that the SAS were set was to take an important enemy position that overlooked the main dissident city of Danaba. This position was codenamed 'Cap Badge' and, once cleared, it was to be used as a drop zone for the Parachute Regiment. A Squadron's 3 Troop was chosen to carry out this mission and it set off on 29 April 1964 under the command of Captain Robin Edwards. It was taken some of the way by armoured cars. These could only go so far and then the patrol had to go the rest of the way on foot. Edwards and his men were toughened soldiers, used to fighting in the harsh conditions of Borneo and Malaya. Even so, they found progress slow in the rough, rocky terrain. To make matters worse, Edward's signaller, Trooper Terry Warburton, was suffering from severe stomach cramps and they had to pause every now and again to allow him to catch up.

At about midnight, Edwards realised that, at the rate at which they were travelling, they were not going to reach their objective before daylight. He made the decision to halt and seek shelter. Nearby were two old rock-built sangars and Edwards decided that they should spend the rest of the night and the following day holed up there to allow Warburton time to recover. They radioed the SAS squadron commander, informed him of the situation and then settled down for a long wait.

Sometime the next morning their position was discovered by a goatherd. Fearing he would run off and tell the rebels where they were, the SAS patrol shot him. Unfortunately, the shot was heard in the nearby village of Shab Tem and very soon they were surrounded by rebel tribesmen. A long-range sniping battle broke out, with the rebels soon becoming bolder, climbing the slopes and coming ever nearer to the sangars. The position was out of range of the artillery but Edwards managed to call in air support in the form of Hunter aircraft from both 43 and 208 Squadrons.

The Hunters held the rebels off for some time, but the aircraft eventually had to return to base, leaving Edwards and his men without their valuable protection. Rescue plans were put forward and considered at the SAS base in Thumier, but in the end it was considered too risky to send in another patrol. Edwards and his men were now on their own, facing an enemy that outnumbered them by eight to one. Deciding to make a break for it, Warburton sent a signal to say they were moving off. Then the radio went dead. Edwards rushed to his signaller's position to find that he had been killed by a single shot to the head.

Leaving Warburton's body where it had fallen, the patrol moved off, hoping to outmanoeuvre the gunmen. They had not gone far when a savage barrage of fire swept their position. Edwards was hit several times and died instantly. During the escape two of the other men had also been hit – in the legs. The patrol's position was now desperate. Corporal Paddy Baker took over the leadership and the patrol, moving slowly because of the injured men, managed to clear the immediate danger area.

The tribesmen, now confident of victory, moved forward and recovered the bodies of Warburton and Edwards. They then set off after the rest of the patrol. Baker, knowing that the patrol couldn't hope to outrun their pursuers, set the two slower, wounded soldiers to wait in ambush. As the first rebels appeared, they ran into the trap and were shot dead. This tactic was repeated a number of times until the rebels thought it prudent to halt the pursuit. Finally, the remnants of the patrol made it back to the Dhala road where they were picked up by armoured cars and taken safely back to base.

The Edwards patrol was soon to become a major news story when, some days later, a report filtered into Aden that the heads of two British soldiers had been displayed impaled on stakes in the main square of Taiz, a rebel stronghold in Yemen. This was confirmed when a British Army patrol reached the area where Edwards and his men had made their stand and found two headless bodies buried in a shallow grave. The headless bodies were recovered and were reburied with full military honours.

52. MAJOR ALASTAIR MORRISON

Having previously served with the Scots Guards, Captain Alastair Morrison joined the SAS in 1968. He was first placed in command of G Squadron's Mobility Troop, but before long was made acting Squadron OC because of difficulties with the then commander. In this role, he and his unit went to the assistance of the beleaguered BATT team at Mirbat. His reputation grew and he soon became second-in-command of 22 SAS.

During this era hijackings were extremely popular with terrorists and the SAS were training hard to counter the practice. Wadi Haddad's PFLP (Popular Front for the Liberation of Palestine) specialised in hijacking and until 1976 they were doing very well. Then the Israelis started fighting back. In a superb military operation, a special anti-terrorist team flew thousands of miles in a daring rescue operation – and it worked. Entebbe remains to this day the beginning of the end for hijackings.

Haddad was not deterred, despite his ailing health (he was dying of cancer). It was less than a year later that he tried again. This time he hijacked a German Lufthansa 737 returning from the holiday resort of Palma. His team were all Palestinian, two men and two women. They had been trained in Aden but had flown to Palma from Baghdad. Although the hijackers were Palestinian, the operation was jointly coordinated with the German Baader-Meinhof gang, who by this time had become known as the RAF (Red Army Faction). For their part, the Red Army Faction had kidnapped a top German industrialist, Hans-Martin Schleyer, a month before. As it later transpired, both this kidnapping and the Lufthansa hijack were linked to the same demands.

The hijack team had spent several days in the holiday resort acting as tourists and selecting a flight that would take them to Germany. After visiting several travel companies in Palma, they eventually booked seats on Lufthansa to Frankfurt. Later, it is said, three of the group returned to the airport where they met with a German woman who was pushing a child's buggy. This woman handed over a biscuit tin that contained the hijackers' guns and grenades. Such was the sloppy security of Palma's airport that the hijack team entered the aircraft armed and ready to go.

Lufthansa flight number LH181 took off from Palma, Majorca for Frankfurt on the afternoon of Thursday, 13 October. It contained 87 passengers and 5 crew. Taking off at 12.57 p.m., the journey should have been completed within two hours. But shortly after the in-flight meal had been served the hijackers struck. Brandishing pistols and hand grenades the four terrorists soon took control of the aeroplane.

Refuelling at Rome and at Larnaca in Cyprus, the plane flew on to Bahrain. Here it refuelled yet again before making its way to Dubai in the United Arab Emirates. The terrorists were demanding the release of members of the Baader-Meinhof gang currently held in a top-security German prison as well as of two other terrorists held in Turkish jails. They also demanded fifteen million dollars. The demand note was identical to that setting out the terms for the release of Hans-Martin Schleyer.

During the first 48 hours of negotiation the Bonn Government took a firm line, refusing any concessions to the terrorists and maintaining an approach of continuous dialogue to achieve the hostages' release safely and without harm. At the same time the German government looked to other European countries for support in their stand against terrorism, receiving assurances from France and Britain. The British Prime Minister offered to assist the German government by sending two SAS personnel to aid their own GSG9 anti-terrorist force. Major Alastair Morrison and Sergeant Barry Davies (author of this book) were chosen for this mission. From the start Morrison took his orders literally, determined that the pair should see the hijack through to the end.

It was at this point that I became directly involved.

The country was shrouded in thick fog and transport was in some disarray. The British Prime Minister was stuck in a shoe factory in the north of England when the call came from the German Chancellor. The outcome was an offer of assistance to the Germans which resulted ultimately in the SAS being activated.

The week prior to the hijack, I was on duty at Heathrow with eight other members of the SAS anti-terrorist team. We were training on various types of aircraft, familiarising ourselves with their basic internal layouts and the procedural variations used by different airlines. Most of our training was done during the periods allowed for cleaning between scheduled flights.

On the afternoon of Friday, 14 October I returned with my crew to Hereford through the fog that was thickening dramatically hour by hour. On arrival at Stirling Lines I found the team commander, who informed me that the British and German governments had agreed on the need for a joint anti-terrorist effort, and that the two of us were to leave immediately for London. The fog was so thick that we took the command helicopter, which flew us directly to Battersea Heliport.

Unfortunately, the heliport had been closed by the fog. When we landed, we had no option but to climb over the heliport gates to get into the street. Luckily, one of the first vehicles we saw was a police panda car, which we flagged down. We asked the driver to take us to Whitehall. He was, not surprisingly, doubtful about such a request from two scruffy individuals, but our manner, backed up by our ID cards, persuaded him to check with his control. They played it safe, telling the PC to give us a lift to see if we were genuine – and to bring us in if we weren't!

Arriving outside No. 10 Downing Street, we were met by senior military personnel, who briefed us on the current situation. Major Morrison, who was then second-in-command of the Regiment and had been at SAS HQ in London, also joined us there. During the week at Heathrow we had loosely monitored the hijack situation, and were aware that the aircraft was now in Dubai – a place both Alastair and I knew well. We were told that a couple of politicians from Bonn had arrived, together with two members of a unit barely known to us at the time, GSG9 (*Grenzschutzgruppe 9*, a division of the border police trained in anti-terrorism). After a meeting in the Cabinet Office we were taken deeper inside No. 10 and introduced to the Germans.

Within minutes both Alastair and I realised that GSG9 and the SAS had much in common when it came to anti-terrorist drills. It was fascinating to see the look on the senior civil servants' faces when we started to talk about stun grenades and MP5 machine-guns. The Germans were particularly interested in the stun grenade, which detonates almost instantaneously when thrown, effectively stunning anyone in close proximity. The grenade emits a very loud bang and a very bright flash of light in a set sequence – not dissimilar to the effect of strobes in a disco as they flash on and off. The effectiveness of these grenades together with our expertise and knowledge gathered from the Middle East plus our recent training on aircraft interiors were of such great potential value to the Germans in dealing with the hijack that we were immediately asked to return with them to Germany. They also suggested that once we had talked to the people in Germany, we would, if requested, fly on to Dubai to give further assistance. Alastair and I were selected to accompany GSG9 and we arranged for eight stun grenades to be sent from Hereford so that we could collect them at the airport at Brize Norton.

The weather made the journey from London extremely slow and also meant that we had to fly to Germany by C130 rather than by helicopter. We landed at Bonn in Germany in the early hours of Saturday morning (15 October) and were taken immediately to GSG9 HQ. Here we had a very short discussion with the GSG9 second-in-command. (The commander, Ulrich Wegener, was already in Dubai.)

Alastair decided that a demonstration of the British stun grenades might impress the Germans and instructed me to find a convenient space. A long corridor in the cellars of the HQ building that was similar in size and shape to the interior of an aircraft fitted the need. A dozen GSG9 soldiers took up positions in various recessed doorways. With the lights out, I tossed in a stun grenade. The language was pretty blue as some very shocked GSG9 soldiers emerged from the cellar corridor. Nevertheless, it proved how effective the grenades were. The German second-in-command then made an instant decision to send both Alastair and me on to Dubai by the fastest means. Unfortunately, this meant getting the 12.12 plane out of Frankfurt and changing aircraft in Kuwait for Dubai.

All went smoothly until we arrived in Kuwait. Predictably, the entire Middle East was alarmed by the hijack in Dubai. For this reason, Kuwait Airport was on full military alert, and even passengers in transit had their luggage rechecked before being allowed back aboard the plane for Dubai. Although Alastair and I hung further and further back in the queue, it was inevitable that we would eventually have to put our bag containing the boxes of stun grenades through the X-ray machine. I can still visualise the screen clearly showing those grenades – and I can still recall, very vividly, the commotion it caused. We were at once slapped under heavy guard and manhandled quite ruthlessly by Kuwaiti soldiers into the main Security Officer's room, followed by our hand luggage.

The bag was opened for examination – a procedure that I had to terminate when one of the Arabs tried to remove the pin from a grenade. At this stage, realisation dawned on everybody in the room that we were taking the grenades from Germany to Dubai. Luckily for us, at that moment the General Manager for Lufthansa in Kuwait came into the security room. He left the Kuwaiti Security Officer in no doubt that unless we were released immediately, together with our grenades, to rejoin our original flight to Dubai, no other Lufthansa aircraft would ever again fly into Kuwait Airport. It worked and we were hustled across the tarmac to the waiting plane, before being physically pushed into our seats. The bag with the stun grenades was dropped into my lap for me to nurse.

We arrived in Dubai at around 3 a.m. on Sunday, 16 October – only to be arrested at the airport for lack of documentation. Our passports were taken from us. This action allowed one of the western news reporters covering the hijack to pick up our names and the fact that we were SAS. Alastair made numerous attempts during the early hours of the morning to contact the British Embassy but got no further than the gateman who was manning the night phone.

Then luck came our way in the form of an ex-SAS officer called David Bullig. He had left the Regiment and had been seconded as an instructor to the Dubai Palace Guard. As he walked past, we both shouted to get his attention. From that moment events took a completely different turn. Within minutes we were able to roam freely about the airport to assess the situation for ourselves. David was extremely helpful in many other ways – not least because he had already primed some of the best soldiers from the Palace

Guard to be ready to attempt an immediate-action assault on the aircraft should the terrorists actually start killing the hostages.

We toured the airport, and then spoke to the German minister, Wischnewski, who was the acting representative for the West German government. We also met and talked with the Defence Minister of Dubai, who had taken charge of the situation directly. (This was the second hijack he had dealt with.) Having fully assessed the situation, we went with David Bullig to talk directly to Colonel Ulrich Wegener, head of the GSG9 anti-terrorist unit, who was resting with several other Germans in the airport hotel. We all agreed that there was very little we could do until the morning. We would be better off refreshing ourselves with a little sleep and meeting later.

David Bullig took Alastair and me to his home where his charming wife plied us with sandwiches and coffee while we laid out our plan of action. David scribbled notes, listing our demands for kit and equipment. Our most expensive request was for the use of a 737 for training and practice purposes. At about 5 a.m. both Alastair and I fell asleep. After a couple of hours' dozing, we were awakened by Mrs Bullig, with the news that David had managed to fulfil most of our demands. All three of us left for the airport to meet with the GSG9 people and three other white officers David had found from various units in Dubai. In addition, he had selected eight of the best men from the Dubai Palace Guard.

Alastair gave me free rein to set up and instruct a team so that in the worst possible scenario (if the terrorists started shooting the hostages) we could enact an immediate-action drill. That would be when we would have had no choice but to attack the plane with the limited force available. Of course, the more time we had available, the more our plan would improve. By now most of the kit and equipment we needed had arrived – shotguns, masking tape, walkie-talkies, various ladders, padding and myriad other items. We had two quartermasters standing by with four jeeps and an apparently endless supply of cash to obtain anything else required. Most importantly, a Gulf Air 737 had been loaned to us and was parked at the far end of the airfield, out of sight of the hijacked plane. I was about to start a crash course in anti-terrorist techniques.

On the personnel side, my resources were limited to a hard core of five men who had received at least some professional CQB – Close-Quarter Battle training or anti-terrorist training. These included Alastair, David, myself and the two GSG9 officers. Additionally, I had three other white officers and the eight soldiers from the Palace Guard. I concentrated our first efforts on the immediate-action drill needed to counter any terrorist deadline.

The Boeing 737 is a simple little animal as far as anti-terrorist drills are concerned. There are only three options for entry: tail, wing and front catering area. We thought that if the terrorists began to carry out any threatened shootings, they would naturally take the precaution of covering the main doors. It seemed less likely that they would cover the two emergency-exit doors leading on to the wings, so the plan that basically fell into shape was to attack through these. The fact that the wing emergency exits were designed to be opened easily from the outside was another strong factor in favour of adopting this mode of attack – and there were others. We had also discovered a blind spot were the wing joined the aircraft body. Two men could sit beneath the emergency doors and not be visible from any of the windows. By comparison the entry and exit points at the front and rear would require considerable manhandling and some time to get them open.

Our basic plan was to make a single-file approach to the aircraft from its blind spot at the rear. Once under the aircraft we would assemble our ladders quietly and raise them to the wings and the rear door. (The assault teams would comprise Alastair and me, the GSG9 and members of the Dubai Palace Guard.) When everyone was in position and the 'GO' word was given, the leading assault teams were to stand, punch the emergency exit panels and drop the doors into the laps of the passengers in the mid-section of the cabin. The teams would then enter, the port side pair clearing to the front of the cabin, the starboard team clearing to the rear. The leading teams were to receive immediate back-up from the second assault pairs entering behind them from their stations at the tops of the ladders to maintain control of the centre of the aircraft.

Simultaneous with the assault, the outside squads were to open both front and rear doors and enter the plane. The intention here was to provide further back-up in case of any problems and also to provide routes for the hostages to leave the plane, which by this time would be full of smoke from the stun grenades. Once entry to the centre of the aircraft had been effected, the starboard assault team could gain a clear line of sight to the toilet doors at the rear of the cabin. The port team, moving forward through the economy area, would arrive in the first-class section that led into the front catering area. Directly beyond this was the flight deck, the door to which was usually closed. The only obstacles the team would encounter were this door and the curtains that separated economy and first class.

Although this basic plan was quite uncomplicated, we calculated that it would require a great deal of practice to get the timing right – particularly the time it would take the assault teams to effect their entry and make their way to the front and rear of the passenger cabin. We reckoned that as soon as we controlled these points, the only people in serious danger would be the crew in the cockpit.

The training got off to a good start with everyone extremely enthusiastic. Around 2 p.m. we took a lunch break, using the time to iron out every detail, searching for anything that might increase the odds in our favour. Both Alastair and I now felt confident that if the terrorists started to shoot hostages we had a better than fifty-fifty chance of getting into the aircraft and stopping them. We refined our assault plan by devising a suitable distraction for the terrorists, one that would possibly also give us some advantage. If we attacked at night, when we got underneath the aircraft it would help to shut down the APU (Auxiliary Power Unit), plunging everything into darkness. Once we were inside the aircraft the lights could be switched back on.

At about 3.30 p.m. Alastair, having talked at some length, persuaded the Dubai Defence Minister to leave his position in the control tower and come to observe our plan. We went through our operation using the Gulf Air 737, and I have to admit that it looked pretty impressive. Then, just as we finished our demonstration, the unexpected happened. LH181 came to life and took off, taking with her any hope that the hijack would end in Dubai. Fortunately the Germans had a Boeing 707 at their disposal in Dubai and everyone concerned with the hijack, including Alastair and myself, got aboard and gave chase.

First indications were that LH181 was going to land at Salala, Southern Oman. This sounded like good news, for the SAS had men with anti-hijack skills stationed in the area. Our expectations were dashed, however, when we learned that LH181 had in fact landed at Khormaksa Airport in Aden. Captain Schumann, the plane's pilot, had been too low on fuel to fly anywhere else and he skilfully put the aircraft down on the hard sand alongside the runway. Our 707 had to fly on to the international airport in Saudi Arabia. Here, confined in the aircraft, we sat on the ground awaiting further developments. During this waiting period, the negotiating psychologists attempted to persuade the hijackers to release the hostages in exchange for $15 million, which we held in a large suitcase in our plane.

Then came the shocking news that brought an immediate end to negotiations. Captain Schumann had been shot dead aboard LH181. The decision was now made for us. Wherever LH181 was, wherever she was forced to fly, we would make our rescue attempt. For the first time I saw the true determination of our German partners concerning their own nationals. The killing of Captain Schumann had decided the matter. Any further ideas of peaceful negotiation were dismissed.

Our next news was that LH181 had again taken off from Aden, with the dead pilot aboard, and had flown to Mogadishu, capital of the Somali Republic. We got airborne in the 707 and sought permission to land there also. Our flight from Saudi Arabia to Mogadishu took us directly across the war zone lying between Ethiopia and Somalia. At Alastair's suggestion everyone seated near a window was instructed to watch out for hostile fighters, which were a real threat.

Luckily we managed to reach Mogadishu without incident and were given permission to land. The situation was, however, complicated by the presence of LH181 sitting in the middle of the main runway. Our pilot was equal to the challenge. Using only a short length of runway, he brought off a superb landing, using every yard of concrete available and rolling to a halt literally within feet of buildings and houses on the airfield perimeter.

On the ground two top Somali officials collected all passports – and were surprised to discover two of the British variety among them. They were most courteous and friendly. The German minister went off to meet the Somali Prime Minister to discuss the developing political aspects of the hijack. The rest of us were taken to one of Mogadishu's top hotels and given accommodation and a meal. We were kept continually informed about the hijack situation through the Mogadishu security services who were very friendly and helpful.

The terrorists now announced that their deadline was 3.00 p.m. on that same day, Monday, 17 October. Negotiators from Mogadishu air-traffic control tower asked for an extension, explaining that the Baader-Meinhof terrorists jailed in Germany, together with the two Palestinians held in Turkey, would be released. They could not, however, be flown to Mogadishu in less than ten hours. After prolonged discussion, the terrorist leader Captain Mahmud Martyr agreed on a final deadline of 3.00 a.m. the next morning, Tuesday, 18 October.

In the meantime, Minister Wischnewski obtained permission to bring in the German anti-terrorist team who would fly to Mogadishu in case they were needed in any assault on LH181. While awaiting their arrival, we all worked together to modify the assault plan to match it with the current situation. Joining us in our planning was a colonel from the Somalia Special Forces.

We refined the basic procedure developed in Dubai by planning to distract the attention of the terrorist leader by talking to him over the cockpit phone. We also thought we might encourage several other terrorists into the cockpit by lighting a very large fire at the far end of the runway. This later diversion was entrusted to the Somali soldiers who were also responsible for ground defence around the aircraft.

The GSG9 team arrived in a second Boeing 707 at five minutes past eight on the evening of 17 October. Immediately, their commander briefed them and they set about preparing their equipment for the assault. We ran through a quick rehearsal, using the GSG9 707, which was parked out of sight of LH181. By 11.30 p.m. the whole group were in position about seventy metres to the rear of the plane. In single file we approached the plane, and in complete silence the ladders were put in position at each wing root and against the chosen doors. Alastair and I were on either side of the fuselage, at the rear of the wing roots. Our initial task was to throw stun grenades over the fuselage just as the doors were opened: this would achieve the penetrating effect of noise and light in the cabin.

The approach to the aircraft was very slick and smooth. The only problem we had was that the airfield lighting around the control tower created long shadows. Had the window blinds been up, any one of the terrorists looking out could have seen them. But this was not the case. The commander of GSG9 was in direct contact with the control tower. Just before the operation began he transmitted to all his assault teams the information that the two male terrorists had been heard in the cockpit. At this moment, the fire was ignited at the end of the runway. In spite of the tension, this caused some amusement, for it was plain that the Somali soldiers had let their enthusiasm run away with them. It looked as if they had set fire to a complete tanker-load of petrol.

The GSG9 commander counted down and gave the 'Go' signal. Everything happened at once. The quiet African night erupted. The front and rear doors opened as the left-hand ladder-men swung on them: their right-hand partners heaved themselves out of sight into the plane. The wing assault teams stood up, punched in the emergency-exit panels and vaulted in as the doors fell into the cabin – all these actions accompanied by the bangs and flashes from the stun grenades. Immediately the rear starboard door swung open the first terrorist was sighted, absolutely amazed by this turn of events. She was shot instantly by a GSG9 soldier, who then threw himself flat into the rear catering area alongside the toilets, firing up the aisle where the other female terrorist had been spotted. The front assault team were involved in a brief firefight with the two male terrorists. Lasting for about a minute, it ended when they had both been fatally shot. During the firefight we heard two dull explosions inside LH181. These were hand grenades exploding as the mortally wounded terrorists' strength drained away and their grip on the firing levers of the grenades relaxed involuntarily.

As soon as the firing died away, the passengers began to disembark. They were climbing out of every exit available and this led to an unforeseen difficulty that could have caused quite serious injury among the passengers, who seemed convinced that every plane was equipped with those inflatable rubber chutes into which they could jump and slide happily down to the ground. In this case they didn't exist, but several of the passengers, young and old alike, tried to slide down the assault ladders. To say that this caused us some concern would be an understatement. The thought of the passengers injuring themselves this late in the game was too much to take.

The GSG9 men on the ground took swift and firm command of the exits, guiding people down the assault ladders or assisting them through the mid-section emergency exits down to the ground via the wings. The passengers were in a state of sheer bewilderment. They had, after all, spent five long days cooped up in a very confined space, in hot, filthy conditions and with failing sanitary facilities. On top of all this physical discomfort, every hour would have been heavily weighted by fear feeding on their uncertainty about their immediate future. The climactic few minutes of the assault, involving loud explosions, flashes, smoke, rapid movement, gunfire and raw danger must have disoriented many of them. As they disembarked they were ushered to the rear, where a fleet of ambulances and other vehicles ferried them to the passenger lounge in the terminal building. As the first few minutes of Tuesday, 18 October ticked away, so ended the hijacking of Flight LH181.

The casualty list showed three of the terrorists dead, with the second woman terrorist severely wounded. As she was taken away for medical treatment she gave the victory V-sign while screaming out an assortment of slogans. On our side we had the dead pilot, plus one member of GSG9 and one member of the aircrew slightly wounded. After receiving necessary medical attention, the passengers were soon taken aboard the negotiators' 707 while the negotiators, the GSG9 men and we two SAS soldiers boarded the GSG9 707 to be flown back to Germany.

Although apparently over, the saga of the hijack of LH181 still had a twist in its tail. During the flight back to Germany Alastair and I were told that the leading members of the Baader-Meinhof terrorist gang had simultaneously committed suicide at Stammheim Jail in Stuttgart. Somehow, within a few hours of the actual event they had received news that the hijack was over. Andreas Baader and Jan-Carle Raspe had shot themselves and Gudrun Ensslin had hanged herself, while Irmgard Muller had made an unsuccessful attempt to kill herself, using a stolen bread knife. These terrorists, all locked in separate cells in a maximum-security prison, had somehow learned of Germany's success in Mogadishu – 3,500 miles away – within a very few hours of the ending of the hijack. Pistols, ammunition, knives and rope had suddenly found their way into the terrorists' cells, and somehow they had managed to convince each other to take their own lives. A mystery that remains unexplained to this day.

The success of the joint operation was only marred by the death of Captain Jurgen Schumann, shot in Aden. He was a very brave man and, like so many other aircraft captains, upheld his professional responsibilities to the end in seeking to protect all those in his care, passengers and crew alike. News of the German government's success also signalled the end for the kidnapped Dr Schleyer, who was still held by Baader-Meinhof gang members. A few days after the rescue Dr Schleyer's body was found in a car boot – he had three bullets in his head.

After a full army career, Alastair Morrison retired from the SAS in 1979 and went to work for the German weapon manufacturers Heckler & Koch. After a spell with them, he set up his own company, Defence Systems Limited (DSL), that has grown into one of the largest private security companies in the world. Many newspaper articles about Alastair Morrison and DSL have been published, but in my sincere opinion he is a real gentleman and much admired by those who really know him.

53. THE PATROL OF BRAVO TWO ZERO

Author's note: Much has been said and written about the troubled patrol call sign Bravo Two Zero. The best of this material can be found in the books written by two of the patrol members, Andy McNab and Chris Ryan. While I have, of course, read both books, another member of the SAS who had actually talked first-hand to both men shortly after the events concerned related the following version of them to me. Whatever version you believe, no one can take away from the courage and tenacity of those patrol members of Bravo Two Zero. They took the right decisions and in the end they took the beatings. As it turned out, the other two Bravo patrols, one of which had two vehicles to move their equipment, decided that they were not going to stop in Iraq. One patrol just got back on the chopper and flew back to Saudi while the other, realising that the type of operation was not viable, drove out within a few days. They were both given a real hard time and, in some cases, were called cowards. As it turned out, they were just very far-sighted.

Andy McNab (pseudonym), Sergeant and patrol commander
Sergeant Vince Phillips – second-in-command*
Trooper Robert 'Bob' Consiglio*
Lance Corporal Chris Ryan (pseudonym)
Mark (a New Zealander)
Stan (born in South Africa and a qualified doctor)
Lance Corporal Dinger
Trooper Steven 'Legs' Lane*

Having arrived in Saudi Arabia later than the rest of the SAS, the men of Bravo Two Zero were told that there would be no move for two days. Andy was placed in overall charge of an eight-man team, made up of his own four-man patrol and Vince's. They, like two other patrols, were to be inserted to watch the three Main Supply Routes coming out of Baghdad. These MSRs not only carried the bulk of the Scuds and Iraqi military equipment but they also connected the six main bridges that spanned the river Tigris in central Baghdad, all of which were still intact. These bridges connected the two halves of the city and also carried the landlines that were vital in connecting Baghdad's communication system with the rest of the country and with the Iraqi army in Kuwait. These landlines ran alongside the three MSRs running west to east, mainly into Jordan. It would be the patrol's task to find and sabotage these landlines in the northern area. Like the other two Bravo patrols, they would have to operate for fourteen days before any resupply.

The patrol was heavily armed for this mission. Four carried 203s, the American M16 Armalite rifle with a grenade-launcher attached to fire a 40mm bomb; the others had Minimis, a light machine-gun. The patrol had no slings on their guns, preferring to keep them ready for use in their hands. In addition to a rifle or a light-support machine-gun and plenty of ammo, each man carried a disposable 66mm rocket and white-phosphorus and ordinary L2 explosive grenades. Some had 203s that they checked were ready and loaded with grenades.

The team spent twelve hours in exhaustive planning, until preparations were completed and they were finally inserted. They did this at last light, being ferried to their drop-off point by a camouflaged Chinook. Their first attempt was aborted, but on the morning of 23 January the patrol reboarded the helicopter for another try. Their safety depended on the skill of the pilot and there were anti-aircraft missiles all along the route. Still, since they were going in under the cover of three Coalition air raids there would be little actual danger of enemy fire.

Stopping at the same refuelling point as on the previous insertion attempt, the pilot was given the go-ahead and they flew on into Iraq. En route, things became hectic when they were spotted by an Iraqi missile crew. The missile locked on and in desperation the pilot threw his aircraft all over the sky. His efforts were rewarded and the missile was evaded. Half an hour later, the pilot gave a two-minute warning in preparation for landing.

At 2100 hours the helicopter lifted off and the team were on their own. The whole immediate area was desolate and it was bloody cold. Although Andy had been in the Middle East many times before, this type of terrain was new to him. But they were well armed and very confident. When things went quiet, Andy and Vince called their guys together. Andy told them where they were, where they were going, and confirmed the RV ahead for the next twenty-four hours. This was just in case there was a crisis and the party got split up. They were to aim north for a half-buried petroleum pipeline that should lead to a major ridge line where the RV point was located. Carrying their huge amount of kit they set off. The going was slow but by 0445 hours they had reached the bend in the MSR. Vince and his men waited while Andy did a CTR (Close Target Recce) and looked for a place to hide.

After about half an hour they found a perfect site for the LUP: a small cave about five metres high, cut into rock and protected by an overhang that would hide them from view and, if necessary, provide cover from fire. The team moved all the equipment into the cave while Andy went out to check the terrain. It was flat ground, mostly, but about 1,500 metres away there was a plantation with a water tower and buildings. According to the map and the OC's briefing, that plantation should not have been there. It was much too close for comfort. Back at the cave they tried to transmit a report – only to discover that the radio was fucked! This meant returning to the landing site the following night to RV with a helicopter at 0400 hours and exchange radios.

At first light Andy risked a daytime look over the brim of the wadi. To his surprise there was a military encampment just three hundred metres from the cave. During his recce patrol the previous night they had missed the Iraqis by about a mere fifty metres! There was still no joy with the radio so, according to the lost-comms procedure, they would have to return to the helicopter drop-off point. They prepared to wait the time out, sitting in the cave and observing the surrounding area. Though vehicles moved on the nearby MSR, there were no problems until mid-afternoon. A boy herding goats looked over into the wadi and saw the team. He promptly bolted to raise the alarm. Andy thought the cave was useless for defence, and preparations were made to bug out.

If forced to fight, they would stand a much better chance in the open. Although it was not yet last light, Andy decided to move. They would go west, trying to avoid the Iraqi positions, then head south towards the helicopter RV. They took only their bergens and belt kit, leaving everything else behind. With *shamaghs* over their faces – to make themselves look more like the locals – they left in single file.

Just when it seemed that they'd got away with it, they heard tracked vehicles to their left. Knowing that a fight was inevitable, they got down in a defensive position with weapons at the ready. An APC (armoured personnel carrier) with a 7.62 machine-gun came down the small depression towards them, with another bringing up the rear. Both Vince and Legs fired off their 66mm rockets, and a pretty unequal fight ensued. As an Iraqi truck arrived on the scene, a third 66mm rocket took it out. What to do next? If they remained in a stand-off fight they would soon run out of ammunition. Chris said that at this stage everybody was psyched up and they decided to attack.

Andy, Chris and two men from Vince's team ran forward, while the others provided covering fire. Then, as the vanguard group dropped down, the covering party advanced. It was a classic example of fire and movement towards the enemy. Andy let those with the Minimis get ahead to utilise their superior firepower. When they got to within fifty metres of the APCs, the nearest one pulled back. The guys could hardly believe it – they had driven off an enemy who had vastly superior numbers and hardware. The patrol was now on top of the situation, with a whole mess of Iraqi bodies lying everywhere. Still, Andy realised that they needed to get away before reinforcements arrived. Grabbing their bergens they moved off, followed at a distance by a now-cautious enemy.

Now that they'd been 'compromised' (the military term for having one's presence unexpectedly detected by the enemy) and their mission was impossible, their one aim was to get out. They would soon have the cover of darkness in their favour, so they moved quickly. As they ran, two trucks carrying about forty infantry came from the east and started firing. The team retreated up a gradual slope to the west. At the brow of the hill they came under fire from the AA (anti-aircraft) guns to the north-west. Things were not looking good and it was generally agreed that the team should ditch their bergens in order to move faster. The enemy finally lost contact as darkness fell and the team faded into the night. Andy stopped at a rallying point and counted the heads and was pleased to find they were still together. Although the radio was gone, they still had four

TACBEs (Tactical Beacons for signalling friendly forces) and decided to use one. There was no reply and no chance of contact unless a Coalition jet flew overhead, when they would call on the emergency frequency.

Andy decided to head for Syria, 120 kilometres to the west. As the enemy would expect them to head south towards Saudi they figured they might make it by moving south and then boxing to the north-west. The main problem now was the cold and all the running they had been doing. Their shirts were wet with sweat, and the cold cut through the damp cloth. A check with the satellite navigation system showed that they had travelled 25 kilometres from the cave: it was time to start boxing and cross the MSR before first light.

They travelled on a compass bearing, stopping for five minutes every hour to drink and rest since some of the guys were close to total exhaustion. The night became very black and the temperature dropped even further. After another fifteen kilometres, they turned north. Around this time Andy noticed that they had slowed down and that there were gaps in the line. Vince had injured his leg escaping from the firefight and Stan was dangerously dehydrated. Chris, the medic, helped a little by putting two sachets of electrolyte into Stan's water bottle. Before they set off once more, Andy changed the order of the march, putting Chris as lead scout with Stan and Vince behind him, followed by Andy and the rest of the patrol. They moved off once more, but Chris said the pace was getting even slower. Both Vince's and Stan's conditions worsened, but everyone was feeling the effects of the cold and the night's marching.

Once, on hearing an aircraft approaching from the north, Andy risked trying the TACBE again. They gathered around as an American voice answered, albeit somewhat garbled. The signal was weakening as the jet flew out of range but the pilot had repeated their call sign, which gave them hope. They staggered off once more. Those who were slow opened the group up and this caused the patrol to become split.

Chris, Stan and Vince, who had been at the front, were suddenly missing. Andy's group waited a while, afraid to shout or show white light, not knowing if there were any enemy around. When no one appeared, they could only hope that they would RV eventually. They moved on and two hours later Andy's party crossed the MSR.

When daylight came they found a small knoll with a cairn surrounded by a low wall on the top. By building this up slightly, they formed a half-decent shelter. As they huddled together Andy got out his map and did some calculations: he reckoned they had travelled some 85 kilometres in the last twelve hours. An outstanding achievement, helped by the fact that they were running for their very lives. With the dawn came icy cold rain and they huddled together to share their body warmth. All code sheets were burned and everyone checked their pockets for compromising material. There were vehicle sounds in the distance and they spotted two APCs about one kilometre to the south. The rain turned to snow. Totally exhausted, the men were exposed to an icy wind in soaking clothes and survival now became top priority. Andy scraped a small hole and lit a fuel block. Brewing up a hot drink meant the difference between life and death.

Stan, Vince and Chris were having it just as hard. After losing contact they had pushed on, by daybreak finding themselves out in the open. The only cover they could find was a deep tank-track. There the three of them lay throughout the day, battered by the wind and covered with snow. As darkness fell, they could hardly move. The cold had eaten into their bones. That night, as they moved off, Vince was in desperate trouble. Time after time he staggered and fell, and at last he simply wandered away. When they realised that he was missing, Stan and Chris searched for over an hour, but there was no sign of Vince. He died all alone, of hypothermia.

Andy knew that it was all becoming simply a matter of survival. Mark was in a very bad way, so both Andy and

Bob gave him their body heat while Dinger and Legs prepared some hot food. The danger of death from hypothermia was now greater than that of being captured. After two hours they got going again, struggling on through the darkness.

At midnight, the patrol realised that they were following a dried-up river bed, which was a little sheltered and warmer. But a near miss with two Iraqis forced them to climb up again. By the early hours it was obvious that Mark was on the verge of collapse. So they returned to the river bed and found a depression in the ground where once more they huddled together for warmth. They would try again tomorrow. At dawn next day the weather had changed to clear skies and sunshine, though it was still bitterly cold. Things looked better, and although they were short of water, another twelve hours' hard tabbing would see them at the border that night.

The same sunshine had also given Stan and Chris a new lease of life. They had fallen exhausted into a small dried-up river bed and now sat against a wall. As the sun warmed them, they sorted out their equipment and cleaned their weapons. About midday they spotted a goatherd out with his flock. Stan thought it best if they tried to get the boy to give them a lift on a tractor or something and, against Chris's advice, set off with the boy. Chris waited until it was dark, by which time Stan had not shown. Fearful that Stan might have been captured Chris started walking. He was now on his own.

Strangely enough, later that day Andy's group also encountered a goatherd out with his flock. He was a friendly character in his seventies who sat down with the group to enjoy food and conversation. Everyone enjoyed his goats' milk and as he seemed to think that Andy's team were connected with the Iraqi army he was allowed to go on his way unharmed. As a precaution, the team headed south for a while, before turning west once more. With only two days' food left and almost no water, they decided to hijack a vehicle. They planned to creep down to the road, where Bob would play the cripple with Andy supporting him. The others would hide, ready to pounce when some Good Samaritan stopped. It was half an hour's tab to the road and they were soon in position. After about twenty minutes a vehicle approached, slowing down when Bob and Andy appeared in its headlights. It was, of all things, a 1950s New York yellow cab, tarted up with typical Arab decoration. The passengers in the back were father and son. They and the driver were quickly tied up and left unharmed in a ditch.

Andy drove off, with Legs beside him giving directions with a compass. The taxi had half a tank of fuel which, all being well, would be enough to get them over the border by morning. They planned to drive as far as possible, dump the vehicle and then cross on foot. Their map, being an air chart, was not very helpful and the roads were very confusing. As they moved through villages and countryside, they came to a slow-moving traffic jam. Iraqi soldiers were checking all vehicles and eventually they were sussed. Legs shot one man with his rifle while the others opened up with the Minimis, killing two more Iraqi squaddies. At this point they were forced to abandon the taxi and go on foot. Once they were clear of the checkpoint, the firing died down.

Andy made a quick check but none of the team had been hit. He quickly checked the Magellan. They were about thirteen kilometres from the border and they had nine hours of darkness left. They travelled close to another road with a heavily built-up area to their left, taking cover every time a car passed. At last, coming over a crest, they looked down on the lights of Abu Kamal and Krabilah, the two built-up areas that straddled the border. There was a hell of a noise coming from the nearest town as Coalition jets carried out an air raid. The population had been thoroughly disturbed. There were lots of lights and much shouting and slamming of doors. The team walked on, using the confusion to cover their escape.

They were now almost at the Euphrates, taking cover at the edge of a plantation. Mark used the Magellan: ten kilometres to the border. They travelled slowly, stopping every five minutes, checking buildings before skirting them: seven kilometres to go. But their luck did not hold. They were seen and in the ensuing exchange of fire Mark and Andy became separated from the others.

They were on the river bank, some ten to fifteen metres above the water, hiding among the bushes on the first of a series of small plateaux that lay between them and the ploughed land that they had just crossed. The Iraqis were on the opposite bank, hunting for them with torches. Tracers and bullets were still flying on their side of the wadi. It was impossible to cross the river: it was too icy and in full flow. The only way out was through the enemy positions. Following the ploughed field, parallel to the river, the two men crawled along the muddy furrows for twenty minutes. Suddenly they were challenged. Mark fired and shot one Iraqi soldier, then both SAS men were running once more. The enemy seemed to think that it was a full-scale invasion and Andy hoped that Mark and he might slip through unnoticed in the confusion. They had two and a half hours of darkness left in which to reach the border.

There was a three-strand barbed-wire fence that they would have to cross. It led to an Iraqi truck compound. They cleared the fence between two canvas-topped trucks, but the wire twanged as Mark went over. A soldier in one of the trucks heard and started jabbering. Andy shot him and, going up to the truck, raked it with fire before lobbing a grenade into the other vehicle. Mark and Andy both fired their last rounds. They were now out of ammo. Dropping their weapons, they bolted.

Just before first light, as the two men ploughed through the muck of a large rubbish dump, two AKs opened up at close range. Both soldiers instinctively dropped down but Mark didn't get up again. Andy ran on alone but he felt that the worst was over: just a quick tab to the border and he would be free. He was in pretty poor physical condition, with deep cuts to hands, knees and elbows, bruising on the sides of both legs, scratches and gashes from thorns and wire. His feet were icy cold and soaking wet, and his boots were caked with mud that weighed a ton.

Stopping for food and drink, Andy weighed up the situation. Navigation was easy, as the communications mast on the Iraqi side of the border was visible ahead. He could still hear firing coming from behind him and, on balance, it seemed best to lie up and wait one more night. He was very hungry and devoured his last sachet of food, washing it down by sucking up a little water from the ditch he was hiding in. He then lay back and waited.

The morning was bright and cold as Andy awoke to the sound of gunfire coming from a nearby steel bridge. Just then, a soldier who was searching under the bridge saw him. Seconds later, men jumped into the ditch and hauled him out by his feet. What followed next was a savage beating as all the Iraqi troopers joined in a concerted attack with their feet and fists. Andy was hit and kicked on both his body and his head but somehow he remained conscious. Then, forcing him to his knees, the Iraqis tied his hands and hauled him to a vehicle. As the soldiers passed through a town, they shot their AK47s into the air and the vehicle was soon surrounded by a howling mob. They swarmed all over the vehicle to get at the prisoner, spitting, slapping, punching and kicking. It seemed that a lynching was likely. Eventually the soldiers drove the crowd away. Those soldiers were the heroes of the hour to the local population!

Andy was taken into a barracks, dragged once more from the vehicle and thrown to the ground. The first thing he saw was another body lying with hands and feet tied together and in a dreadful state. It was covered in blood and dirt, with the head a horribly swollen shape. But he knew it was Dinger. So at least one other member of the patrol was alive. There then followed a continuous round of beatings and interrogations. Both Andy and Dinger took everything the Iraqis could give them and, painful as it was, they survived.

After a while it became obvious that the interrogations were not for any specific purpose and that the brutality was just for fun. Having been moved to several different locations, the British soldiers finally found themselves being driven to Baghdad. When the vehicle stopped, they were dragged across a cobbled courtyard. This was agony for Andy as the wounds to his injured feet broke open and began to bleed again. They were made to sit cross-legged on the floor of a semi-dark room with damp stone walls. The blindfolds were ripped off and for the first time Andy saw Dinger close enough to make eye contact. Talking was not allowed, but it was not necessary: the eye contact alone was worth a thousand words and bolstered their morale.

The interrogations did not become violent again but continued for a long time. Andy stuck to his cover story and acted broken and pathetic. He was put in the same cell as Dinger, where they shared a blanket on the floor. Andy learned what had happened to his patrol. Dinger, Legs and Bob got into a firefight after the group split up. Bob had been shot. Only Legs and Dinger made it to the river. They searched but no boats were available, so they swam. The water, which was bitterly cold, almost finished Legs off. Dinger had dragged him out of the water to a small pump-hut where he lay exhausted. By morning, Dinger could see that Legs would die without medical attention, so he beckoned a nearby farmer. Dinger then slipped away leaving Legs, who was still dozing, to a better fate. However, the locals spotted Dinger and pounced, using his *shamagh* to tie his hands. When Dinger had last seen Legs he had been on a stretcher and appeared to be dead.

Some days later, as Andy was looking past the guards into the corridor, he saw Stan being dragged past. Stan was in a dreadful state, covered in blood and apparently lifeless. But when he saw Stan for a second time, at least he was still alive, albeit in a bad way. On the afternoon of 6 February

Andy was blindfolded, handcuffed and put into the back of a vehicle. The English-speaking guards in front teased and chatted. They said that they could see Dinger and Stan in the car ahead. Andy was taken to the military prison and led to a cell, with a blanket over his head. Presently someone came and asked if he would like to be with his friends, and at last the three were reunited in another cell.

Once more they compared notes and speculated that all the others were probably dead. Vince had died of exposure, Stan was fairly sure of that: Vince had been in a pretty bad way the evening they had lost him. Then, after they had met up with the goatherd who had seemed friendly, Stan had gone with him to see if he could get hold of a vehicle. All seemed well, though there were two vehicles outside the destination hut instead of one. The boy wandered off and Stan watched the place for about twenty minutes. He planned to take a vehicle if the keys had been left in the ignition.

As Stan approached the vehicles, an Iraqi soldier came out of the house. He tried to pull a weapon out of the nearest vehicle but Stan shot him. Several Iraqi squaddies then rushed out of the house, less than twenty metres away. Stan shot three, then his gun jammed. He tried to get away in one of the vehicles but the five remaining soldiers attacked him with rifle butts, knocking him down. Once they'd tied him up they took him to a military installation near the Euphrates. His interrogation had followed the usual pattern.

One night an injured airman in the American Marines was dragged in. He gave them the news that the ground war was nearly over. On the morning of 3 March, Stan and Dinger were told that they were going home. It appeared that Andy was being kept back as a hostage. On 5 March the remaining prisoners in the block, including Andy, were told that they were going home too.

When at last they were free the whole story of Bravo Two Zero came out. Chris had been without water for two days.

He had made his way down to the river where he sank in deep mud to his waist. He then lay up in a small wadi until nightfall, moving off again as darkness fell. After staggering around for several days, his body feeling as if it was falling apart, Chris came upon an illuminated road sign. He was still fifty kilometres from the border. He had estimated his position badly. With his water gone, he was dehydrating fast. Luck was with him when he found a stream. With septic cuts on his hands, and his feet in an appalling condition, Chris struggled forward until he eventually crossed into Syria. A few days later he was reunited with the Squadron in Saudi Arabia.

54. CAPTAIN ROBIN LETTS

C aptain Robin Letts was not everyone's idea of an SAS hero: self-effacing, shy, short-sighted and a great lover of books and music, he also showed great initiative and bravery during the Borneo confrontation. In 1965 he was put in charge of a patrol detailed with collecting intelligence on Indonesian communication routes across the border. The rest of his patrol consisted of Corporal 'Taff' Springles, the signaller, medic and soldier with the most experience, Trooper Brown and Trooper Hogg.

The area in question, consisting mostly of swamp, had already been mapped out by members of B Squadron, making navigation easier for Letts and his men. Nevertheless, the going was still slow as they were trying to keep their movements as quiet as possible. After six days of living in mud and water, the sound of an outboard motor drew them to a twelve-foot-wide stream, one of the main tributaries of the swamp, draining into the River Sentimo.

Finding an area of dry land about forty yards back from the stream, Letts and Hogg took off their bergens and left them with the other two men, intending to do a little reconnaissance. To lessen the likelihood of their tracks being spotted by the enemy, they took to the stream, walking and sometimes swimming along it. A small way downstream they saw a domestic water buffalo and heard voices, a sign that there was a village not far away. Letts realised that their progress through the river had been just a bit too easy: none of the usual debris of underwater logs or vegetation had blocked their way at any point – which could only mean that the river was regularly cleared to allow water traffic through. This realisation meant that the men had to get out of the stream, and fast. At any moment a boat could come along and they would be sitting ducks.

Back with Springles and Brown, an observation point was soon found that was ideal for the purpose of monitoring traffic on the waterway. It was set on a loop in the stream where the visibility was clear sixty yards to the left and thirty yards to the right. Late in the afternoon their patience was rewarded as two boats, each containing two armed soldiers, paddled past them, heading downstream.

Leaving Hogg at the observation point, Letts and the others returned to the LUP to signal base and ask for permission to engage the enemy if the chance recurred. While they were gone, two more boats appeared unexpectedly. Hogg, who was standing and still watching after the first two boats, was caught unawares, his head exposed. He feared for his life, thinking that he had been seen, but the two boats passed by without incident. Luckily for him, the crews were unobservant of their surroundings.

By the morning there had still been no word back from base giving the patrol the approval they needed to attack the enemy. Letts decided that the opportunity was too good to pass up and that they would act anyway. The stream was obviously more important than it had previously appeared, and probably served as a main supply route for conveying men and equipment to the enemy forward base at Achan.

The village that Letts and Hogg had discovered earlier possibly served as a staging point, which meant that any attack would bring swift retaliation.

A plan was drawn up and at dawn Letts positioned his men at various positions around the loop. The stream, at this point, seemed difficult for the boatmen to navigate and took all their concentration, leaving them less alert to attack than normal. The position of the loop also meant that once a boat had passed a certain point it was no longer visible to those behind, thus creating the perfect conditions for an ambush. With Letts at the apex of the loop, Brown to his left and Springles to his right, the men were ready to take on any boat, no matter what direction it came from. However, as most of the water traffic seemed to be coming from the left, Letts positioned Hogg along that side too, to give warning of any problems. Letts also worked out an escape route; if his assumption about the village was correct, they would need to get out of the area as quickly as possible.

At eight-fifteen, a boat came into view, but this time it carried three armed soldiers instead of two. The extra man sat in the stern, acting as sentry, alert to any dangers ahead. The next boat was the same: two armed men, paddling, sat in the front and another, cradling a weapon, crouched in the stern. This new situation upped the stakes.

The first boat passed by Brown, as planned, but the second one managed to crash into the bank right next to him. Luckily, the crew was too busy trying to rectify the situation to notice him. As the boat struggled to get back on course, a third boat came into view. As with the others, it also carried three armed soldiers. Eventually the first boat reached Springles's position and Letts gave the signal to attack. He took aim on his first target, the armed sentry in the second boat, but was surprised when one of the paddlers grabbed for his gun with what seemed like amazing speed and lined Letts up in *his* sights. At this close range, Letts really had no chance to get out of the way and to change his aim to the man in the bow in such a short space of time. It looked as though he was about to be killed when Springles fired at the Indonesian and killed him.

All of the patrol opened up on the boats with their weapons in a fury of fire. During the firefight, the crews of two of the boats managed to flip them over, throwing themselves into the water. Later, it was surmised that this was part of an anti-ambush drill, as some of the Indonesians soon emerged on the bank with their weapons.

Seeing the boat go over, Letts fired into the water, hoping to hit some of them. At the same time, the only man remaining alive in the second boat managed to take aim at Letts. The captain realised his predicament, almost too late, and jumped to one side before turning his weapon on the man and firing. The Indonesian fell forward into the boat. For a split second, Letts looked away to see how Brown was coping with his boat when the man he had just shot seemingly came back from the dead. Although wounded, he raised himself up and took aim at Letts again. Luckily, Letts saw the action in time and shot him twice. This time the wounds were definitely fatal.

While Letts had been distracted, he had failed to notice that he had become a target for another of the Indonesian soldiers. One of the men from Springles's overturned boat had finally managed to reach the near bank and had immediately taken aim at Letts. Once more Springles saved Letts's life by shooting the man dead. Instantly, another soldier emerged from the water and made a grab for the dead man's weapon. Of course, he never had a chance and was killed alongside his companion.

Brown had dealt with the occupants of his boat relatively easily. They all lay dead. A fourth boat now came into view but as the occupants realised what was happening, they quickly reached the bank and pulled their boat backwards, out of sight. Hogg fired off a few rounds but the enemy were already gone. The firefight was over: the whole thing had taken only four minutes.

Dead Indonesians littered the water, the bank and the boats. Only one had managed to escape the ferocity of the patrol's onslaught with their SLRs. Letts gave the order to retreat and the patrol made haste to their LUP, picked up their bergens and headed back in the direction of the border. With the Indonesians now alerted to their presence, they knew they had little time before the search parties were sent out. The hunters had now become the hunted and Letts decided that they would have far more chance if they relied on speed rather than concealment.

The SAS men's extreme fitness served them well and they managed to cover a great deal of ground before the enemy mortared the ambush position. Apart from speed, the other advantage that Letts and his men had was that the Indonesians had no idea how big a force they were up against and, seeing the damage done, probably thought the numbers of British infiltrators were greater than they were. Therefore they would have expected such a large force to be moving more slowly through the jungle, their misjudgement giving Letts's patrol a much-needed head start.

The patrol covered much of the nine kilometres back to the border by the time dusk fell. Springles set up his radio and contacted base to tell them of their success. Before he could, he was told that permission had been granted for them to attack the enemy. Luckily for them, the *fait accompli* had worked out well, especially as they had forgotten, in the heat of the moment, that they had still been waiting for that permission to be given.

In the morning they continued their journey and cautiously made their way back over the border. They called for an 'extraction' and were winched out by helicopter through a break in the forest canopy. The helicopter arrived far quicker than usual, much to their surprise, and they had to forgo a tasty dinner cooked by Hogg. Hogg's bad luck didn't end there: while being winched up by the helicopter a jungle vine became tangled around his neck and he was almost strangled in mid-air and mid-rescue.

Nevertheless, the whole operation had been a complete success and a few months later Letts was awarded the Military Cross for his part. Soon after, Letts joined the Australian SAS so that he could take part in the Vietnam War.

55. CAPTAIN MALCOLM MCGILLIVRAY

Captain Malcolm McGillivray had arrived in the ranks of the SAS via the Black Watch. At first his superiors had not wanted to let him go but he had managed to persuade them anyway. First of all, he completed selection easily, even without having obtained permission to do so. Then, when his regiment persisted in its reluctance, he showed his displeasure by eating nothing but porridge, day after day. Finally his fellow officers could stand his obstinate protest no more and agreed to let him go. His qualities soon served him well in the SAS and he was given the command of 2 Troop during the emergency in Borneo. His mission was to search Mount Kalimantan for Indonesian units and destroy them.

His team consisted of ten SAS men, including Corporal Roberts, Troopers Franks, Henry, Bilbao, Condie, Callan and Shipley, as well as 21 scouts gathered from local tribesmen. Air-reconnaissance photographs showed that there were a number of huts high up on the mountain, situated in a clearing. Regarding this as a good target,

McGillivray had a full-size replica of the huts built and made his team practise an assault on them again and again until he was convinced they had it right.

Preparations complete, McGillivray and his men set out on 9 July 1965, crossing the River Bemban and trekking up through the foothills. This first part of the journey took five days. On the sixth day McGillivray split the men into six patrols to search the area for any signs of enemy occupation. At first, the intelligence that they had been working on seemed to be right on target as a patrol of scouts returned with the news that they had found bootprints and had smelled cooking. After a long conversation complicated by the language barrier between the SAS and the scouts, McGillivray finally worked out where the enemy force was likely to be found. He gathered his team together again and they set off.

Unfortunately, by the time they reached the place where the scouts had found the camp there was no sign of it: every evidence of human occupation, if there had ever been any, had been removed. Either the enemy was very clever or else all their intelligence had been wrong and the scouts had imagined what they had seen and smelled. McGillivray looked about him, visualising mentally the landmarks he had memorised from the photographs and other intelligence, and found that they matched what he could actually see in the surrounding landscape. This was definitely the place, but minus the camp.

No matter how hard they searched, the camp could not be found. However, they were near a track that was obviously used by the enemy as a supply route to Batu Hitam. At least they should be able to mount an ambush on any Indonesian troops who came their way. After a spot of reconnaissance, McGillivray decided that the best ambush point was at a gully just north-west of the river. Here the gully was spanned by a large log. On the north side, where they were, the ground flattened out to provide a broad, flat space, good enough to fire across from the safety of cover.

Anyone trapped on the log when the shooting began wouldn't stand much of a chance.

McGillivray's signaller, 'Rover' Slater, usually worked with the captain. They argued about every decision and although it seemed sometimes that they were always at odds with each other, in fact they managed to work as a team in some strange antagonistic way. Disputing matters as they did, no idea was unchallenged and no possibility was left unexplored.

McGillivray took Slater and two others with him to keep a watch on the ambush point. A group of locals appeared, carrying heavy bundles, and crossed over the gully using the log. Convinced now that this was definitely the place for the ambush, McGillivray sent the two other men back to round up the rest of the team while he stayed at the point with Slater. Soon after, a group of about eleven armed enemy soldiers came into view. However, at such close range and with such odds it was deemed unwise to take them on.

The rest of McGillivray's men arrived and deployed initially to the LUP where he and Slater met up with them. He selected fifteen men, including Corporal Roberts, to form the first watch. This group was divided into three separate sections, each with a different responsibility during any attack. The men were all then placed individually in one long line, five to twenty yards away from the track. The 'killer' team, consisting of Roberts, Franks, Bilbao and three scouts was placed alongside the log. The group on the right-hand side, consisting of Condie, Callan, Shipley and three scouts, was responsible for keeping a watch for the enemy approaching and informing the others by means of pulling on a cord that ran down the line. They were also charged with stopping any escapees and warning of the likelihood of a counter-attack. The left-hand side group assumed a similar role to that of the right.

It was by now the afternoon and no one expected the enemy to return before dusk, so McGillivray carried on with his preparations. Back at the rendezvous area he realised that he was not happy with the position he had picked and so had the men move the bergens to a new place. As usual, Slater pointed out the downside – that the ambush party would not know where to retreat to, and even if they were told, they still might not be able to find it in all the confusion after a contact. However, McGillivray was not unduly worried: he felt he had plenty of time in which he would change the watch over and that would ensure that all the men were fully aware of the new rendezvous location.

An hour later it began to rain heavily, the storm creating difficult conditions for the watchers. Then, without warning, halfway through the afternoon, the soldiers who had passed through before returned. They were obviously wet and uncomfortable as they travelled at a very quick pace. Nevertheless, they were spotted by Shipley, out on the right-hand flank, who gave five tugs on the cord. The message was passed down the line in the same fashion until it reached Roberts. Roberts alerted his men just as five of the soldiers stepped onto the log. The 'killer' group all took aim and fired, sending the Indonesians tumbling into the gully below. Roberts, thinking that all of them had been killed, gave the order to stop firing. Bilbao, however, spotted one of them trying to crawl away and fired off two more rounds to stop him, as he had been previously instructed.

However, the five men on the log had only been one element of the returning soldiers, as the men on the right flank were about to find out. Alerted by the gunfire, a second enemy group disappeared into cover next to the track and let loose with their rifles and machine-gun towards the ambushers. It looked as though they were about to storm the position from the right flank. Condie, who was a little further back, called out to them to fall back to his position. Shipley, Callan and their scouts needed no second urging and retreated. Realising that the area of ground to the rear provided good cover from the enemy fire, they ran to it but in the process completely missed Condie who had taken it upon himself to move forward to check that they had got away and not been wounded or killed. Once Shipley and Callan reached the dead ground they continued on to the old rendezvous point, standard procedure after a contact, expecting to find others there. Of course, due to McGillivray's move, they were the only ones there – a fact that caused them great frustration.

McGillivray was also feeling frustrated by having to follow standard operating procedures. They prohibited him from joining the action, although he could hear it at such close quarters. Slater, still at his side, reminded him that the ambush party still knew nothing about the position of the new rendezvous point. Stirred into action again, McGillivray tasked two of his scouts to go to the old location and guide anyone they found there to the new one. Guiding them part of the way there himself, the captain was suddenly confronted by the first of the scouts coming back from the ambush. Once again, communication proved a bit of problem but McGillivray was sure they said Roberts was in trouble. Standard operating procedures or no, McGillivray decided that he couldn't hang back any longer so he made his way to Roberts's position. In fact, he had heard the scouts wrongly; the corporal wasn't hurt at all and was profoundly displeased that his commanding officer had risked going against procedure so recklessly.

The thick jungle cover slowed the battle and although the gunfire continued from the enemy's position, they did not seem as willing to advance as they had been before. The bodies of two Indonesian soldiers lay under a log close to Roberts's position, but as yet they had not been searched for weapons or papers. McGillivray turned to two scouts standing nearby and asked them to carry out the task, something which they seemed to be only too glad to do. McGillivray then went to all of his men's positions to check that they had retreated safely before retreating himself.

At the new rendezvous location, the group gathered together to prepare for the journey out. The scouts that

McGillivray had sent to search the bodies returned, not only with weapons and papers from their enemies but also with their heads. The British men stared, shocked that the tribesmen still took heads as trophies: they thought the practice had stopped long ago. Even some of the most hardened men there were taken aback by the grisly sight and the apparent jubilation of the tribesmen that accompanied it.

Although revolted by the practice, McGillivray and his men made no attempt to stop it or to dampen the tribesmen's celebration in any way. It seemed an important thing to the Iban, a ritual that appeared to raise their morale. And, as McGillivray and his men readily recognised, if it raised the Ibans' morale, such an act was likely to lower the Indonesians' once they found the headless bodies of their comrades in the jungle. Nevertheless, the headhunting incident would be wonderful news for any hostile propagandists if it got out so it was decided that the whole affair should be kept quiet. And despite rumours, during his future years in the Regiment McGillivray always denied that he had ever witnessed any headhunting.

57. CAPTAIN THE EARL GEORGE JELLICOE

The Earl George Jellicoe already had a lot to live up to when he became one of the first members of the SAS: his father had been the famous First World War admiral who had fought at the Battle of Jutland in 1916. When the Second World War started, the young earl was studying at Cambridge. Leaving his books behind, he soon joined the fledgling SAS and became one of Stirling's best officers in the desert, showing a great sense of bravery and inventiveness.

In 1942, George Jellicoe, now a captain, was sent by Stirling to raid Heraklion airfield in Crete. The raid was to be launched from a schooner, and the men, some of the SAS's best canoeists, were to cover the last stretch of water in two captured German inflatable dinghies. They landed on a beach near Heraklion and sank their dinghies offshore so that they would not be discovered. Gathering their equipment, they walked to their pre-established rendezvous point: a cave above the port itself. Here they met up with their Greek guide, Lieutenant Costi, and four French commandos.

The next evening, Costi and one of the commandos did a reconnaissance of the airfield and counted 66 aircraft. Jellicoe immediately organised his men and they set off for the airfield to attack and destroy as many of the aircraft as they could. Their first obstacle was the barbed wire of the outer perimeter fence. They had just managed to cut their way through when a German patrol appeared and noticed the bodies lying down by the wire. The shouted challenge was answered by a stroke of genius from one of the Frenchmen: he let out what sounded like a drunken snore. The Germans, thinking that the prone bodies were no more than a group of Cretan peasants, all the worse for drink, decided they weren't worth bothering with and passed on. Of course, when they passed back the same way a little later, the bodies had gone and there was a large gaping hole in the wire. The alarm was raised.

Jellicoe's men were now in trouble. With their presence on the airfield known it was only a matter of time before they would be caught. Then, as if in answer to their prayers, three Stukas landed on the runway, closely followed by two RAF Blenheim bomber aircraft. They had obviously been shadowing the German aircraft so carefully that the Germans had not seen them on their tails. The Blenheims swooped low and dropped their bombs, which hit the runway with destructive force. This event completely overshadowed the fact that there were intruders on the airfield and as soldiers ran about in aimless circles Jellicoe and his men were able to complete their job in comparative safety, placing explosive devices on as many aircraft as they could manage. The infiltrators were still inside the perimeter fence ninety minutes later when the first charge went off, destroying its target. Jellicoe decided it was time to leave, but it was no longer wise to use the hole they had cut as it was probably being guarded by the enemy. Instead, he spotted a German patrol making its way towards the main gate. He told his men to step in behind them, keep in time and remain calm. It was dawn, and in the half-light there was a good chance that they wouldn't be looked at too closely. After all, who would expect an enemy raiding force to take such a risk?

Against all odds, the ruse worked and the SAS men marched their way off the airfield. As soon as they could, they dropped away one by one into bushes and behind rocks at the side of the road. Incredibly, the German patrol still didn't seem to notice anything. Once they were sure they were in the clear, the Allied force made their way back to the cave. In all, 24 planes – a Feisler *Storch* and 23 JU-88s – were destroyed in the attack. The Germans were infuriated and took reprisals against the local population, executing eighty hostages, including the Greek governor of the island.

Three days later the whole operation nearly ended in disaster when the French commandos were invited for dinner at the house of a nearby Greek and were betrayed to the enemy. Luckily, Jellicoe and Costi managed to escape and made it to their pick-up point 190 kilometres from Heraklion.

Jellicoe's exceptional qualities as a leader were rewarded in 1943 when he was given command of the Special Boat Squadron. During this time he was asked by his superiors to travel to Rhodes and attempt to persuade the Italian C-in-C there to come over to the Allied side. An armistice with the Italians had just been agreed, but Rhodes still had a strong German contingent on the island, including seventy tanks. It would be a brave Italian commander who would cross the line in those circumstances. Jellicoe was told of this operation at a meeting in Cairo full of generals and brigadiers. Their plan to get there seemed pretty hopeless, involving transporting them all in a couple of RAF crash boats and relying on the services of an SOE (Special Operations Executive) operative on the German side of the island whose wireless hadn't worked for weeks.

Despite being a junior officer by comparison with those sitting around him, Jellicoe stood up and told them what he thought of the plan. Instead, he suggested that a small party should be dropped by parachute that very evening. Although this idea obviously hadn't occurred to the senior officers, they agreed. A major called Dalby, who spoke good Italian, offered to go as Jellicoe's interpreter, but it wasn't until they were in the aircraft that he admitted he had had no parachute training whatsoever. This unfortunately proved a serious flaw: when he landed, he fell awkwardly and broke his leg badly.

Jellicoe almost didn't do any better. He fell close to an Italian AA battery that had opened up as soon as they saw the parachutes falling to earth. Fearing he might be captured at any moment, he took the letter he had been given – from General Wilson and addressed to Admiral Campioni – out of his pocket. His orders were that if he found himself in any sort of danger he was to destroy it. Not having any immediate means of destruction to hand, Jellicoe ate it instead, not an easy task because the paper was embossed. As it turned out, he discovered later he had been in less danger than he had thought.

He and his wireless operator made their way to Rhodes and were extremely surprised to find that Dalby had got there before them, despite the bone sticking out of his leg. The two of them spent time with Admiral Campioni, trying to persuade him to hold the port to allow the landing of a British force. The Admiral, although sympathetic to the Allied cause, feared the force of the German tanks and aircraft that could be brought against his troops if he complied. Nevertheless, he did all that he could for Jellicoe and his men. He had Dalby evacuated to Cyprus by one of his seaplanes and later sent Jellicoe off in an Italian MTB (motor torpedo-boat) with plans of every Italian minefield in the Aegean. Despite the failure on Rhodes, Jellicoe went on to take Cos and had a main role in the fight for Leros.

He continued as commander of the SBS until 1945, when he was sent to the British Army's Staff College.

57. LIEUTENANT ROBERT 'BOB' BURY – SPECIAL BOAT SQUADRON

L ieutenant Bob Bury, a patrol commander in the SBS, led a raid on the German- and Italian-held island of Simi, in the Dodecanese, on 20 November 1943. He and his men were up against one hundred enemy soldiers, with only the element of surprise in their favour. Landing on the nearest beach, they made their way to the capital, Castello, heading for the Governor's house. They entered the house stealthily and Bury soon came across a room where men from one of the light-machine-gun detachments were quartered. He threw in a grenade, killing them all outright. Meanwhile, other members of his raiding party were not idle; one of them, Sergeant 'Tanky' Geary, killed a patrol of eight Germans while standing guard at the entrance to the house. Bury himself, upon retreating from the premises, shot another German before placing a 25-pound explosive charge in the next-door building. Making sure his men were clear of the area, he detonated the charge, destroying the building he had placed it in as well as demolishing half of the Governor's house. Bury and his party now withdrew, laying a booby trap for enemy soldiers in the street. They hadn't gone far before they heard it go off.

In 1944, on the night of 13 July, Simi was attacked by Allied forces again. This time a large force consisting of 81 men from the SB Squadron and 159 from the Greek Sacred Squadron landed on the island without being seen by the enemy. From dawn onwards they attacked the German forces on the island with their machine-guns and mortars. Bury led his assault party against German positions situated at the old monastery, the force of their attack pressing the enemy back until they became trapped on a headland where, having no means of escape, they were forced to surrender. The entire operation proved to be a great success with the surrender of all the German forces: 185 prisoners taken as well as the destruction of ammunition and fuel dumps. Allied losses had been comparatively light: two Greek officers had been killed and six other soldiers wounded.

Three months later, Bury undertook a reconnaissance mission, sailing along the coastline of the island of Spetsia. Unfortunately, what he did not know was that a nearby bay concealed Loyalist partisan troops who were expecting an attack by their arch-rivals, the Communist guerrilla group ELAS. These men mistook Bury's caique for a boat carrying ELAS members and opened fire. The helmsman was hit immediately, leaving Bury to take over. He knew that they were not being fired upon by German weapons and assumed, rightly, that it was a case of mistaken identity. To try and show that they were friendly forces, he steered the boat closer to the shore, intending to land it. Before this was possible, he was wounded by partisan fire and died soon after. The mistake by the partisans was now realised but it was too late for Bury. The next day, both the partisan force and his own men carried him to a spot on the island where he was buried.

58. MAJOR ANDERS LASSEN

Anders Lassen was an exceptional, dedicated soldier, a member of both the SAS and the SBS. The stories told of his exploits during the Second World War have earned him respect and renown down through each new generation joining the Regiment.

Lassen came from Denmark originally but the beginning of the Second World War found him joining first the Merchant Navy, then SOE. During his training in SOE, it was decided that he was better at fighting than spying so he was sent to the Small-Scale Raiding Force (SSRF) under Captain Gus March-Phillips. He took part in raids on the French coast, his actions earning him the Military Cross. The operations of the SSRF were finally halted by the British Secret Intelligence Service (SIS) on the grounds that the raids endangered its own operatives in France.

Lassen, never one to stay out of the action for long, joined 1 SAS instead, as part of D Squadron which was in action in the Middle East. Soon after, 1 SAS split into two, one part becoming the Special Boat Squadron, of which Lassen became a member. His first major operation with the SBS, Operation Albumen, was in 1943, in a raid on enemy airfields in Crete. On 22 June, three patrols led by Lieutenants Kenneth Lamonby, Ronnie Rowe and Anders Lassen were sent to destroy aircraft at the enemy airfields of Heraklion, Timbakion and Kastelli. Lassen's patrol was the most successful, managing to destroy four Stukas, an armoured vehicle and a fuel dump, despite coming under fire from sentries. Lassen and one of his men were almost captured soon after when they were betrayed to the enemy forces by a Cretan, but fortunately they managed to escape and return safely to base. The other patrols had done less well: Rowe had found 'his' airfield empty while Lamonby too had found 'his' airfield devoid of aircraft – but he managed to destroy a fuel dump instead.

At this time the SBS were under the command of Major the Earl Jellicoe. Their range of operations in the Aegean included the large group of islands known collectively as the Dodecanese. These islands, including Crete, Kos, Leros, Simi, Karpathos and Tilos, were occupied by German forces and were therefore a rich target for special-warfare units. Aircraft and airfields were especially high on the list of targets to be destroyed since German dive-bombers were a constant threat to the Allied forces in the area. The SBS therefore set up several floating bases, all heavily camouflaged, around the islands, from which operations could be launched. Jellicoe, as the commanding officer, was not allowed to take part personally in the actions, usually much to his frustration, but instead directed them from the *Tewvic*, a small schooner. The men of the SBS used a variety of vessels, including caiques, inflatables and motor launches, to carry out their raids, although the boats were generally used as a ferry service to the islands rather than as fighting platforms in their own right.

The main German base was on the island of Rhodes and from there the Nazi regime spread its influence through the Dodecanese and the Aegean, occupying as many islands as possible. Kos fell easily, leaving the British forces without any air support or air cover, a situation that left the Allied forces in a very dangerous position. The Germans then turned their attention to other islands in the vicinity, including the small island of Simi. Lassen and his men landed on Simi, intending to take it back, and found it occupied by a small Italian contingent. Seeing the Germans arriving to rescue their allies, Lassen held a gun to the head of the Italian commander and 'persuaded' him to turn his men against their former comrades. Under the combined firepower of the SBS and the Italians, the Germans finally withdrew.

The next island that Lassen and his men landed on was Calchi. Here, he was told, a small group of Fascists had taken over the police station and were holding out from there. They refused absolutely to surrender. Irritated, to say the least, Lassen was not going to put up with this kind of time-wasting. He went straight to the police station, kicked down the door and put an end to the resistance immediately. As if this wasn't enough to deal with, a small German supply boat was observed making its way into the harbour. With a bit of quick planning, Lassen and his men launched an ambush against the vessel, capturing the German crew as well as the supplies on board.

Soon after, Lassen was made commander of M Detachment, SB Squadron and sent to the Greek mainland where the Germans were slowly withdrawing. He arrived in Salonika only to have the communist partisan group ELAS forbid him to make any attacks on the German forces. Of course, Lassen took no notice; his orders did not come from ELAS and he was keen to get on with what he did best, namely, making German lives a misery. Some of his men seemed even keener: his second-in-command, Lieutenant Henshaw, and the Naval Liaison Officer, Lieutenant Soloman, took the detachment's one jeep and drove up to an enemy battery position. Here, with an incredible amount of nerve, and maybe a touch of insanity as well, they tried to persuade two tanks, a battery of self-propelled guns and sixty men to surrender. Of course, the ruse didn't work and they were forced to beat a hasty retreat.

Lassen, however, was undaunted and soon discovered a new way to teach the German rearguard a lesson. The next day, he commandeered four fire engines, loaded his men into them and drove into the centre of Salonika. The locals, glad to see the arrival of Allied forces, flocked around the engines and clambered on board. The next minute they were scattering for cover as German weapons opened up on the intruders. A firefight followed, which the Germans got the worst of. At the end of the battle, over sixty German soldiers lay dead, eight killed by Lassen himself. Lassen's detachment lost no one and they returned to the town square, victorious.

Despite their achievements, Lassen and M Detachment were next sent back to Crete, instead of going on to take part in the Battle of Athens. Here, Lassen was ordered to keep the 13,000-strong German garrison on the island under observation as well as to try and persuade the obstinate ELAS to make attacks on them. As usual, ELAS proved uncooperative and Lassen, frustrated beyond measure, reported that he could do no more there. It wasn't long before his detachment, like all others from SB Squadron, were ordered to Italy. It was now mid-January 1945.

In early April, the last SBS action of the war took place at Lake Comacchio, north of Ravenna. The Germans had withdrawn to the northern shores of the lake and Lassen was detailed to do a reconnaissance of the German rear units to see whether they could be outflanked by a large commando raid. Lake Comacchio was a problematic area to cross as it was more swamp than lake. This meant that it was not deep enough to use assault boats and yet it was too waterlogged for tank or infantry movement. With the Germans controlling all but the south shore it also meant that anyone going that route would be likely to run into a hail of bullets and artillery fire. All in all, a great deal rested on the work of the SBS.

Together with one of his best men, Guardsman O'Reilly, Lassen achieved a great deal of the preliminary recces for 2 Commando Brigade, mapping the areas best suited for an assault. As part of the operations leading up to the main attack, Lassen also captured four of the islands in the lake. On 9 April, the main commando assault began while Lassen led a diversionary raiding party from one of the captured islands. The object was to make the Germans think that the objective was Comacchio itself.

After landing on the far shore, Lassen's party soon met heavy German fire from a series of pillboxes. Almost immediately, one SB man was killed and O'Reilly was seriously injured. Lassen charged the position responsible and destroyed it with a grenade, as he did with three others after that. At the fifth pillbox a white flag of surrender was hung out and from inside someone called 'Kamerad'. Lassen moved forward to the entrance but was met by a hail of fire and sustained mortal wounds. Despite his injuries, he managed to crawl back to his men but died not long after. He was only 25. Lassen had already been awarded two more Military Crosses to add to his first one. His actions at Comacchio also earned him a posthumous Victoria Cross.

59. MAJOR ROY FARRAN

Major Roy Farran, a commander with 2 SAS, was involved in many successful operations behind enemy lines during the Second World War. November 1943 found Farran and sixteen of his men on their way to Italy in an Italian submarine commanded by a Royal Navy officer. Dodging a German U-boat on the surface, the submarine stopped at the mouth of the River Tronto, 35 miles north of Pescara. Here, Farran and his men disembarked and paddled ashore in inflatable dinghies. Splitting up into four-man patrols commanded by Farran, Captain Grant Hibbert, Sergeant Rawes and Sergeant Seddon, they set out in the pitch darkness. By dawn, they were only about five hundred yards from their target, the railway line between Ancona and Giulianova, so they decided to find a place to lie up for the day.

As dusk fell, they prepared themselves and sent out a recce party. Two sentries patrolled a bridge but that seemed to be all; Farran decided to carry out the attack that night. The four groups set off for a predetermined rendezvous point but in the terrible weather conditions only three groups made it. Sergeant Rawes and his men were missing. With things going against them, Farran called off the attack, postponing it until the following night. The three patrols then separated to prepare LUPs for the coming day.

The following night, Rawes and his men finally made it to the rendezvous and everything now seemed set for the assault. Three of the patrols headed for the railway line with their explosives and managed to blow it in sixteen places, Rawes's patrol also destroying three enemy trucks. The fourth patrol, led by Sergeant Seddon, mined the roads around their area and succeeded in destroying seven telegraph poles. With a successful mission behind them, the men now had to face a seventy-mile walk to their pick-up point on the coast.

Things went from bad to worse, especially the weather. The heavy rain made the ground under the men's feet sodden and slowed them down. One of Farran's men was also seriously ill with malaria. But the local populace were usually friendly and provided them with shelter and food as they lay up during the day. Travelling at night, however, and with such handicaps, meant that the group was losing time; at the rate they were going they weren't going to meet the pick-up with the MTB. Farran decided that, dangerous as it was, they were going to have to move in daylight as well. The plan worked and they made it to the appointed beach in time. However, there was no sign of the MTB so they were forced to find a place to lie up and wait. The following night, much to their relief, the submarine that had originally brought them appeared and picked them up.

During 1944, Farran and 2 SAS were in action in France in what was known as Operation Wallace. On 19 August, Farran, sixty men and twenty jeeps were flown into an American-controlled airfield at Rennes. The first fifty miles behind enemy lines were straightforward, without any hostile encounters. This was mostly due to the help given by the local Maquis. Farran's objective was to reach the base of Operation Hardy on the Plateau de Langres, north of Dijon. A number of men and jeeps had been dropped previously and it was Farran's aim to join up with them as soon as he could.

To this end Farran tried to move mostly at night but soon abandoned this after he found out that more Germans were on the move at that time than during the day. This was largely the result of the supremacy of British air power: any Germans caught travelling on the roads in daylight were more than likely to get shot up or bombed. Hence, Farran changed his plans and started to travel in the daytime, splitting his men into three groups who were to travel thirty minutes apart. Despite his orders to avoid enemy forces at all costs, the leading group drove straight through a village full of German soldiers at Mailly-le-Château. Apart from one jeep, the group got through without loss. The second group, containing Farran, unaware of what had happened, drove straight into a hail of fire. Hastily turning his men around, Farran and the third group detoured to the south, eventually meeting up with the lead vehicles again in the Forêt de St Jean.

The next morning, the lead group repeated its previous folly by running into German forces again. On this occasion, all the jeeps were destroyed and all the men killed or captured except for one: the leader. Even so, he was not able to get to Farran to warn him of what had happened. Consequently, Farran's group once more drove into a firefight. Their own rate of fire managed to keep the Germans at bay for a short while, then it became clear that they were about to be outflanked. Driving in a wide arc to the south, Farran and his men managed to escape again. However, this time they had lost a jeep and a radio set. The third group, unaware of the fate of the other two, drove into the same ambush. Most of the men, including the officer commanding, were killed but a few survivors eventually managed to make their way to Paris, which by now had been liberated.

Farran's convoy had been cut down to seven jeeps but he remained undaunted. Carrying on to meet up with the Hardy party, he came across a goods train slowly making its way toward their position. Finding it too good an opportunity to miss, he positioned his men at the gates of a level crossing and, as the train drew level, gave the order to fire. The fury they unleashed with their Vickers-K guns was enough to stop the train in its tracks with a punctured boiler. All the Germans on the train had been killed but, by some good luck, the French engine driver managed to escape unharmed.

Farran's next encounter was at the Forêt de Châtillon. Close to a radar station, his group came under heavy enemy fire. Knowing themselves to be outnumbered, they hastily withdrew. Puzzlingly, so did the Germans. Later on it was discovered that the Germans had retreated because they thought they had come across the advance guard of General Patton's Third Army. Of course, Farran pressed the advantage and pursued the retreating troops, killing 35.

Not long after, Farran met up with the other men from the Hardy Base camp and took command. He now had ten jeeps, a truck and sixty men. Operation Hardy had already been making a name for itself in the area – almost too much of a name. Farran decided it was best if they now removed their camp to another location. Throughout the following days, Farran split his squadron into three so as to cause disruption over as large an area as possible. On 17 September, a month after they had parachuted into France, Farran's operation came to an end when the American Seventh Army arrived and liberated the area. Operation Wallace/Hardy had proved itself to be one of the most successful SAS operations of the war, with 95 vehicles, a train and 100,000 gallons of petrol destroyed and with 500 enemy casualties. Of course, it had not been without cost: sixteen members of 2 SAS and sixteen jeeps had been lost to enemy action. Nevertheless, Farran was proud of what his men had achieved and rewarded their efforts by sending them off to Paris for a week.

A few weeks later, Farran and his unit were dropped into France again, this time near the small village of Moussey near the Vosges mountains in eastern France. After landing, the men quickly got into cover in the woods surrounding the village. They made contact with the villagers who befriended them and gave them every assistance they needed. General Patton's advance into the area had been stalled by lack of supplies, giving the Germans time to move reinforcements along the River Meurthe nearby. Farran's men used this opportunity to carry out raids on the German forces, raids that in the end brought down German wrath on the population of Moussey. Every person in the village was rounded up and interrogated. Still loyal to the Allied men they had befriended, not one villager betrayed them. Frustrated by their silence, the Germans sent 210 men, most of the male population, to concentration camps. Of this number only seventy returned alive after the war. Moussey's great sacrifice had saved Farran and his men from discovery, something that would never be forgotten. Today Moussey is still a village, spread out for about a mile with a few houses scattered alongside the road. Near the centre is a church with a military graveyard. Many of the men buried there are from 2 SAS.

Moussey was Farran's last major operation in France. He was ordered to Italy where he took on a new command: 3 Squadron 2 SAS. This was a newly raised Squadron consisting mainly of volunteers from 1 and 6 Airborne and was, or so Farran considered, better disciplined than the men he had served with before. From mid-December 1944 onwards, Farran and 3 Squadron took part in several operations, with Farran himself taking part in as many as he could get permission for. However, more than once he entered into the action when he shouldn't have: he narrowly escaped a court martial for his active role in Operation Tombola where he played a great part in coordinating local partisan groups in attacks on German positions.

One such attack took place on 24 March at the German 51 Corps headquarters, south of Reggio. The Germans were based in two villas – Villa Rossi and Villa Calvi – in the village of Albinea in the Po valley. Just before the attack, as the men were en route to the target, Army Headquarters changed its mind and forbade the whole operation. In his usual manner, Farran decided to ignore it. His argument was that he had built up a good relationship with the partisans in his group; if he called the whole thing off now, he would lose all credibility with them, as would the entire British Army.

Finding a farm near the villas, Farran and his men lay up during the day and planned to attack the following night in three groups. One group would attack the Villa Rossi, the headquarters of the corps commander, Generalleutnant Hauk, while another group would attack the Villa Calvi, accommodation for the corps chief of staff as well as the operations room for the area. The third group would be responsible for making sure that none of the troops from the neighbouring garrison interfered in what was going on.

That night, all three groups set off from the farm, making their way over open ground to the two villas. Their actions went undetected by the enemy. The group detailed to attack Villa Calvi, led by nineteen-year-old Lieutenant Ken Harvey, soon reached the front door of their target. The door was locked so they tried to blow it in using a rocket launcher. Unfortunately the rocket misfired, creating enough noise to alert four German sentries. Harvey killed them with his Bren gun but by now the enemy had been forewarned and had started firing back at the attackers.

With the partisans providing covering fire, Harvey and nine of his men stormed the ground floor, killing four Germans, the chief of staff included. The Germans on the upper floors held off Harvey's attempts to gain access by rolling grenades down the stairs. Seeing that there was no other way, Harvey set the building alight before rejoining the rest of Farran's group. For his actions in the raid, Harvey was awarded the Distinguished Service Order.

The attack on the Villa Calvi had started before the Villa Rossi attackers were in place. As a result, the Germans were alerted by the noise and were ready. Once again, the men from 2 SAS gained the ground floor but were thwarted from going any further by the actions of those on the upper floors. Realising that time was getting short, the attackers set the kitchen quarters alight and retreated.

The third group was also coming under heavy fire; the troops in the garrison had now realised what was afoot and were fighting back. Nevertheless, the SAS and the partisans managed to hold them at bay until the job was done and then, as Farran fired off a red Very light, all retreated to the rendezvous point. During the fighting, despite inflicting high casualties on the Germans and causing much destruction, only three British soldiers were killed and eight British and Italian men wounded. The whole party retreated across the valley plain to their base in the mountains, managing to avoid the German search parties sent out to locate them.

60. KEITH (PSEUDONYM)

Author's note: There is a man whom I shall call Keith. He arrived in Hereford during 1967 from one of the Guards battalions and went on to follow an active career in the SAS. Now Keith is commissioned and still serving – in fact, he holds a very important position in the SAS hierarchy. I telephoned my friend Jock Logan the other day and he recommended that I recount a story in which Keith and I were the principal players. Jock reckons it will do Keith good to remember his roots. Although I have not seen Keith for many years I still class him as a friend, and I hope he will recall this little scenario with as much enthusiasm as I still do.

Acting on behalf of the RUC Special Branch in Northern Ireland, we were tasked to observe the daily routine of a certain hairdresser. There were two angles to this operation. First, it was believed that he was a courier for the IRA. Second, it was also claimed that he was having an affair with the wife of an IRA man who was currently languishing in the Maze prison. If this second part of the story could be proved it would make him very eager to work with the security forces. A word in the right ear that he was sleeping with the wife of an IRA prisoner would not be well received. (How else do you think we got our information?)

Keith and I spent several nights trying to establish the best observation position. This was difficult as we needed to see in through the windows of the hairdresser's – which were on the second floor – in order to take pictures. We reached the necessary vantage point by climbing up the walls of a very large building (now you know why the SAS places so much emphasis on mountaineering) and eventually found a brilliant location in the ceiling of the town hall that could be accessed via a small trapdoor. Inside we would be working in the space between the inner ornate roof and the buildings outer roof. The front fascia housed the back of the town clock with a small platform measuring six feet by four feet for whoever replaced the bulbs and carried out maintenance. At each side of the clock there was a sloping air vent. By placing the camera into the left-hand vent, we could take clear pictures of the hairdresser's shop across the street.

As there was only room for two men, this meant that one would sleep while the other manned the camera. The chances of being detected in such a location were very low but, even so, in accordance with SOPs cooking was not allowed. Any smell could easily have drifted down into the town hall and alerted the staff, most of whom where Catholics. So Keith and I had to survive on hot soup provided in thermos flasks, together with a two-day supply of cold chicken and egg sandwiches. These supplies would be delivered during the early hours of the morning by a back-up team. During such times we would get out through the small trapdoor that led onto the outside roof and lower a line down into the shadows of the town hall yard. Messages, exposed film and waste were sent down, while fresh supplies would be hauled up.

The small platform at the back of the clock was cramped, but large enough for one man to sleep while the other kept watch and took photographs. As the hairdresser's closed at around six p.m., Keith and I would pass the long dark evenings listening to a variety of functions taking place in the town hall below. This ranged from classical music to bingo. For the latter Keith and I would make out our own bingo cards – would you believe it? – and on several occasions we actually had a 'line'. Once when the hall was closed we lowered ourselves down from the roof space, no mean feat considering the height, and did a recce of the hall.

The cold chicken and egg sandwiches did little for our digestion and flatulence was a real problem. Luckily, we had the two air vents beside the clock. A narrow catwalk ran from our small platform down the entire length of the inner domed roof. To provide a little modesty, a bin liner was placed in the gloom halfway along it. When using this we had to be careful not to slip off the catwalk and put our feet through the ornate ceiling, which was made of plaster. The weather at the time was extremely sunny and, after about five days, the heat that became trapped between the inner and outer roofs was unbearable.

Around four o'clock one afternoon I was in need of the toilet so I negotiated my way along the catwalk. About halfway along, something caught my eye and I stopped. Shock and alarm gripped all my senses as something in the gloom before me started to move. The shock and alarm turned to horror as I realised I was facing the biggest spider man had ever seen. Without exaggeration, its body was two feet across, and the large eyes in its head glistened. One pounce and it would have me. I panicked, unable to move, fearful that the beast would attack me.

It took nerves of steel and several moments of rational thinking to get a grip on my fear. Spiders of this size only existed in the movies. Then came the flood of relief as I realised what it was. The black bin liner used as our toilet had been twisted and sealed up with an elastic band in order to cut down the smell. As the heat had increased, the gases had expanded, creating in the gloom a lookalike giant spider. I was so euphoric at not having being savaged by the beast that I made the mistake of opening the bag, fearing that it might explode if I did not. The smell hit me like a sledgehammer and I reeled on the catwalk. Finally, I managed to crawl back to where Keith was keeping watch, only to find him face up against the vent trying to suck in pure air. Later that night we lowered the offending bag to the back-up crew.

Although funny, this story demonstrates the daily hardships that SAS men encounter in the war against terrorism. Keith and I stayed in the location undetected for two weeks.

61. CORPORAL ALASTAIR 'JOCK' LOGAN

A uthor's note: The final biographical entry in this book is for one of my oldest and dearest friends, a man who pulled me out of the shit on more than one occasion.

Jock Logan joined the SAS in 1965, arriving via the Scots Guards. He was an excellent soldier but above all he was an outstanding mechanic. It was nothing to see the barrack room where we all lived strewn with a wide variety of car parts. On one occasion the Squadron Sergeant Major came to inspect the room, only to find a complete engine hanging from the rafters while Jock worked merrily away on it. 'What the hell's going on – whose is that engine?' came the demand. Jock just looked up and smiled: 'It's yours, sir, you asked me to fix your car.'

Like so many, Jock became disillusioned with the inactivity during the late 1960s and decided to leave the SAS. He did not go far. In fact, he went to work in a garage no more than a few hundred metres from the camp which was then called Bradbury Lines. However, at the outbreak of war in

Oman Jock was soon back with his old Squadron. His arrival on the Jebel Massif was accompanied by the comment 'What the hell am I doing here?' as he came face to face with the ferocity of Adoo firepower.

He and I survived many small battles, the first of which was at a small escarpment. A small group of BATT and Firqat ventured forward, moving off the high ground into the thick bush and scrub that covered the lip of the escarpment. Mac McAuliffe (see Chapter 27) stayed on the high ground, controlling a team manning two mortars with the barrels 'laid' neatly on the escarpment. Unbeknown to us, the Adoo were on their way up from the valley below in order to ambush us. Both sides met in the heavy bush, slap bang on the lip of the escarpment.

The silence and the darkness erupted into a crashing cacophony of light and sound as the enactment of hell on earth began. Men on both sides were running or diving for scant cover. Others were caught in the brutal crossfire, jumping and bouncing like rag dolls. The air was filled with *zip! zip!* sounds as small copper-coated bullets passed overhead. Both Jock and I dropped to the ground and desperately brought our weapons into play. Training and conditioning overcame fear as we both searched the long grass for targets. Abruptly the steadfast sound of a 'gimpy' (GPMG) machine-gun chattered to our left and from the rear came the steady 'plop, plopping' sound as Mac dispatched the mortars.

I shouted for Jock to cover me and made to rise and run for a large mound of earth several metres away. Jock grabbed the belt of ammo from around my neck, pulling me back down. He needed ammunition. I dropped back as he raised the top cover of the gun, allowing me to feed in the belt. Without thinking, I slammed down the cover, trapping Jock's fingers and cutting one through to the bone. If he noticed it never showed. Next second we were both up and running hard, hell-bent and determined.

We dropped into the relative shelter of the mound only to find that there were two Adoo lying on the other side of it.

I think that at that moment all four of us went into a frenzy. I tried to pull the pin out of a grenade but was hindered by Jock who was trying to speed up the process. So we lay there, flat on our backs, with the grenade bouncing around as if we were playing ball. It seemed like a lifetime but was no more than a few seconds – eventually Jock lobbed the grenade over his head. It landed about three metres away on the other side of the mound. We waited. *Crump*. The grenade exploded. A split second later Jock was up and over the top. I rolled onto my stomach, peering over the top of the mound. One Adoo lay wounded and Jock was running forward. He did a little dance as a stream of bullets kicked up dust around his feet. Next second he was flat beside me. 'Fuck this for a game of soldiers.' He was laughing.

The battle died down and we started seeing to the wounded and policing the bodies. Nearby one of the Adoo was being attended to by an SAS medic. He had taken four bullets diagonally across the chest, and the blood bubbled frothily from the wounds. He was no longer the enemy, just a wounded human being who, despite the best efforts of the medic, was going to die. This was the first time I had seen the enemy close-up and we were all surprised to see how neat and tidy the man was. He was dressed in dark green shorts and shirt, long socks and desert boots. The blue beret with its red communist star was still on his head, and we later found a small copy of the *Thoughts of Chairman Mao Tse-tung* in his pocket.

Ken, the medic, was busy stuffing the Adoo's wounds and covering his chest with plastic sheet. Ken then administered a very large dose of morphine: the guy was going to die, but at least he would die happy. What happened next was most bizarre. The dying Adoo was smiling in gratitude for Ken's ministrations when the expression on his face turned to one of absolute terror. The cause of this change was one of our own Firqat who now stood by the wounded man's feet with a large knife in his hand. We all thought the same thing: he's going to cut the wounded man's throat. Before we could stop him, he dropped to his knees – to cut away at the man's laces and remove his boots. We all stood there in amazement as more Firqat arrived and proceeded literally to strip the man of his clothing. Jock and I walked away in disgust.

The battles continued each day until we found ourselves at the location known as 'White City'. Here, with the establishment of good defences and an airstrip, more adventurous patrols were undertaken. One such task was the Jebel Aram mission.

It was cold and dark as the patrol set off from White City at around 8 p.m. The patrol consisted of some fifteen SAS (including Jock and me), thirty Firqat and a platoon of SAF. The weight of necessary equipment carried by each man made our progress very slow. The bulky rucksacks contained mostly ammunition and water, but in addition Jock, Frank Bilcliffe (see Chapter 10) and I carried an 81mm mortar. Our small group made up the tail end of the lead group and behind us came the SAF platoon, each carrying two mortar bombs. This was all the support we would have until we reached the Jebel Aram and established a firm base.

At last we came to a halt, and the chance came to take a break from the merciless weight we carried. After about ten minutes all the SAS men, apart from our mortar crew, together with the Firqat went forward for a recce. It was estimated that we were about five hundred metres from our objective. The recce had almost reached the old tree that was to serve as our goal (old trees in the desert are almost always used as landmarks) and there was no sign of the Adoo. Suddenly one of the Firqat dropped down on one knee and pointed: 'Adoo,' he whispered. Mat (the patrol commander) used his nightscope to survey the ground ahead: there, at the edge of his night vision, stood the ancient tree. He signalled for the remainder of the group to close up and indicated the direction by pointing into the darkness. Then he quietly relayed the information back to the SAF commander. When he had finished he gave us instructions to set up the mortar. As this was done, the SAF platoon dropped their mortar bombs off at our location, then spread out in defence, covering the rear. Once everyone was ready, the SAS and Firqat moved to the base of the tree.

Then it happened. As so many times before, the darkness became a crashing firestorm of light and sound. Within seconds we had the mortar thundering into action, the ground beneath our feet thumping as the bombs hit the pin at the base of the barrel and the propellant charge exploded.

As quickly as it began, the shooting stopped. We all waited tensely but the Adoo had gone. An hour later it was full daylight and the patrol had settled down, having set up a defensive position overlooking the Jebel Aram. Jock, Frank and I set about building a mortar pit, checking the ammunition since it would be some hours before we would get resupplied. Later that day several short patrols were sent down into the wadi that ran at the back of the Jebel Aram. These patrols could rely on excellent coverage from the mortars and GPMGs, which had spectacular views from our position. On the second day of occupation one of the SAS patrols came under heavy fire. They had been caught by the Adoo in a bush-covered wadi some 1,500 metres to the front of the SAS position. A relief patrol was formed of which Jock and I were part. Together with several Firqat we started forward.

The ground sloped downhill and was covered with knee-high dried grass and littered with medium-sized rocks. One of the Omani soldiers ran a little ahead of me and about a metre to my left. The Adoo bullet took him directly through the heart, freezing his body momentarily in time and space – it was as if he had hit an invisible wall. I distinctly remember the exit wound exploding from the centre of his back, spraying dark blood in a funnel effect. (Why does time stand still during such moments?)

I ran on, only to see the Adoo no more than fifteen metres in front of me. As he lay prone behind a large rock, with only his head visible through the long grass, I saw him re-sight at me. There was little I could do, and no time to do it – I saw him shoot. Next moment I was being thrown upwards, as if tumbling through the air like some rag doll.

I slammed back to earth with a massive thud. Luckily for me, I had fallen into a shallow dip where, for a few seconds, I lay numbed. Fear, pain and distress prompted me to open my lungs and yell – scream was more like it – for help. Jock Logan, with whom I had spent almost every living moment on the Jebel, crashed down beside me in a cloud of dust. He blasted off a long belt of machine-gun ammo in the direction of the Adoo and proceeded to fix me up. His voice was full of confidence and assurance as he ripped away my trouser leg. 'Lucky bastard, it's not gone through.' Five minutes later the medivac choppers came in and shipped me to the FST (Field Surgical Team) where I was patched up nicely and sent home to England. The squadron returned, as did Jock. As the war came to an end, Jock left the army once more, this time for good.

Author's note: The SAS rely heavily on the 'buddy' system. There is no greater buddy than my friend Jock Logan. He now lives on the north coast of Scotland where he runs his own successful business. Despite the miles that separate us we still find time to meet up once every couple of years and reminisce about our past.

62. WHAT HAPPENS TO EX-SAS SOLDIERS?

At the start of this book I tried to tell the reader what makes the average SAS soldier, as far as one can call them 'average'. The end of the book is the logical place to tell you what happens to SAS soldiers when they leave the Regiment. It is fairly true to say that most soldiers who arrive at Hereford normally stay there for the rest of their military careers. The exception to this rule is either being killed or RTU'd (Returned To Unit).

The SAS is not a large Regiment and the death of an individual soldier is a great loss. It is an unfortunate fact of SAS life that many soldiers do die, some while in training and others during operations. One only has to take a look in the SAS graveyard at Saint Martin's church in Hereford to see the cost. Here lie many young men, good men, men full of life and promise, dead before their time. It is not that the Regiment is careless or 'Gung-Ho'. On the contrary, those graves are there because these men dared to face foe and adversity head on – they 'Dared to Win'.

The other premature way of leaving the SAS is through being RTU'd. Anyone, officers, NCOs and soldiers alike, can be RTU'd for a number of misdemeanours, but generally the soldier in question must have made a serious error of judgement. For example, there was a sergeant who had served with the Regiment for around ten years: his error of judgement was getting caught. At the time the guy was operating in Northern Ireland and, being one for the ladies, had taken up with a Catholic girl. He had used one of the undercover cars for his first date, driving his girlfriend out into the countryside. His chat-up line had been 'naff', actually claiming that he was a spy, the real James Bond, etc. The encounter progressed from the undressing stage through to the relaxing cigarette afterwards.

This incident might not have come to light except for one small detail. All the undercover cars were fitted with miniature 'press-to-talk' buttons hidden around the car. The operators pressed these in order to talk to the base unit. On this particular car there was a presser switch hidden near the foot of the passenger – and the girl had somehow locked it down. Unfortunately, while our erring sergeant was having his wicked way a full-blown operation involving the various security agencies was taking place, the communications for which were routed through the SAS base station. The rogue transmission blocked out the entire operation and was heard by everyone. In addition, it was recorded on the master back-up. Result: RTU the moment Sergeant Romeo arrived back at base.

Those who spend several years in the Regiment begin to understand fully its workings, which, I might add, are complex, and therein lies another dimension. Many SAS soldiers rise through the ranks to the point where they are offered a commission. Those who take up this option, and many do, make excellent officers, although their employment is normally restricted to the role of training or stationary command positions. Those who serve out their time, which is at the completion of 22 years' military service, leave with three attributes: SAS expertise, mystique and confidence.

The uses to which SAS 'graduates' put their expertise will depend partly on which subject they specialised in, but for the majority it will be some form of training or bodyguard work. There are several large security companies, many of which have been started and staffed by ex-SAS personnel. From time to time these companies make headlines when, for one reason or another, they are accused of some unlawful transgression. In reality their ex-SAS members are only providing a service based on their skills learned while in the Regiment, and which for the most part is beneficial to the stabilisation of society. For example, many ex-SAS soldiers went back to Oman, working in a training capacity for a company called KMS. And why not? Oman is extremely friendly to Britain, so such training is in our own national interest. Some years later, also with the blessing of the British government, the same company sent a team to Sri Lanka.

It is not just governments that require the services of ex-SAS soldiers. If a 'blue chip' company has one of its diamond mines overrun with rebels in some remote corner of the world, who do they turn to? Oil is a commodity on which the western world is reliant: what happens when rebellious villagers hijack the company helicopter and hold several senior oil workers hostage in Nigeria? I will tell you. The blue chip companies call for expert help and, lo and behold, a few days later a couple of casual-looking guys will turn up and assess the situation. Their solution to the problem will not normally advocate the use of arms, more likely they will negotiate a peaceful and lasting settlement with the rebels or malcontents. I am not saying that all of these security companies are whiter than white – indeed, many become actively involved in the military and political situations of smaller countries. Their services in helping to establish a more settled situation in these emerging countries are usually paid for in the form of mining and drilling concessions. For good or bad, if corporate and commercial interests are threatened you can be assured that ex-SAS personnel will usually be involved in resolving the problem.

As for the mystique, well, I hope that this book has shown you that this does not exist. 'Mystique' is what the media sell; in reality, the SAS only has *secrecy*. If the SAS are deployed to Bosnia, then everyone will know about it. What they will *not* know is how or where the regiment is operating. Therefore the answer for the media is to look back at past encounters and fabricate a story. As the years go by, fabrications are built on fabrications: thus we have mystique. Who has benefited from this mystique? Well, I have for one, so have the handful of other 'SAS authors', but we are few, and for the most part all of us have told you the truth. Sometimes there may be a different version of the same story: that is to be expected. On the whole, all the SAS books I have read impart no mystique. They simply tell the reader how it was.

Confidence is a different matter altogether. For example, I can pick a lock, make home-made explosive using a variety of items found in any kitchen cupboard, and shoot the eye out of a rabbit at one hundred metres. These skills are not very handy in civilian life, unless you are a crook – and, yes, the SAS has had a few of these.

By far the greatest quality one gets from service with the SAS is confidence. This virtue has always been a Regimental characteristic since the formation of the SAS way back in the early 1940s. It is bred from working with men who are undaunted when faced with insurmountable and life-threatening problems. From the discovery that you are as capable as the next man, including heads of state, Prime Ministers and millionaires. This confidence comes from facing yourself, a process that starts when any soldier volunteers for SAS selection. It is this confidence that helps many adapt to civilian life once they have left the SAS – which can be difficult. Imagine you are a forty-year-old Squadron Sergeant Major with all the privileges and responsibility the rank carries. Suddenly you find yourself in a civilian suit applying for a job and the interviewer is half your age. Luckily that scenario is a rare one, as most SAS soldiers have guaranteed employment before they leave. SAS skills come in very handy for a number of government agencies, including the Secret Intelligence Service, Customs and Excise (drugs division) and the prison service (anti-riot). Then there are the mavericks. Mavericks are those soldiers who choose to go it alone. They become publicans, post-men, professional gamblers, private investigators, adventurers and smugglers.

One such person left the SAS to work in Saudi Arabia. He set up a company dragging scrapped cars from the side of the road and fitting new tyres to those that had had a blow-out. That business failed, so he went to work for a security company protecting a British High Commission in some African state. He married the Commissioner's daughter, but both the marriage and the job failed. He next found employment as a bodyguard, protecting a female millionaire who owned half a Dutch oil company. He married her (at her invitation, I might add) and the last I heard they were happy together.

Others have crossed seas, climbed mountains, and set numerous world records. No matter what road an ex-SAS soldier takes or what attribute he exploits, it is done in the knowledge that he has survived life in the Regiment – for many do not. From time to time, an ex-SAS man will meet a fellow survivor and for a brief moment over a pint the flame of the past is rekindled.

REGIMENTAL COLLECT OF THE SPECIAL AIR SERVICE

Oh Lord, who didst call on Thy disciples to venture all to win all men to Thee, grant that we, the chosen members of the Special Air Service Regiment, may by our works and our ways dare all to win all and, in so doing, render special service to Thee and our fellow men in all the world, through the same Jesus Christ Our Lord, Amen.